THE CURRENT AFFAIRS MINDSET

THE CURRENT AFFAIRS
MINDSET

Published by:
CURRENT AFFAIRS PRESS
631 St. Charles Ave
New Orleans, LA 70130
currentaffairs.org

First U.S. Edition

Distributed on the West Coast by
WATERS & SMITH, LTD
MONSTER CITY, CA

ISBN 978-0-9978447-2-6

LIBRARY OF CONGRESS CATALOG-IN-PUBLICATION DATA
Robinson, Nathan J. (ed.)
The Current Affairs Mindset / Nathan J. Robinson
p. cm
Includes bibliographical references
ISBN 978-0997844771
1. Cultural analysis 2. Political science 3. Libertarian socialism
4. Social Philosophy 1. Title

CONTENTS

THE CURRENT AFFAIRS
MINDSET

ESSAYS ON POLITICS, PEOPLE, AND CULTURE

EDITED BY NATHAN J. ROBINSON

CURRENT
AFFAIRS
currentaffairs.org

CONTRIBUTORS

FELIX BIEDERMAN
co-hosts the highly-regarded *Chapo Trap House* podcast.

ERIC M. FINK
teaches labor and employment law at Elon University.

AMBER A'LEE FROST
co-hosts *Chapo Trap House* and
writes the "Your Sorry Ass" advice column for *The Baffler*.

BRIAHNA JOY GRAY
co-hosts the Someone's Wrong On The Internet (SWOTI) Podcast.

DAVID KINDER
is a civil rights attorney from Michigan.

ANGELA NAGLE
is the author of *Kill All Normies: Online Culture Wars From 4Chan And
Tumblr To Trump And The Alt-Right*.

YASMIN NAIR
is a writer and activist based in Chicago, and co-founder of Against Equality.

ALEX NICHOLS
is a musician and writer based in Western Massachusetts.

OREN NIMNI
is a Boston attorney and co-author of *Blueprints for a Sparkling Tomorrow*.

BRIANNA RENNIX
is a third-year student at Harvard Law School.

EMILY ROBINSON
is a writer and activist from Virginia living in Scotland.

NATHAN J. ROBINSON
edits the New Orleans-based political periodical *Current Affairs*.

LUKE SAVAGE
is a Toronto-based writer whose work frequently appears in *Jacobin*.

ZACH WEHRWEIN
is a PhD student in sociology at Harvard University.

INTRODUCTION

by Nathan J. Robinson

FOR THOSE OF US ON THE LEFT, it is both an encouraging time and a horrifying time. The horrifying aspects don't really need much elaboration. Two days before this writing, hundreds of white supremacists wielding flaming tiki torches descended on the University of Virginia, before one of them used his car to murder a leftist counter-protester. Donald J. Trump, who immediately felt compelled to insist that some of the neo-Nazis might have been quite nice people, has somehow ended up becoming President of the United States, a fact that still seems difficult to fully accept even seven months into his term of office. Environmental catastrophe, nuclear war, mass deportation, police shootings, increasing economic inequality: we seem to be living in a time of terrible intractable problems that can only get worse. And with the Republican Party holding total control of government at the federal level, and consolidating their power in the states, the future for left policies looks—to put it mildly—moderately grim.

And yet I really do think it's also an "encouraging" time. In the United States, it feels as if even as the left has been pushed out of political office, it also has an incredible moment of political opportunity. The presidential campaign of Bernie Sanders brought energized millions of young people. Membership in the Democratic Socialists of America has ballooned in the last year. The left may be small, and it may not be in power, but there are many signs of hope. As the traditional political establishment becomes more discredited and despised, more and more people are receptive to fresh and radical political ideas. Donald Trump is obviously a catastrophe for the country and the world. But if the left can get its act together, his presidency may also help galvanize a new opposition movement that can propose a compelling political alternative.

But taking advantage of the moment requires having a clear political vision. If the left doesn't know what it wants, what it stands for and doesn't stand for, then it won't be able to persuade people to join it. Clarifying what it actually *means* to be on the left is therefore incredibly important. We must have a well-defined understanding of who we are and what we believe. That, in turn, will require thinking about and discussing our values, aspirations, and strategies.

This is where good left-wing writing should come in. Writers perform an incredibly valuable function in politics: they not only spread information and ideas, but they can help people come to know themselves better and give people helpful intellectual tools for considering how to act in the world. I've never believed that there should be a caste of "intellectuals" whose job it is to do people's thinking for them. But I do believe that writers should use their skills in order to improve the public conversation as much as possible, by clearing up misconceptions, shining light on neglected topics, adding important facts that complicate existing narratives, and ironing out problems with various ideologies. At their worst, writers can confuse and delude people, leading them toward foggier or more rigid thinking. But when writers do their jobs well, they are essential, guiding people toward more humane and nuanced political beliefs and proposing useful courses of action toward the improvement of human social life.

Current Affairs was founded in order to provide an outlet for the kind of thoughtful, non-dogmatic, lively, and accessible left-wing writing that I think will be indispensible in helping us reverse our side's political fortunes. So much leftist writing has always been boring, sanctimonious, and inscrutable. But there's no reason it needs to be. If we believe what we say we do, namely that we want to *make the world a better place,* that necessarily involves making sure the world has fewer boring or inscrutable things in it, because a world without such things is better than a world with them. If leftist writing is dull and preachy, this suggests that the kind of society we would build would be dull and preachy, and I for one do not want to live in that kind of society.

In *Current Affairs,* then, we've tried to produce the seemingly impossible: left-wing writing that people might actually enjoy reading. We try not to be predictably dogmatic. We try to incorporate humor and satirical bite, and to always treat the reader as if her time matters. We aim to be fair-minded, willing to criticize the left as well as the right, and committed to factual accuracy, never distorting reality in order to serve ideological ends.

We're a young magazine, and I am not sure how well we have managed to attain these goals so far. Certainly, we are continuing to try to improve. But so far I am proud of the results: the essays in this book, by a diverse range of authors on a variety of subjects, are the beginning of an attempt to provide a new kind of fun, smart, and engaging political commentary from a left perspective.

The Current Affairs Mindset mixes the silly and provocative with the deadly serious. Sometimes, we're trying to puncture pomposity and dreariness, as when we take on beloved liberal cultural products like *The West Wing* and the *Hamilton* musical. In other writings, we're trying to increase readers' understandings of various undiscussed forms of human suffering, such as the plight of refugees at the Texas border or the economically desperate people who make up a portion of America's 40,000 annual suicides.

In everything we write, we try to combine a sharp critical eye with a deep moral seriousness. The one thing we are not is nihilists: we believe very sincerely and unashamedly in trying to help give people better and more fulfilling lives, and in reducing the world's quantities of evil and misfortune. From time to time it may appear as if we are cynics blowing spitballs. This is not the case. We do blow plenty of spitballs. But we are not cynics. Everything we say is undergirded by a clear set of committments.

The essays in this book also represent an attempt to increase people's discussion of *ideas*. Even when our writers are talking about particular events or people, they are also implicitly addressing broader themes. When David Kinder writes about Ruth Bader Ginsburg, he is not just writing about Ginsburg herself, but about the way in which celebrity and legal culture can function to distract people from injustices. When Alex Nichols writes about *Hamilton*, he is writing about the way that self-congratulatory celebrations of diversity can ultimately whitewash other kinds of systemic inequalities. When Yasmin Nair talks about Ziad Ahmed's hashtag-based college application, she is really talking about problems with both the contemporary university and the world of liberal activism. Even when our writers cover seemingly minor subjects, they are attempting to get people thinking about serious political questions.

I am proud of what we have accomplished so far with *Current Affairs*. Our team of writers, artists, and editors have produced an exceptional body of work during the short period of our magazine's existence. I am also incredibly grateful to our magazine's readers and subscribers, without whose support our publication (and this book) would have been impossible. Even though it is an unusually promising moment for left-wing media and political activism, everything depends on public support and involvement.

A lot of people I know feel a terrible sense of hopelessness and doom. I feel it myself, a lot of the time. And you'll find plenty of seemingly depressing and hopeless things over the course of this book—the first essay is about the ubiquity of slavery. But *Current Affairs* does not peddle hopelessness. We are a group of people who believe life can be fun, and that human problems can be solved. Nobody should turn away from the pain and violence that afflict so many parts of society. But nor should anyone give up. It's a moment of both crisis and possibility, and our little magazine will do its best to help people see it through.

SLAVERY IS EVERYWHERE

by Brianna Rennix & Oren Nimni

ALL HUMAN BEINGS ARE ENSLAVED, though some are more enslaved than others. Our typical binary distinction between freedom and slavery (I am either free, or I am enslaved; I cannot be enslaved but free, or free but enslaved) is false, for coercive conditions exist on a spectrum. At the extreme end of that spectrum is the typical scenario of slavery, the antebellum South with its whippings and overseers. But myriad other conditions bear striking similarities to this kind of slavery, even as they lack what we think of as its central features (auctions, manor houses, white-suited masters with sluggish drawls).

For example, say you were to take Highway 61 out of Baton Rouge, and head north toward the Mississippi border. If, after about 35 miles, you turned off into the country, you would soon find yourself at the Louisiana State Penitentiary, known informally as "Angola." There, you would notice something striking. You would see open fields, filled with cotton and other crops. And in these fields, you would see row after row of black men, young and old, tilling the fields and picking the cotton. It might seem like a scene from the 1850's. But then, as you looked closer, you would notice something else, something even more disquieting: these rows of black men were being watched over, overseen, by other men. Men with guns. And it would quickly become clear to you that if the men picking cotton decided they were tired of picking cotton, and began to pack up and wander off, these men with guns would have something quite emphatic to say about it.

The Angola prison facility began as a slave plantation, and little has changed about it since its earliest days.[1] Perhaps the only difference is that it has since installed a gift shop, where tourists can purchase T-shirts and koozies emblazoned with cheery confinement-themed slogans ("Angola: There's No Escapin' It" and "Angola: A Gated Community"). In all but the most superficial aspects, the facility is the same: black men in chains, working the fields from dawn to dusk, their every personal liberty surrendered, every wish granted solely at the discretion of the fat old white man who runs the place.

It's certainly very strange to see slavery so alive and well in a country so convinced it has abolished it. But for a nation of lawyers, Americans are startlingly oblivious to a gaping loophole in their formally codified rights: they've never actually prohibited slavery at all. That sounds like somewhat of a conspiratorial exaggeration, but it's indisputably the case. The 13th Amendment, the one that supposedly abolished slavery, reads as follows:

> *"Neither slavery nor involuntary servitude, except as a punishment for crime whereof the party shall have been duly convicted, shall exist within the United States, or any place subject to their jurisdiction."*

Did you notice the loophole? It's alright if you didn't; it seems to have passed the rest of the nation by for 150 years. But there it is: slavery is prohibited, *except...*

It's perfectly fine to enslave someone, then. The only condition is that it be punishment for a crime. The 13th Amendment therefore does not prohibit slavery; it doesn't even pretend to. What it does is offer a procedural guarantee that nobody will be enslaved without first undergoing a legal proceeding to determine whether they deserve it.

In practice, this does very little. After all, nearly anything can be made

SLAVERY IS EVERYWHERE   17

a crime; by some estimates, the average American commits three felonies per day without knowing it. And the State of Louisiana has taken full advantage of the 13th Amendment's useful little caveat; it officially sentences people to "years at hard labor" rather than "years in prison," and it often assigns people to decades of labor for even petty crimes like marijuana possession.

Now, fortunately, for most people, there is little risk of falling in the loophole and ending up enslaved. But this shouldn't be especially comforting; if we had been told in 1850 not to worry, because most people have no risk of ending up as slaves, this would be irrelevant to the moral horror of the institution.

The fact that for most people the risk of slavery is low, but the law sanctions it for others, turns rights into little more than a myth. The question of whether or not a person becomes enslaved depends on whether they stay on the correct side of the law, a law that is destined to be crafted far more by the powerful than the powerless (that is, after all what power means to begin with).

Indeed, in the years after the Civil War, white Southern elites figured out how to take full advantage of this opportunity. Frustrated by the prohibition on the buying and selling of human beings, they turned to the criminal law to obtain a continuing supply of cost-free black labor. As Douglas Blackmon documents in *Slavery By Another Name*, a system of "neoslavery" arose, in which being poor effectively became a crime, and since crime could be punished by enslavement, black people could be reenslaved.[2] It was a neat trick, almost effortless. The ease with which the South simply replaced slavery with Jim Crow is a cautionary tale for those who act as if the existence of legal procedural rights is a sufficient guarantor of social equality.

As a word and a concept, slavery is troublesome. It's etymologically arbitrary, deriving from the word "Slav," since a number of Slavic people were captured and enslaved during the Middle Ages. Slavery therefore does not have some kind of easy inherent connotation, the way that a word like "prisoner" might (from the Latin prensionem, "a taking," thus "one who is taken"). Of course, all words are arbitrary at their core, but some have more intelligible conceptual underpinnings than others, and "Slav"-ery doesn't do much to help us answer the question of what slavery *is*.

The 1926 International Slavery Convention defined slavery as "the status or condition of a person over whom any or all the powers attaching to the right of ownership are exercised,"[3] and most other definitions are similar; slavery is what happens when person becomes a commodity. But determining whether the "powers of the right of ownership" are being used is less clear than might initially be supposed. In legal theory, property is a kind of "bundle" of rights; the right to use something, the right to alienate (sell) it, the right to proceeds from it, and the right to destroy it. Now, a person can't sell me or destroy me, so he can't have the full rights of ownership, but people are given the right to use others all the time. Getting the right to use without the right to sell is called a lease; and people regularly lease land, cars, and people. A labor market is just a market for people-leases.

Focusing on slavery as a set of theoretical property rights constructions is therefore somewhat bizarre. It considers the types of legal rights the owner holds or exercises, rather than the person in question's actual experiences. Thus the same two experiences could be slavery or not, depending on how they arose. If we see a row of men doing back-breaking work picking cotton, whipped and beaten, working 12 hour days, they might be enslaved. But what if we learn that they're employees, that they've signed up for this since it's the only job in the area? Well, according to all the theories we're not dealing with slavery anymore, but it sure looks pretty similar.

That's one of the reasons the phrase "wage slavery" arose to describe industrial toil. By the people-as-property definition of slavery, it's an oxymoron; if everybody in the factory is being paid, nobody is being enslaved. But workers' rights campaigners used the term "wage slavery" to illustrate a crucial point: being given wages so pitiful you couldn't afford to move elsewhere meant that a wage system and a slave system could end up feeling exactly the same for the worker. Some even argued that wage-systems were worse; a capitalist who rented his labor could brutalize and destroy workers' bodies and simply replace them one they wore out, while a slaveowner had some incentive to protect his investment. Most people treat rental cars with less care than cars they own, thus leased wage-workers could be even more poorly treated than slaves in many cases. (Rather than justifying slavery, that fact indicts wage work.)

Because the boundaries of slavery are difficult to pinpoint, and people tend to associate it so strongly with the slave regime of the American South and the Transatlantic slave trade (far more than they think of Greek slaves, slaves in the Middle Ages, or, well, Slavs), many situations resembling slavery in "all but name" are ignored or treated as normal.

Yet if we honestly examine what sort of experiences constitute slavery or its equivalent, we find that the experience of brutal and effectively involuntary work, is everywhere. Slavery is invisibly present in the architecture of our lives. In fact, we are surrounded by innumerable symbols of slavery, cunningly-disguised, made anodyne by ubiquity and routine.

The experience of slavery is present in countless products we unthinkingly purchase, consume, and discard every day. These items were created or harvested, in whole or in part, by fellow human beings who have been conveniently hidden from our sight. Such workers are not paid a living wage. Their lives are devoid of the most basic necessities. They live under conditions of abject misery and fear. And so once we get ourselves out of the conceptual muddle, and look below the surface, we are faced with the disquieting reality that we are all actively participating in a slave economy: today, right now, this minute.

It's a simple enough matter to prove. Take, for example, your morning cup of coffee. If you drink an inexpensive brand like Folgers, your brew is a hodgepodge of beans from all over the world: there's no way to know exactly where they came from. So there's a good chance that some of your coffee came from the Ivory Coast, and that those beans were picked by children under the age of 15. These children were trafficked and made to work long hours, as many as eighty a week.[4] They groaned under the weight of loads so heavy that their burdens left them with open sores on their bodies. When their pace slackened, they were beaten with branches or bicycle chains.

If you source your coffee regionally, say from Honduras or Brazil, the story is a bit better, but not much.[5] [6] Many children quit school to work the fields, depressing wages for the entire workforce. If your coffee-picker is an adult, he or she still likely earns next to nothing, was forced to pay inflated prices for goods at the estate shop, and was then bound to the plantation by ever-mounting debts. The coffee industry, overflowing with the milk of human kindness, has performed a Cost-Benefit Analysis, but says that ensuring that child labor and forced labor are absent from their supply chains would be "onerous and especially costly to implement."[7]

"Alright, so coffee is slavery. I'll stick to tea." Ah, don't be so quick. Workers on tea plantations endeavor to live on about 17 cents a day.[8] Sex trafficking of tea pickers' children, with or without their parents' knowledge, is rampant, because parents cannot afford to feed and educate children on the wages they earn.[9] The pattern repeats across products in dozens of industries. There are similar stories behind your sweets, your clothes, your electronics. Nor is this confined to remote corners of the world: right here in the United States, slaves and child laborers are part of the labor force that picks the fruits and vegetables we eat every day.

All of this is the realm of the quasi-known. Everyone knows it, but they don't really know it, or they pretend not to know it so everyone can get on with life without feeling miserably, uselessly guilty. It is one of those things that seems better not to think too much about. Yet think about it we must, if we are not to be monsters.

Contemporary slavery comes in several varieties. Some occurs on a lucrative black market, while other forms are perfectly legal components of the economy. The old-fashioned kind of slavery, kidnapping people by force or trickery, who are then bonded into performing labor against their will—is common, and becoming more common every day. There are twice as many in this kind of enslavement today as there were during the entire 350 year duration of the transatlantic slave trade.[10] [11]

But there are legal horrors to match the illegal ones. Shockingly enough, for example, your American-grown blueberries may have been picked by an elementary- or middle school-aged child, who then had to go wearily to class and try to learn their multiplication tables. This is because, since 1938, using children for agricultural labor has been permitted by law, and the National Farmworker Ministry estimates that there are 500,000 agricultural workers under the age of 18.[12] In 2014, Human Rights Watch released a report on U.S. child tobacco farm workers, some of whom are as young as 11 and work full 10 or 12 hour days.[13] On the tobacco farms, many of these kids develop nicotine poisoning, experiencing "vomiting, nausea, headache, dizziness, skin rashes and burning eyes." Yet for migrant families struggling to survive on meager wages, sending a schoolchild to work for a local farmer may be the only way to stay afloat. If you thought child labor had disappeared from the United States, you haven't seen the agricultural sector.

And then there are countries like Bangladesh, where the main source of employment is the garment manufacturing industry, which pays about 14% of a living wage, and where factory working conditions are infamously unsafe.[14] (Should we be surprised that Bangladeshis comprise a significant percentage of the refugees fleeing to South Asia and Europe, as desperate for escape as if their country were irreparably ravaged by violence and war?)

There's a tendency to cast Bangladesh's story as the growing pains of economic development, or cast the U.S. story as a consequence of irregular immigration. Of course, one shouldn't downplay the complexity of the economic and logistical issues implicated by global trade, or large food systems. There may be some truth in saying that misery is a fact of human life, that we cannot simply will it away by disliking it. But let's be honest with ourselves: we all instinctively know that to harness the misery of humans in one part of the world to provide comfort and entertainment for humans in another part of the world is a perverse and inexcusable form of evil.

If the choice were available, no person on earth would voluntarily toil away all the years of their life, on starvation wages or worse, with no hope of improving their lot, manufacturing useless luxuries to be fleetingly enjoyed by others upon whom the accident of birth has bestowed greater fortune. That is injustice itself. To respond to exposés of worker exploitation with statements like, "Well, they'd be worse off if they weren't making our products" is to employ the logic of a slaver. It means shrugging and accepting obvious moral evils simply because they would be difficult to address, because altering the prevailing system will likely have complicated economic and political consequences. This is the kind of thinking that perpetuated the institution of slavery in this country throughout multiple centuries during which many people of both conscience and influence were fully aware that it was wrong. During those intervening years, thousands of human lives were trampled, degraded, mutilated, both spiritually and physically; and the ruination of those lives can never now be repaired. For those who believe that justice is not a mere category defined and circumscribed by our legal system, but is rather a holistic moral worldview that should inform all the decisions of our daily lives, it is impossible to accept a status quo that makes us all into the mirror image of an earlier generation of American elites: "masters who do not know how to free their slaves."

The prevailing wisdom in some circles is that the bad PR surrounding labor abuses can compel multinationals to voluntarily improve their standards; or that multinationals, which are major regional players in most developing economies, will self-regulate in increasingly a humane direction due to the growing popularity of the "corporate responsibility" ethos. Perhaps that's true. But this requires us to repose a large amount of trust in the personal goodness (or, at any rate, care for reputation) of company executives; and to trust also that this mindset will be handed down as a sacred charge to each new generation of managers. History should make us skeptical about the resilience of this sort of hereditary ethics. It would be preferable to have a somewhat more solid assurance than mere *noblesse oblige*.

On an individual level, the "conscientious objection" approach is ethical consumerism: to boycott companies that engage in unfair labor practices (including unpaid or minimally-compensated labor, use of child labor, bans on or retaliation against unionization, inadequate sanitation and safety standards, tolerance of sexual assault and harassment, and environmental destruction) and patronize companies that use good practices. But this is necessarily an approach with severe limitations. For starters, making ethically-informed choices can be extremely difficult due to the differences between the amount of information known by companies and by consumers, and the misleading or unverifiable nature of most "fair trade" labels. (Most companies claim themselves not to know what is happening on the contractor or sub-contractor levels of their supply chains, which may well be true, though it's hard to believe that they could not possibly bestir themselves to find out if they so chose.)

And while it's comparatively easy to be an ethical consumer of certain common food products, it's next to impossible when it comes to necessities such as clothing and (what is now effectively a necessity in modern society) technology. Ethically-produced garments are nearly impossible to find; ethically-produced electronics are entirely impossible. You can buy used items, but that's as close as you get. The "free market" approach is to buy the products that one wishes to see the market moved towards, but it's hard to move the market towards a product that doesn't exist.

Ethical consumerism is also something a middle- or upper-class gambit, because most ethical products are specialty products, difficult for low- and fixed-income people to afford. Companies like Wal-Mart have had great success with the reverse-Robin Hood approach, whereby, in charging rock-bottom prices for cheaply-manufactured goods, they rob the poor to feed the poor. And this is all to say nothing of the economic ravages and immediate hardship to vulnerable workers that would occur if all companies were to suddenly pull their operations wholesale from countries where exploitation is perceived to be "endemic."

But what of the law? Can it save us? Until very recently, the answer was a resounding no. The law was, as it usually is, a pretty pitiful guarantor of basic human liberties, and slave conditions have persisted for centuries with statutory blessing.

However, a modest new legal tool may now be at our disposal. This February, with very little fanfare, Congress passed, and President Obama signed into law, a bill with the potential to significantly impact the extent to which companies are held accountable for the presence of slave labor in their supply chains. Section 901 of the Trade Facilitation and Trade Enforcement Act, introduced by Republican Congressman Tom Reed and co-sponsored by seven other Republicans, mandates the "elimination of the consumptive demand exception to prohibition on importation of goods made with convict labor, forced labor, or indentured labor."

The "consumptive demand exception" refers to a provision of the 1930 Tariff Act that forbade the import of "all goods, wares, articles, and merchandise mined, produced or manufactured wholly or in part in any foreign country by convict labor and/or forced labor and/or indentured labor," except for those items "not mined, produced or manufactured in such quantities in the United States as to meet the consumptive demands of the United States."[15]

In other words: you couldn't import slave-made goods into the U.S. unless, you know, people really, really wanted to buy them. The exception rendered the Tariff Act's prohibition on slave-made goods effectively meaningless. It was an almost sublimely-constructed piece of self-negation: we don't import slave-made goods from abroad unless we don't have enough of such goods here; but almost by definition, the goods we import are the goods we don't already have.

Predictably, the law was rarely invoked. Many goods highly likely to contain slave labor in their supply chains—including coffee from the Ivory Coast, electronics manufactured in Malaysia, and garments woven from Uzbeki cotton—are regularly imported into the U.S. Theoretically, with the passage of the new law, the import of all such goods is completely prohibited. But many questions remain. How far down its supply chain does a company's obligation extend—all the way to the raw materials stage? What penalties will companies face for attempting to import slave-made goods? How will the enforcement effort be funded? Who will undertake the difficult, research-intensive work of supply chain investigation, which will be necessary to prove specific violations? As is so often the case, without public pressure, the law will likely be a dead letter.

But if people concerned about the eradication of slavery come together to demand an articulate legal framework and substantial funding for enforcement, we may finally see the penalties for slave labor allocated onto the actors who drive the market for prices, the actors who are best equipped to bear economic risk: large multinationals. The closing of the "consumptive demand" loophole, even if well-enforced, will admittedly not directly improve the lots of those workers whose dire situation does not meet the technical definition of "slavery." But you've got to start somewhere, and steady improvements to the laws should never be rejected even as they remain inadequate.

Slavery has actually been in the news quite a bit recently. It's come up repeatedly in debates over removal of the Confederate flag. At Harvard University, student activists successfully advocated to eliminate the title "house master" from residential dormitories,[16] and to remove a slaveowner's family crest from the Harvard Law School shield.[17] As national debates examine the role of race in our justice and our correctional systems, in our social structures, in housing and employment and education, the U.S. is confronting the ways that the underlying evil of slavery has metamorphosed and reappeared in many guises throughout the subsequent life of our nation.

But slavery does not just exist as the continuing reverberation of a tragic past, and by focusing on rooting out the symbolic and material consequences of historical slavery, we risk missing something quite important: the world is still full of actual, literal slaves. From the penitentiaries of Louisiana to the garment factories of Bangladesh to the coffee plantations of the Ivory Coast, slavery is ubiquitous but invisible. Faced with this disconcerting fact, each person must decide whether she is comfortable in continuing to passively participate, or whether she will accept the conclusion of our 19th century abolitionist predecessors: that one cannot coexist quietly alongside a slave system, and that it is one's basic moral duty to find every available means of eliminating slavery from the earth for good.

THE PATHOLOGIES OF PRIVILEGE

by Zach Wehrwein

LONG BEFORE HE FLED TO MEXICO sporting a hastily dyed goatee, Ethan Couch was already a deeply unsympathetic figure. One night in 2013, when he was 16 years old, Couch drunkenly plowed a truck into a group of people, killing four of them.[1] Hauled before a Texas judge, Couch offered one of the most notorious excuses for a brutal crime since "If the glove doesn't fit" or the "Twinkie defense": Couch's crime was caused by an ailment known as *affluenza*.

Affluenza, a disease not recognized by any of the prominent medical manuals, is a novelty portmanteau of the words "affluent" and "influenza," and refers to a phenomenon whereby rich children become so spoiled that they become incapable of restraining themselves from indulging their every impulse. As the psychologist testifying in Couch's defense explained, from the earliest days of his upbringing, Couch had been raised without limits. Couch's father, who owned a prosperous suburban roofing company, had let his son do precisely as he pleased. At the tender age of 13, Ethan was allowed to drive himself to school alone in his father's truck. When the principal of the Anderson Private School pointed out to the older Couch that this might be unwise, the father "threatened to buy the school."[2] Couch's mother was no less indulgent, reportedly supplying her son regularly with Vicodin.[3]

All of this, argued the psychologist, turned Couch into a creature incapable of understanding that people "should" or "shouldn't" do certain things, that there are acts, such as causing deadly accidents while driving drunk, that are considered "wrong." Indeed, witnesses at the scene of the crash reportedly heard Couch bragging to his passengers that he could get them out of any legal trouble, and the victims' families were shocked when he expressed no remorse whatsoever for killing four people.[4] Raised in an environment where none of his actions had ever brought him so much as a scolding, Couch must have been puzzled by the very idea that people would hold him responsible for causing the deaths.

And so when Couch was sentenced, the judge appeared to take the "affluenza" diagnosis into account, letting Ethan off with probation and a required stint in a rehab facility. Nationwide outrage ensued, with Couch's punishment being seen as absurdly light, and Couch himself becoming the poster boy for the rich, white, and privileged. The decision had been made, though, and Couch went free.

But Ethan Couch couldn't even satisfy the extremely generous terms of his probation; after two years, a video surfaced of Couch playing beer pong at a party. Faced with the possibility of serving a prison sentence for failing to comply with the requirement that he not drink, Couch then went on the lam. He and his mother fled to a resort town in Mexico, where he was finally caught after reportedly spending thousands of dollars at local strip clubs.[5] Three years after his crime, Couch finally faced the possibility of serious prison time.

It is tempting to see Ethan Couch as being emblematic of every inequality in the American justice system. Couch was the ultimate unaccountable brat, hurting people in whatever ways he pleases and then accepting no responsibility whatsoever. However we slice the thing, it is difficult to care about him.

In the language of progressivism, Couch seems like an extreme case of "white privilege." "Privilege" is a popular term referring to the "set of unearned benefits" that accrue to someone because of their membership in an advantaged group. If you're white, you're simply more likely to catch a break than if you're not. Many of us probably suspect that if Couch had been a poor black teenager, he would have been far less likely to receive a probationary sentence after killing four people.

The available evidence strongly suggests that this is indeed the case. By now, the horrifying statistics on black incarceration rates have long since ceased to actually horrify. A black man has somewhere between a 1 in 4 and 1 in 3 chance of being imprisoned in his lifetime, as compared with 1 in 17 for a white man,[6] and there are more black men under the custodial control of the state (including probation and parole) than were enslaved in 1850, with a total of nearly one million African Americans imprisoned.[7]

In criminal courtrooms, race is depressingly salient in sentencing decisions. The United States Sentencing Commission found that "prison sentences of black men were nearly 20% longer than those of white men for similar crimes."[8] While blacks are no more likely than whites to sell or use drugs (about 10% of both racial groups consumes illicit substances), blacks are 3.6 times more likely to be arrested.[9] In capital cases, the race of the victim and the race of the defendant are two of the most important variables predicting whether the death penalty will be imposed. Statistics like these cannot be explained away by differences in the rate at which people of different races commit crimes; the precise same level of criminality results in different levels of punishment.

But it's a mistake to just look at a single institution, like the criminal court system, in order to understand the continuing salience of race in American life. The heap of privileges that accrues based on skin color has a multitude of components, and the small instances of discrimination are pervasive. Researchers have found that a white job applicant who states he is a convicted felon is more likely to receive a callback for an interview than a black applicant with a clean record.[10] And black applicants from Ivy League schools are less likely to receive callbacks than white applicants from less socially prestigious institutions. Landlords, too, were much less likely to respond to African American applicants.[11]

Similar studies have shown race-based differences in how doctors judge the degree to which a patient is responsible for their health outcomes.[12] (If you're black, you're irresponsible. If you're white, you're helplessly afflicted.) Two political scientists even found that white state legislators were far less likely to respond to emails from black constituents (the finding applied to legislators in both major political parties).[13]

Looming over all the other disadvantages is wealth. Black Americans have lower median incomes than white Americans.[14] But the difference becomes far more extreme when we look at the wealth people hold rather than just the incomes they receive. According to the Pew Research Center, the median white family in the United States was about 13 times wealthier than the median black family in 2014.[15] A typical white family has over $100,000 in assets, while a typical black family has only $7,000.

The term "white privilege" is useful insofar as it captures the way the sum total of these differences creates a kind of "web" of disadvantage, in which being white just tends to make life much easier in a multitude of ways, both large and small. The theory does not say that for certain, without a doubt, in all circumstances that one's life is going to better of if one is a straight white male. There are homeless white veterans and phenomenally wealthy black women. There are white defendants that receive unfairly heavy sentences, and black defendants who receive leniency.

But the existence of exceptions doesn't disprove a tendency, and to be black in America means experiencing constant daily reminders that You Do Not Belong. It means being followed around and searched in your local deli even when you are one of the most recognizable world-renowned actors (as in the case of Forest Whitaker[16]). Or it means coming home from an academic conference celebrating your scholarly achievements, only to be suspected as a burglar and arrested on the doorstep of your own home (as happened to Harvard Professor Henry Louis Gates[17]). Ta-Nehisi Coates describes racism in modern America as a day-to-day experience of physical exhaustion that bores deep down into the soul. "White privilege" means being free from all of this.

Given the differential system of racial privileges, then, it is understandable that "white privilege" has taken on such resonance among progressives. Activist literature is full of exhortations to "check" one's privilege, and privilege itself is treated as a fundamentally unfair and unjust entitlement, a mechanism by which one race maintains its dominance over the others.

But in this respect, "privilege" has a serious drawback as a way of helpfully explaining the social world. Privilege, because it is the fount of racial injustice, becomes self-evidently bad, something that one should be against. To possess privilege is to participate in the reproduction of inequality. Yet many of the social assets classified as "white privilege" are actually good things, to which human beings ought to be entitled. That which is granted to white people as a "privilege" should not be treated as a "privilege" at all, but as part of the basic dignity of all human-to-human interaction and taken-for-granted courtesy.

Consider a recent article from "EverydayFeminism.com," a fairly typical exemplar of progressive discourse.[18] The author describes six indicators that one has "class privilege." These include: 1. Waking up well-rested. 2. Paying for a convenience (such as deciding to buy a coffee so as not to have to make it). 3. The ability to call in sick. 4. Having reliable transportation. 5. Being paid for all of the hours that one works. 6. Being able to buy healthy food.

The author is, of course, right that poor people can't be assured of these things, and that to have money confers an extraordinary amount of additional comfort and security in ways that often go unrecognized. But there is something disturbing about using the word "privilege" to describe something as basic as getting a good night's sleep. Being well-rested seems like something that all human beings ought to deserve as a right. By classifying something as basic as "not having one's wages stolen by one's employer" as a "privilege" instead of a right, one erodes the degree to which such a guarantee should be universally expected by all.

Take the Ethan Couch case. Couch's "lenient" sentence was met with outrage, because he was given rehab and probation after causing four deaths. This was seen as a clear case of privilege. And indeed it was, insofar as Couch would have been less likely to get such a sentence if he had not been of such a moneyed background and such a marshmallowy complexion. But hatred of Couch easily blurs the difference between "his sentence was unfair because he received it on account of his race" and "his sentence was unfair because it was too lenient." In fact, the sentence Couch received was perfectly fair. Couch was a teenager who had driven drunk. There were horrendous consequences to his irresponsibility, but Couch killed people negligently rather than premeditatedly. Sending him to rehab, and then giving him a full decade of probation (during which time any offense would result in his imprisonment), seems an entirely appropriate punishment for someone whose actions were grossly reckless rather than actually malicious.

Couch's punishment *was* an injustice, of course. But it was an injustice because only Couch and people like him get the benefit of leniency, not because leniency is itself inappropriate. It is not unfair that Ethan Couch was given probation, it is unfair that Ethan Couch's black counterpart would likely have been sentenced to spend half his life in a cage.

The same was true in several other recent cases of "white privilege" in the criminal justice system. Last June, after a 22-year-old white supremacist murdered nine black parishioners at the Emanuel African Methodist Episcopal Church in Charleston, he was treated with courtesy by arresting officers. When transporting the shooter to the station, police placed him in a bulletproof vest (in case he was attacked).[19] Then, and most controversially, police bought him a hamburger from Burger King, because he had not eaten.[20]

The police's treatment of the Charleston shooter was instantly taken as a case of "white privilege." If the shooter had been black, ran the criticism, he would have been slammed against the police car and tossed into the backseat like a sack of mulch. If the shooter's black equivalent had asked for a bulletproof vest and a hamburger, officers would have laughed in his face, and possibly administered a beating.

All of that was true. But it's also the case that criminal defendants deserve to be treated as the Charleston shooter was. If they haven't eaten, somebody should bring them some food. A humane country feeds its prisoners. If they could be in danger because their crime was high-profile, measures should be taken to protect them. In the Charleston case, the injustice committed was not the granting of a hamburger to one individual, but the denial of hamburgers to others.

It can be hard to admit this. The Charleston AME shooting was so horrendous, and the defendant such a monstrous and hateful individual, that it is easy to feel rage upon thinking of him munching on a Whopper compliments of the Charleston Police Department. Imagining him smugly devouring it, one cannot help but want to knock it out of his hand and pummel him to a crimson pulp. These are understandable instincts. But they are also our worst instincts; it is our least rational self that fantasizes about vengeance. And to be scandalized by injustices against black defendants does not mean one should wish it on white defendants instead.

That concerning tendency became very clear in a recent case involving a Stanford University athlete, who was witnessed raping an unconscious woman. The athlete, Brock Turner, was given a six-month sentence (plus probation) and required to register as a sex offender. Prosecutors had asked for Turner to receive six years in prison, but the judge, Aaron Persky (himself a former Stanford lacrosse player[21]), rejected the recommendation.

When Turner's victim released a harrowing statement describing the assault, and Turner's lack of remorse, the case became a nationwide scandal.[22] An effort was launched to recall Judge Persky for his "undue leniency."[23] Turner became the latest poster boy for "white privilege," an individual who believes himself free to violate and dominate whomever he pleases without having to fear any major consequence. Turner's father was derided for his alarming statement that Turner was having his life ruined over "20 minutes of action" and for remarking that prison would have a "severe impact" on Turner.[24]

But while the Turner case certainly illuminated the existence of "white privilege," it also demonstrated some limits of the "privilege" framework. Those scandalized by Turner's sentence were progressives, but they began voicing sentiments somewhat contrary to the ordinary progressive position on punishment. After all, it is typically rare for those on the left to (1) advocate recalling judges for being too lenient (2) mock the idea that prison has a severely negative impact on defendants and (3) demand more prison time. Very few of those who condemned the judge, and supported Turner's victim, said explicitly how much prison time they wished Turner had been given. But it was an odd position for people on the left to put themselves in. After all, prisons themselves are dens of rape and abuse. To advocate that a young person be sent to prison, no matter how privileged that person may be, is to advocate something that should be meted out only sparingly and with extreme restraint, if at all.

Critiques of white privilege can therefore slip into the very callousness that we are attempting to critique in the first place. If white people are perceived to experience "undeserved" advantage, then creating a world of just deserts will involve removing those advantages. But if those "advantages" are necessities rather than luxuries, we may bizarrely find ourselves advocating to take away things we support. If only white people get fair criminal procedure, with a presumption of innocence, we could remove white privilege by giving everyone an extremely unfair system, but it's hard to believe we would have successfully increased the amount of justice in the world.

In June of 2016, at a Disney resort in Orlando, a small child was killed by an alligator.[25] The boy had been splashing about in the water at the edge of a manmade Disney lagoon (though there were signs warning against swimming), before being snapped up and carried of. The alligator death was a national news story; it was devastating to imagine the pain of the boy's parents, their inevitable trauma and grief and guilt. But one internet commentator put things differently, saying: "I'm so finished with white men's entitlement lately that I'm really not sad about a two-year-old being eaten by a gator because his daddy ignored signs."[26]

That heartless sentiment was only expressed by a select few online. But it shows the moral reasoning toward which "white privilege" analysis can lead, if it is not combined with empathy and a belief in people's common humanity. The Disney toddler's parents would surely trade every last scrap of their racial advantage for another moment with their son; white privilege offers small comfort when your child is being eaten by an alligator.

While "white privilege" is an important concept, then, it can have terrible pitfalls. It can lead to a belief that whiteness versus non-whiteness is the end-all determination of the human experience. At the extreme end, it can let us believe that grief itself can somehow be mitigated by privilege. But the benefits of privilege, as the alligator case shows, are limited. Often, privilege just means getting something, like a good education, that should be guaranteed.

The problem with privilege is not that it is an undue luxury, then. It is that all do not share in it equally. A failure to recognize that causes a doomed political strategy; it results in critiquing those who have privilege rather than granting it to those who do not. That means dragging entitled people down rather than lifting non-entitled people up; it's a bit like responding to the racial disparity in death penalty sentences by resolving to kill more white people rather than to kill fewer black people.[27] Indeed, that's not as absurd as it sounds: Bill Clinton once professed himself very concerned by the racial differences in federal cocaine sentences (majority-African American crack users are more harshly punished than majority-white powder cocaine users), only to later announce that he supported raising powder sentences rather than decreasing sentences for crack.[28] You can always fix inequality by making everyone equally miserable.

Certainly, some kinds of privilege are more "zero-sum." A number of "privileges" operate like positions in a queue, where if I am near the front, you are necessarily near the back and vice versa. If I have $100,000 and you have $7,000, the only way to address my privilege may be to redistribute some wealth from me to you. But for those things, like fair criminal procedure, that can easily be given to all equally, "white privilege" matters less than black disadvantage.

Racial inequalities are pervasive in the United States, and take the form of both micro-level miseries and massive structural obstacles to economic and physical security. But privilege itself is a better thing than is traditionally supposed; everyone deserves privilege in abundance. The question is not how privilege can be eliminated, but how it can be democratized.

THE NECESSITY OF POLITICAL VULGARITY

by Amber A'Lee Frost

MANY WERE SURPRISED TO SEE the notoriously centrist *Vox.com* run a glowing profile of a revolutionary socialist quarterly. In leftist circles *Vox* is generally derided for its bland liberal politics, so when it published a lengthy examination of the popular socialist magazine *Jacobin*, a hatchet job seemed more likely. But astonishingly enough, *Vox* covered *Jacobin* fairly, even generously, in a piece flatteringly titled "Inside *Jacobin*: how a socialist magazine is winning the left's war of ideas."[1]

For a publication inherently antagonistic to capitalism, *Jacobin* felt downright reasonable to *Vox* writer Dylan Matthews. Matthews described it as the "leading intellectual voice of the American left, the most vibrant and relevant socialist publication in a very long time," leaving one to wonder how *Jacobin*'s frequent allusions to violent revolution sat so comfortably with such proudly pragmatist liberals.

One answer is that, however radical *Jacobin*'s political program may be, the magazine is committed to maintaining civility and sobriety in its tone. As Matthews explained:

> *The long-term goal might be a revolutionary working class, but for now [Jacobin publisher Bhaskar Sunkara] is most passionate about trying to get more uniques than the New Republic or*

FiveThirtyEight. He has little patience for left-of-center writers who go out of their way to make enemies, saying of Gawker, "It's less mean and snarky than it used to be. I don't like that kind of mean internet humor. ... Being mean as a way to fight the power is kind of ridiculous."

"Being mean" is an interesting aversion for an impertinently revolutionary magazine that sells posters of guillotines and regularly invokes the specter of Soviet communism. Are not guillotines a bit—dare I say—"mean?"

What Sunkara is talking about here is much more specific than "mean," a rather vague word that he pairs with "snarky" (behead the kings of course, but don't dare snark against them!). What he is *actually* talking about is vulgarity, the crass, ugly dispensation of judgment with little to no regard for propriety. Vulgarity is the rejection of the norms of civilized discourse; to be vulgar is to flout the set of implicit conventions that create our social decorum. The vulgar person uses swears and shouts where reasoned discourse is called for. Someone like Saul Alinsky for example, might be considered vulgar, for considering protest tactics like his famously unrealized "fart-in" at the Rochester Philharmonic. (One might question the efficacy of a flatulent protest during a symphony, but it is certainly the sort of vulgarity that cannot be ignored.)

It is understandable for a magazine aspiring to respectability to eschew vulgarity in its pages. To poach the *New Republic*'s readers may require poaching the *New Republic*'s restraint in tone, and one does not impress *Vox* by childishly taunting the bourgeoisie.

Yet to dismiss vulgarity as a tool for fighting the powerful, to say that being mean is "ridiculous," is to deny history, and to obscure a long and noble tradition of malicious political japery. In fact, "being mean" not only affords unique pleasures to the speaker or writer, but is a crucial rhetorical weapon of the politically excluded.

Vulgarity has always been employed in revolutionary rhetoric, perhaps most notably in the propaganda leading up to *Jacobin*'s own beloved French Revolution. Forget snark, the pamphleteers of France were all too happy to satirize and smear the upper class with the utmost malice. Clergy, royals, and anyone else in power were slandered and depicted visually in all manner of crass and farcical political cartoons.

Of all the public figures subjected to such vicious derision and gossip (often highly inaccurate gossip at that), Marie Antoinette was singled out for especially inventive and vicious taunting.[2] True to French tradition, the slanderous pamphlets, called *libelles*, were fond of wordplay. For the Austrian-born Antoinette, they coined *Austrichienne*, meaning "Austrian bitch," but also resembling the French word for "ostrich." Thus, layering a visual pun upon a verbal one, one artist actually portrayed Antoinette stroking a massive, ostrich-like penis, complete with legs and a saddle. Mounted upon the penile steed was progressive royalist Marquis de Lafayette, who sympathized with the peasants but was eventually denounced as a traitor by Robespierre (revolutionaries tend not to be terribly fond of diplomatic fence-straddlers). In another of the ostrich-themed cartoons (it was evidently a series), Marie actually bared her own genitals to the phallic beast and its rider. It's a stunningly vulgar image, and without a doubt, quite nasty and mean. One couldn't imagine a Beltway professional depicting the ruling class so crudely today; even the most offensive of right-wing political cartoonists haven't yet dared to explore the satirical possibilities for giant ostrich-dicks.

There was also no requirement that a piece of anti-royal propaganda be clever or punny in order to be published. Quite a few of the cartoons regarding Marie were the sort of pure tabloid sensationalism that would make *Gawker* blush. Likely owing to the rumor that the King suffered from sexual dysfunction, leaving his wife to wild bouts of promiscuity, Antoinette was often *in flagrante delicto*—sometimes with Lafayette, sometimes the king's brother—the Count of Artois, and sometimes even with different ladies of the court and her close female friends. These pornographic little pamphlets showed various stages of undress, ranging from a hand up the skirt to full nudity and sexual contact. Cartoonists enjoyed drawing Marie in orgies with both men and women, and the King's own sad and scandalized penis often made an appearance.

The line between farce and rumor was often blurred by the flip ambi-

guity of the *libelles*. It can be difficult to discern today what was speculation and what was just a joke, but some of it was clearly very elaborate
parody.

Take the 1789 *libelle, L'Autrichienne en Goguettes ou l'Orgie Royale* (that's
The Austrian Bitch and her Friends in the Royal Orgy), which is written as
a play. In this ribald little piece of fan-fiction, Louis XIV's brother has
cuckolded the impotent king and sired the royal heirs himself:

Characters:
Louis XVI
The Queen
The Count of Artois
The Duchess of Polignac
Bodyguards

The action takes place in the apartments.

GUARD: To arms, there comes Her Majesty.

ANOTHER GUARD: There will be an orgy tonight. The female
Ganimede is with the Queen.

ANOTHER GUARD: Artois, the beloved one, there he is between
vice and virtue. Guess who the vice is.

GUARD: You do not need to guess. I can only see that this God
is multiplying.

Scene II

THE QUEEN (*to Madame de Polignac, who steps aside to let the
Queen go*): Come, come in my good friend.

THE COUNT OF ARTOIS (*slightly pushing the Queen and pinch-
ing her buttocks*): Come in too. What a nice bottom! So firm!

THE QUEEN (*whispering*): If my heart was as hard, wouldn't we
be good together?

THE COUNT OF ARTOIS: Be quiet you crazy woman, or else my

brother will have another son tonight.

THE QUEEN: Oh no! Let's have some pleasure, but no more fruits.

THE COUNT OF ARTOIS: All right. I will be careful, if I can.

MADAME DE POLIGNAC: Where is the King?

THE QUEEN: What do you worry about? Soon he will be here to annoy us.

Charming, no?

It's important to note that *libelles* like these were highly illegal—just as illegal as the writings of Voltaire or Rousseau, or any explicitly political tract deemed guilty of "heresy, sedition or personal libel"—and that they were sold right alongside their more serious-minded counterparts (under the counter, of course). Illegal pamphlets had to be printed outside the country, producing dozens of printing presses just outside French borders. Hundreds of agents smuggled pamphlets through a secret network to reach the tabloid-hungry French masses. In order to stem the tide of banned pamphlets about Marie Antoinette in particular, the French government actually sent spies to England to buy up the entire stock before they could make it France. It's therefore not particularly difficult to argue (as many historians do) for a causal relationship between nasty political porn and the revolution that followed, especially when the pamphlets posed such a risk to produce and obtain.

Historian Robert Darnton noted in *The Forbidden Best-Sellers of Pre-Revolutionary France*, his fascinating book on the illegal pamphlets and their illicit circulation, that primary documents indicate that booksellers themselves did not distinguish between the intellectual and the prurient, saying, "We consider [Rousseau's] *Du Contrat Social* political theory and *Histoire de Dom B* pornography, perhaps even as something too crude to be considered literature. But the bookmen of the eighteenth century lumped them together as 'philosophical books.'"[3]

So if nasty little *libelles* weren't that much of a threat to power, why suppress them and punish possession with imprisonment as you would revolutionary philosophy? And for that matter, why would a French citizen risk their freedom for a cartoon of Marie Antoinette enjoying an orgy if there wasn't something satisfyingly transgressive in the insolent and forbidden consumption of vulgarity?

Historian Lynn Hunt, author of both *Politics, Culture, and Class in the French Revolution*, and *The Family Romance of the French Revolution*, also holds hard and fast to the significance of meanness and vulgarity in a revolutionary context, saying of the *libelles*, "There's a disagreement about this among historians, but I have argued and others have argued that this was a part undermining the aura of the monarchy and making it easier in the end to arrest the king and execute him—and especially to execute the queen."

One lesson of the French Revolution, then, is that rudeness can be extremely politically useful. There are arguments to be made over who constitutes a valid target, but when crude obscenity is directed at figures of power, their prestige can be tarnished, even in the eyes of the most reverent of subjects. Caricature is designed to exaggerate, and therefore make more noticeable, people's central defining qualities, and can thus be illuminating even at its most indelicate.

And evidence abounds for the galvanizing power of vulgarity in our own time—just look at the appeal of Donald Trump. Trump successfully undermined opponents through the use of innuendos and crudities, and has turned the political process upside-down by gleefully undermining its dignity.

Of course Trump's willingness to be disgusting has been alienating to those who like their politics to come with a sheen of respectability. He so revolted the punctilious and proper conservatives at the *National Review* that he inspired an entire "Against Trump" issue of the magazine. His braggadocio and dick jokes appall the traditional right; he would have made William F. Buckley's eyes bulge (although what didn't?) and he gives Peggy Noonan a traumatic case of the vapors.

But Trump's vulgarity is appealing precisely because it exposes political truths. As others have noted, Trump's policies (wildly inconsistent though they may be) are actually no more extreme than those of other

Republicans; Trump is just willing to strip away the pretense. Other candidates may say "national security is a fundamental priority," whereas Trump will opt for "ban all the Muslims." The latter is far less diplomatic, but in practice the two candidates fundamentally mean the same thing. We should prefer the honest boor, as polite euphemism is constantly used to mask atrocities.

This candor is also the fundamental reason why Old Money types have always detested the *arrivistes*. The *nouveau riche* with their gaudy tastes, their leopardskin carpets and solid gold bathroom fixtures, upset the balance of things by giving the game away. They make wealth look like something nasty and indefensible. Douchebags in Lamborghinis fundamentally undermine the self-conception of the upper classes, which is that they are the appointed stewards of taste and judgment against the vast uncultured hordes. But since the rich of all flavors are a monstrosity and a cancer, it's the flashy, obnoxious kind of wealth that we should hope for, the kind that tells no lies and is more obviously despicable. Civility is destructive because it perpetuates falsehoods, while vulgarity can keep us honest.

In fact, there are times when political vulgarity is not just useful, but vital to convey the passion of messaging. In 1968, a 19-year-old anti-Vietnam protester was arrested in a courthouse for wearing a jacket with the words "Fuck the Draft," leading to a major Supreme Court decision protecting freedom of speech. In 1988, N.W. A. released "Fuck tha Police," a song that instantly became notorious for the bluntness of its confrontational, profanity-laden lyrics.

In both cases, the vulgarity was an unmistakably clear response to political circumstances. The Vietnam war was a moral obscenity of the highest order; there was no polite way of expressing the appropriate depth of revulsion. N.W.A. were saying what every black person had wanted to say for a long time, in the only words strong enough to even begin to communicate the truth. The depravity of the atrocious acts committed by the powerful far exceed the depravity of any swear words one could use to describe those acts. The death and brutality of Vietnam didn't just deserve an f-word or two, but warranted every last curse that could be spoken by the human tongue. And as the 18th-century French knew, monarchy is the real barbarity; it was the *libellistes* who were the true allies of the Enlightenment.

To maintain its potency, vulgarity should certainly be the exception rather than the rule. And there will always be *Jacobin* and its kin for the more genteel set. But there are certain people to whom one must be mean, certain circumstances in which one must be crude. A politically effective propriety means knowing when to use one's manners, and when to tell an ostrich-themed dick joke.

And of course, vulgarity isn't inherently subversive. Even when politicized its effects are often mild and mostly cathartic. When anonymous Twitter trolls deluge establishment journalists with *bon mots* like "I will eat your ass like McRib," it may not be particularly revolutionary. But it is not at all unprecedented; it's not even particularly shocking if you know a little history.

The left will always need its journals and polemic and academic writing, but there are times when it is both right and proper to terrify the bourgeoisie with your own feralness. Reclaiming vulgarity from the Trumps of the world is imperative because if we do not embrace the profane now and again, we will find ourselves handicapped by our own civility. Vulgarity is the language of the people, and so it should be among the grammars of the left, just as it has been historically, to wield righteously against the corrupt and the powerful. We cannot cede vulgarity to the vulgarians; collegial intellectuals will always be niche, but class war need not be.

WHAT DOES FREE SPEECH REQUIRE?

by Eli Massey

LET'S MAKE ONE THING CLEAR RIGHT AWAY: attempts to suppress free speech come from all political camps. The United States has a long and sordid history of attacks on expression, traceable back to John Adams.[1] Wherever there is politics, there are attempts to keep the other side from talking. As the late journalist Phil Kerby used to memorably quip, "censorship is the strongest drive in human nature; sex is a weak second."

In the 21st century, outright government censorship has at least somewhat abated. While you might still land in jail for exposing a war crime or filming a factory farm, American dissent is generally flourishing.[2] Political speech is more delightfully vulgar and hostile than ever, and almost nobody fears prosecution for what they say on their podcast, blog, video blog, or vodcast.

If there is any impending free speech threat to worry about, it probably comes from the unhinged occupant of the White House. Donald Trump, after all, hates the press. He wanted to "open up our libel laws" in order to make it easier to bring lawsuits.[3] He has pondered aloud on Twitter whether individuals who burn the American flag should be imprisoned or have their citizenship revoked.[4] He has also indicated he'll investigate and prosecute leakers at least as aggressively as President

Obama.[5] Journalists writing critical stories about Trump have been told they will have their "lives messed up."[6] And with Trump having inherited a powerful apparatus for surveillance and violence,[7] the country is now counting on his somehow turning out to be a person of good judgment with a sense of inner restraint.

But the country's most visible (as opposed to most consequential) contemporary free speech controversy concerns the actions of left-wing activists on college campuses. In particular, there was considerable anguish over the college tour of—now former—*Breitbart* "tech editor" Milo Yiannopoulos. (It had long been unclear what he actually edited, or what he knew about technology.) Activists on the left tried to have Yiannopoulos's events canceled for promoting hate speech, while conservatives treated the left's response as proof that conservative thought is suppressed on college campuses. At Berkeley, Yiannopoulos was instructed by the police to flee the campus for his own safety when a group of masked anarchists disrupted the peaceful protests outside, setting a large fire and pepper spraying a female attendee.[8]

Debates over free speech are often messy and confused, in part because nobody believes the right is unlimited, yet everybody has a self-interested conception of where that limit is. Should Nazis get to speak on campus, and if they shouldn't, who should get to determine who the Nazis are? Should anti-Semites get to book an open access meeting space?[9] Does the principle of free speech only apply to government repression, or can private acts threaten free speech as well? If powerful corporations like Twitter are the new gatekeepers to the public square, do their decisions affect speech rights? To what extent does having the right to speak necessitate having the capacity to speak? (E.g. if you can speak freely, but you get punched in the face every time you do, is your right meaningful?) What about the fact that the amount of speech you get depends on the amount of money you have? Nobody should think the answers to these questions are easy.

There is also a great deal of hypocrisy and selectivity in outrage over violations of the right of expression. The right-wingers who profess to be so sincerely concerned with free speech only care when it is conservative views that are targeted. On university campuses, criticism of Israel has been stifled for years with frightening zeal.[10] Fordham University, in a blatant case of censorship, recently banned the university's chapter of Students for Justice in Palestine on the grounds that the organization's "sole purpose is advocating political goals of a specific group" which would be too "polarizing."[11]

Nor is censorship from the right limited to college campuses. As part of a competition, a painting by a high schooler—depicting Black Lives Matter protesters being confronted by animals donning police uniforms—was hung in the U.S. Capitol. The painting was taken down repeatedly by Congressional Republicans, who described their actions as a protest against an "offensive" and disrespectful representation of police.[12] [13] The ever-consistent and freedom-loving *Breitbart* sided with the censors, condemning those who were "using the Constitution as an excuse to spread hate."[14] Which side was supposed to have the delicate and easily offended sensibilities again?

At the same time, it's also true that for a substantial portion of the left, the concept of free speech *has* lost a lot of currency. At least some censorship of people whose values we oppose has come to be viewed as acceptable, ethical, and necessary. For decades much of the left has supported the expansion and broadening of prohibitive speech codes at universities.[15] Outside the classroom, people like Catharine MacKinnon lobbied forcefully for legislation that suppressed objectionable materials. Speakers like *Daily Wire* editor and attempted novelist Ben Shapiro have been banned from speaking on campus universities. (In at least one case, university police literally threatened Shapiro with arrest if he entered the university building to attend an event, let alone deliver his lecture.[16] Since when is allying, in effect, with police to achieve our goals consistent with leftist values?) Now, every couple of weeks there's another story of an individual being prevented from speaking at a college campus.[17] [18] [19] If speakers aren't disinvited outright, community members and students protest and disrupt these events, making it impossible for the speaker to proceed.[20]

The arguments that are made for these practices are straightforward:

free speech doesn't mean the freedom to issue hate speech. Free speech doesn't guarantee one a platform. And free speech doesn't mean speech is free of consequences.

All of which may be true, depending on what one means by "consequences," "platform," and "hate speech." But leftists making arguments for why speakers should be disinvited from schools should recognize that every argument they make will soon come back to haunt them. If we continue to advance an agenda that privileges our particular worldview over universal free speech, it won't be long before our own tactics are turned on us as a cudgel. (The last words you may hear as the fascists pummel you to death are: "freedom of speech doesn't mean that speech has no consequences.")

Indeed, we have already seen the use of anti-hate principles of speech suppression against the left. In March of this past year, the University of California Board of Regents, in an overly broad statement of principles, lumped anti-Semitism with anti-Zionism. Both of these, they said, "have no place at the University of California..." They further noted that anti-Zionism "often is" linked to bigotry against Jews. (Facing an outpouring of criticism, the Regents later removed the blanket condemnation of anti-Zionism from their statement.)

Now someone on the left can draw a distinction here: Milo Yiannopoulos, one might insist, is clearly spreading hate speech while a BLM activist or a speaker discussing Palestine clearly is not. But it's nearly impossible to define "hate speech" narrowly and specifically enough to prevent leftist speech from also being caught up in the web. And even if "hate speech" *could* be defined in a sufficiently narrow and specific fashion, any prohibition empowers someone to act in the role of censor.

Time and again, in universities around the country, we have seen signs of how a failure to support a pro-speech culture can harm the left.[21] A year before the University of California debacle, rapper/actor Common was disinvited from Kean University's commencement ceremony after the law enforcement community complained about his song in which Assata Shakur is portrayed sympathetically. Only months before this, a petition was circulated at Texas Tech that attempted to prevent Angela

Davis from speaking. Around the same time, Bill Ayers was subject to a similar attempt by students at Dickinson School of Law. The need to protect the freedom of students to invite whomever they please is therefore crucial, because it protects *our* speakers. Freedom for all means freedom for leftist student groups, a right they absolutely need.

At the same time, Milo Yiannopoulos presented an unusual case. It's particularly understandable why leftists wanted to see his events canceled in particular. Yiannopoulos was no ordinary conservative ideologue. He was often called a "provocateur," but this whitewashes the content of his talks. At them, Yiannopoulos regularly called people "cunts" and "retards." To a Muslim woman who spoke up against him during an event, he replied: "You're wearing a hijab in the United States of America, what is wrong with you?"[22] He gave his audience the phone number for Immigration and Customs Enforcement, encouraging people turn in suspected unauthorized immigrants and "purge your local illegals."[23] Displaying the photograph of a transgender student at the University of Wisconsin, Yiannopoulos said: "I've known some passing trannies in my life... The way that you know he's failing is I'd almost still bang him... It's just a man in a dress, isn't it?"[24] The student in question, who was present in the audience, professed herself to have been terrified and humiliated, writing: "Do you know what it's like to be in a room full of people who are laughing at you as if you're some sort of perverted freak?"[25] Afterward, she "broke down sobbing uncontrollably."

Those who think that calling on universities to cancel these events is simply "suppressing conservative ideas" have a strange notion of what "ideas" are. They are also implicitly conceding that conservative intellectual discourse consists of calling people "cunts" and giving lectures on how feminists are ugly.[26] (By the way, this is what Simon & Schuster were willing to pay $250,000 for.[27])

It's very important not to sanitize Yiannopoulos's conduct if one argues the events should proceed. Yet many liberals, while acknowledging Yiannopoulous as "inflammatory" or "provocative," ended up failing to fully convey the reality. For example, a recent *Huffington Post* column suggested that while you could *disagree* with Yiannopoulos, this was no reason to keep him away from campus:

> *"Milo is not an oppressor, he's a messenger. I don't agree with every aspect of his message... [But] it's important for people from different sides of the isle [sic] to listen to one another...When you listen and engage in a respectful dialogue about your differences, that's called making an argument; something many liberals, the regressives, are forgetting how to do."* [28]

This goes too far in affirming the myth that Yiannopoulos was doing anything close to "respectful dialogue." Actually, what he was doing was extremely clever. His lectures combined dirty jokes, intentionally cruel or bigoted statements, and serious speechifying from a fairly conventional right-wing perspective. The vicious and bullying remarks, such as talking about whether he would bang a particular student, are what made left-wing activists so angry. *Then* when the activists respond as anyone could be expected to, he declared that his true passion was the open exchange of serious ideas, and the rest was just entertainment.

That means that left-wing activists who spent energy opposing Yiannopoulos, instead of ignoring him, fell straight into a trap. He intentionally baited them, and they played right along. After the Berkeley incident, Yiannopoulos's book sales went up by 12,740%. [29] Note what this means: it means that anyone who wishes to stop people like Yiannopoulos from "spreading hate" should *oppose* shutting down their events. Those who claim to be "fighting fascism" by disrupting conservativer talks are doing nothing of the kind. They are directly causing the ideas they hate to become more and more popular, by handing the right an incredible gift. (In the case of Yiannopoulos, they were also fixing their attention on someone who didn't really matter terribly much. It's understandably hard to resist paying attention to a British man in a feather boa shouting about hijabs. But it's not where the true source of political power in this country lies.)

Thus one can make an argument against shutting down Yiannopoulos's events while still acknowledging just how reprehensible some of his "ideas" truly are. When leftists tried to stop Yiannopoulos by force, they ended up allowing him to further the impression that he cares about discourse. It's *only* if people heard what he has to say that they would be able to realize how false this is.

In another context, leftists seem to understand the point that you can't stop the spread of an ideology by trying to smother it. This is precisely the argument made for why a "War on Terror" can never succeed: one can't bomb an ideology; one can only bomb people. We realize that waging war can actually help to spread the fundamentalism that the United States ostensibly seeks to extinguish. Yet we don't recognize that the same can be said of the left's efforts to stifle hateful rhetoric.

It is sometimes claimed that the words of an individual like Milo Yiannopoulos *incite* hatred, contributing to a campus climate where marginalized students already feel, and are in fact, unsafe. That may be true. Nevertheless, it remains true that preventing him from speaking incites *even more hatred*. It's unclear how stopping the event, risking arrest, potentially escalating the violence, turning the individuals who invited Yiannopoulos to speak into a besieged and victimized minority, and further angering an auditorium of people—some of whom were likely attending because they were merely curious—makes anyone any safer. But it certainly makes a lot of people more interested in finding out what Yiannopoulos has to say.

Some on the left have insisted that not just protest, but outright violence, is both a justified and useful way to deal with Yiannopoulos. In a recent article in *Left Voice*, Hart Eagleburger and Jack Rusk issue a rousing call to fighting fascists and racists like Yiannopoulos in America.[30] While they admit they don't believe "that the United States is fascist or descending into fascism" Eagleburger and Rusk make clear that "fascists must be stopped. They must be stopped at all costs. And this includes confronting them violently in the streets..." If they *aren't* violently confronted, the consequences are clear: "the right is empowered, the left is disheartened, and bystanders—including, importantly, vulnerable oppressed groups— become convinced the far-left does not offer them a dependable protection against fascists." It's therefore violence or defeat.

This seems worse than useless. Any battle of force against the American right will end up badly for the left, who tend not to have the guns. As Noam Chomsky observed after the recent punching of a neo-Nazi[31]: "When we move to the arena of violence, the most brutal guys win—and that's not us."[32] Indeed, the most vicious attack during Yiannopoulos's entire tour came from one of his supporters, who shot a demonstrator in the abdomen.[33] [34] (A fact that Yiannopoulos and the right prefer not to discuss.) For leftists, there is simply no alternative to fighting on the terrain of words and thoughts rather than physical force.

Many on the left are understandably skeptical of the power of reasoned discourse and persuasion. But that's partially because we don't really do them very well. Yiannopoulos is an incredibly charismatic speaker, a person who even left-wing feminist writer Laurie Penny conceded was "a charming devil."[35] He succeeds at winning converts entirely through his (sometimes hideous, sometimes beguiling) speech. Our side needs to understand how people are persuaded towards ideas using language, and counter it not just with "facts" and "decency" but with equally persuasive rhetoric and charm. It's essential to fight horrible speech with better and more powerful speech.

A certain school of thought says that to allow a reprehensible person to speak at a prestigious venue is to confer "legitimacy" on them. But legitimacy is not a particularly useful concept. The fact is that when things are popular, they automatically become "legitimate," insofar as they need to be heard, understood, confronted, and dealt with. Once Donald Trump is the President of the United States, it becomes hard to argue that his worldview should or can be kept "non-mainstream." It's already the mainstream, insofar as a lot of people believe it. Sapping Trumpism of "legitimacy" does nothing to diminish its popularity. And it's popularity that we should be focusing on: the question is not whether canceling a speech reduces a speaker's legitimacy, but what it does to the size of their audience.

Ultimately, it's inescapably true that the principle of free speech is an essential component to a well-functioning democracy. That's true (to differing degrees) in both public and private spaces. And it's especially true on university campuses, where students need to be maximally free to listen to whomever they want. That's partially out of principle, and partially because in accepting the censorship of reprehensible individuals, *we pave the way for our own muzzling.* With Donald Trump as this country's president, it's crucial now more than ever that we embrace radical free speech and defend one another's right to say and write things that elicit outrage, disdain, and discomfort. Otherwise, we should not be surprised to find ourselves being stifled by the very techniques we have wielded against our ideological opponents.

HOW IDENTITY BECAME A WEAPON AGAINST THE LEFT

by Briahna Joy Gray

HAVING AN "IDENTITY POLITICS" is incredibly beneficial. Identity politics, which emphasizes the unique concerns of different communities and demographic groups, shows how historical inequities have been distributed across different races, genders, religions, abilities, and sexualities. In doing so, it allows us to better understand how to critique and reform the systems that replicate those inequities. It reveals how the foreclosure crisis disproportionately hurt black homeowners,[1] how health issues manifest differently across populations,[2] and how various forms of "hidden taxes" penalize women in professional life.[3] To ignore identity is to ignore injustice. Yet there are risks to viewing the world through the prism of identity. If people are defined by their demographic characteristics, they can be reduced to those characteristics in a way that obscures differences within groups. If "identity" becomes synonymous with "perspective," dissenting members within the identity group risk having their viewpoints erased and their humanity diminished. And when used cynically, as a political weapon, a simplistic view of identity can allow people of a particular political faction to wrongly imply that they speak for all members of their racial or gender group.

Kamala Harris is black. She is a lot of other things, too: a person of South Asian descent, a woman, a former prosecutor and state Attorney

General, a sitting Senator, and, according to Barack Obama, "the best looking attorney general in the country."[4] (I am your sister in side-eye, Michelle.) Out of nearly 2,000 senators in the country's history, Harris is one of only ten black Americans and two black women to have held the position. Her personal characteristics and political accomplishments, together with the intelligence and tenacity that propelled her to the Senate, have made her a highly visible prospect for the 2020 presidential race. Already, influential Democrats have shown a strong interest in Harris,[5] with prominent former Clinton donors meeting privately with Harris in the Hamptons.[6] *The San Francisco Chronicle* called her the Democrats' "Great Blue Hope,"[7] and a *Guardian* writer suggested that the combination of Harris's race and her centrist platform "could be the party's solution to its identity crisis."[8]

But certain parts of Kamala Harris's political résumé have led to skepticism from the left. As California's Attorney General, with responsibilities for overseeing the second largest prison population in the country,[9] Harris's professional obligation to put people behind bars was seen as being in direct tension with the goals of Black Lives Matter,[10] perhaps the most prominent progressive movement of our time. Harris touted a reform-minded "smart on crime" approach in her prosecutorial role,[11] one that encouraged education and reentry programs for ex-offenders, and in the Senate, she has co-sponsored legislation to improve prison conditions for women.[12] Yet she has also come under heavy criticism from activists for, among other things: defending the state against court orders to reduce its prison population,[13] declining to take a public stand on sentencing reform proposals,[14] attempting to block a court decision requiring the state to provide a transgender inmate with gender reassignment surgery,[15] opposing a measure to require independent inquiries into police uses of force,[16] and obstructing efforts by federal judges to hold California prosecutors accountable for an "epidemic" of misconduct.[17] Harris has been a zealous prosecutor (at times, she said, she has been "as close to a vigilante as you can get"[18]), and certain of her policies—like bringing criminal charges against parents whose children miss school—conflict with the efforts of groups like BLM to reduce the reach of the criminal justice system into people's lives.[19]

Harris has also drawn scrutiny over the crimes she *wasn't* tough on. While serving as Attorney General of California, Harris failed to prosecute now-Treasury Secretary Steven "Foreclosure King" Mnuchin after his OneWest Bank engaged in a notoriously aggressive pattern of home foreclosures. Under Mnuchin, OneWest was a "foreclosure machine" that did everything it could to seize people's houses,[20] inflicting misery on homeowners while failing to properly review foreclosure documents.[21] Harris's consumer law division found that OneWest had engaged in "widespread misconduct" in its treatment of borrowers; the investigators urged Harris to "conduct a full investigation of a national bank's misconduct and provide a public accounting of what happened."[22] Instead, Harris closed the case, not even pursuing the compromise measure of a civil penalty. As David Dayen writes, this "watered-down version of public accountability was seen as the best possible outcome, and Harris didn't even go for that."[23] In failing to hold the bank accountable, Dayen emphasizes, Harris was far from alone among state law enforcement officials. Harris was, however, the only Democratic senatorial candidate to whom Steven Mnuchin felt compelled to give a campaign donation.[24]

There are therefore both principled and pragmatic reasons why people on the left might be skeptical of a Harris candidacy. There's a serious question about whether Harris can be counted on to advance progressive values when doing so might require political sacrifices. But there's also a question of strategy: from a leftist perspective, it's unwise to run yet another presidential candidate whose ties to banks could make them "untrustworthy" in an era of low public trust in elected officials. Given the crushing defeat of November 2016 (which was all but predicted by certain insightful progressives[25]), it would seem obviously beneficial for the Democratic Party to listen to progressive criticism early and adapt candidates and their messaging accordingly.

Yet progressive critiques of Harris were met with swift and unyielding hostility. After a *Mic* article documented the lack of left-wing enthusiasm for a Harris candidacy,[26] investigative journalist Victoria A. Brownsworth suggested that a better headline for the article would be:

"Kamala Harris, biracial senator and former Attorney General of the most populous state, faces misogynist white men defaming her." (This despite the fact that every critic quoted in the piece was female, and one was a woman of color.) Center for American Progress president Neera Tanden, a close Clinton ally and frequent defender of the Democratic Party, declared she found it "odd" that "these folks" (meaning Bernie Sanders supporters) "have [it] in for Kamala Harris and Cory Booker" in particular. "Hmmmm," she said, implying that criticisms of Harris and Booker were racially motivated. MSNBC host Joy Ann Reid said the *Mic* article simply reported the opinions of "3 alt-left activists," "alt-left" being a term used to brand leftists as racist analogues of the neo-Nazi alt-right.[27] In *Cosmopolitan*, Brittney Cooper wrote that the left in general, but in particular the "Sanders Left," "has a black-woman problem,"[28] a charge I've addressed elsewhere.[29] Cooper said that those criticizing Harris "think that black women who care about establishment politics lack vision" and that the debate "isn't about Harris, but about the emotional and political labor that black women are expected to do to save America's soul." "Angry white Sanders voters," she said, must "get off [Harris's] back." In large part, responses to skepticism about Harris have simply dismissed the substance of the analysis, instead suggesting a "targeting" of Harris because of her gender and/or race.

By wielding identity to neutralize political pushback, these commentators were continuing a trend. Throughout the 2016 campaign season, criticism of Hillary Clinton was frequently deflected with claims that her critics were motivated by sexism. And certainly, there *were* a lot of sexist attacks. Allusions to her husband's sexual exploits, scrutiny of her appearance, and a perception of the candidate as "untrustworthy" were all rooted, in part, in gender bias. No one can credibly deny that Clinton's gender has affected the public's perception of her since the very beginning of her career, including the early political hostility she faced in Arkansas when she refused to give up her maiden name,[30] and the time in 1992 when she was publicly pressured into proving that she liked to bake cookies.[31]

But writing off Clinton's leftist critics as necessarily motivated by gender bias was sexist in itself. It reduced Clinton to her gender and implied that she had no agency in her own decision-making. Some people had perfectly defensible grounds for seeing Clinton as "untrustworthy," such her shifting position on subjects like the TPP, welfare "reform," and NAFTA.[32] Others disapproved of Clinton for her hawkishness,[33] her insistence that single-payer would "never ever" happen,[34] her ties to Wall Street, or myriad other legitimate reasons.[35] Those who raised these concerns, however, were often dismissed as either "Bernie Bros" or unpersuadable "deplorables" motivated by bigotry.

The "Bernie Bro" narrative, which attempted to paint Sanders supporters as disproportionately sexist (and Sanders himself as borderline bigoted) was deeply pernicious and effective. Sanders was vulnerable to this kind of attack: in a world in which personal identity has become a shorthand for "progress" (see e.g. Obama), and "white man" has become an epithet, Bernie's identity was an easy target. His unflinching support of women's issues, his history of advocacy for racial justice, his record of support for civil rights and LGBT issues, even his Jewishness were all made secondary to his image as an "angry white male."[36] Sanders was accused of downplaying the political concerns of people of color. Even now, when 73% of African Americans view Sanders favorably (as compared with 52% of white people)[37] he is still treated as having a race problem.

Since more allies are generally made by engaging one's critics than dismissing them as biased deplora-bros, the heckling approach was not a politically savvy one. Just as importantly, though, the "bro" stereotype entirely erased the perspectives of countless women and people of color who did not share the center-left political position. The "Bernie Bro" mythology—that progressives are almost exclusively white, male, and young—will not die, no matter how often women and people of color try to speak up to disprove it. In all the words spilled about the uninterrupted whiteness of Sanders supporters, prominent "Bros" like Rosario Dawson, Ben Jealous, Pramila Jayapal, Eddie Glaude, Spike Lee, Killer Mike, Cornel West, and Nina Turner went largely unmentioned. Hillary supporters were appalled that leftists challenged civil rights hero John

Lewis's commitment to Clinton,[38] but it seems civil rights legend Harry Belafonte was considered less sacrosanct—his endorsement of Bernie Sanders was whited-out of the public discourse along with the perspectives of Michelle Alexander[39] and Ta-Nehisi Coates[40]—both of whom are generally considered among the most respected liberal thought leaders. One of the most powerful pro-Black Lives Matter messages heard during the entire campaign was a Sanders video featuring Erica Garner talking about her father,[41] but Garner was an inconvenient figure for the narrative. As black progressive Leslie Lee III said in March 2016:

> *"Me, myself, and many other POC, people of color, who support Bernie Sanders, feel like we don't get to be a part of the conversation. We get ignored. We get erased. It's assumed that the black vote, the Hispanic vote, and everyone is all behind Hillary Clinton and none of us really get Bernie Sanders or like Bernie Sanders."*[42]

In March of 2016, exasperated Sanders-voting POC even employed the hashtag #BernieMadeMeWhite,[43] joking that a love of the band Journey and pumpkin spiced lattes would accrue with our new race status. Other, more sardonic, tweeters celebrated the immunity from police violence their newfound caucacity might bring.[44] Ironically, whiteness—when attributed to blacks—became a punishment rather than a privilege.

Twitter has been an especially revealing host forum to this ugly friction between identity and ideology: there, unapologetically leftist people of color and women are routinely shouted down, called race traitors, self-hating women, or, incredibly, are accused of being white—even by people with white-presenting avatars.[45] Twitter is where you can find a liberal Democrat referring to Our Revolution president Nina Turner as "Bernie's Omarosa."[46] It's disorienting to see white (and black) liberals calling leftists of color sellouts, Uncle Toms, "coons," house-slaves, and well, white people, all in the name of anti-racism. But the Bernie Bro framework tells us that all the racists are at the fringes of the political spectrum, while the middle remains pure. Progressive women or leftists of color therefore present a kind of glitch in the matrix. The solution? Deny our existence. Leftists of color are regularly told—by white liberals!—that we are white and/or secretly racist. And while stories about the sexism Clinton supporters faced online are familiar, the racism and sexism directed by the center against the left are ignored. Purported anti-racist Democrats stayed largely silent as an Islamophobic smear campaign was waged against progressive black Muslim Representative Keith Ellison,[47] one of the ugliest instances of bigotry to come out of the Democratic Party in recent history.

The same kind of hypocrisy could be seen in Gloria Steinem's inane quip that young women who supported Bernie must be in it for "the boys."[48] A feminist icon struggled so much to make sense of the inconvenient fact that a majority of young women supported Sanders that she fell back on the same basic gender stereotypes she has been fighting since the 1960s.[49] But this is the dissonance created by a certain conception of identity: if we believe that Hillary Clinton is "the candidate of women and people of color," and "women and people of color" are defined entirely by those identities, it becomes impossible to understand how anyone who shares the identity could reject the candidate. Once the distinction between perspective and identity is erased, voters of color become an undifferentiated hive mind incapable of political independence.

It's strange that we're at the point where this needs to be said: a black politician is not necessarily the best politician to promote black interests, and a female politician will not necessarily serve women's interests better than a man would. Race produces a set of lived experiences that inform our political perspective, but identity cannot be used as a mitigating factor for political shortcomings. A glance at the unusually diverse 2016 Republican primary field illustrates as much. If we believe that a political candidate's identity overrides their substantive beliefs and policy prescriptions, then a Ben Carson/Carly Fiorina ticket would have been a progressive dream. Brittney Cooper of *Cosmopolitan*, in her defense of Harris, makes a good point here: Cooper says that, despite a history of performing the role, black people should not be cast as "the conscience of the nation." The burden is too heavy for any group, and it certainly exceeds the capacity of any single politician. Belonging to a protected class does not immunize a politician from error, nor should it insulate her from criticism.

During the 2012 presidential race, Cory Booker went on *Meet The Press* and defended—of all people—Mitt Romney against criticism of Romney's work for Bain Capital.[50] Booker, evincing more sympathy for the financial industry than for the disproportionate number of black people affected by the financial industry's bad acts, told voters to "stop attacking private equity." Booker was wrong to do so. During the 2016 primary, Representative John Lewis unfairly impugned Bernie Sanders' character, implying that because Lewis hadn't personally seen Sanders in the crowd of hundreds of thousands at the 1963 March on Washington, Sanders was probably lying about having gone.[51] Lewis, likewise, was wrong to do so. Democrats defending Hillary Clinton's support of the 1994 Crime Bill relish pointing out that two-thirds of the Congressional Black Caucus voted in favor of it.[52] But those members, too, were wrong—despite being black. The other members of the CBC, the ones who opposed the bill, were right. Likewise, the contemporary equivalent of that dissenting third—the black voters who supported Bernie Sanders in the primary—should not be erased because *other* quantities of black people disagree. Any statement about what "black people" think or support automatically discounts the perspective of very large numbers of us, because—as is often said but rarely internalized—*black people are not a monolith*. Identity is, at best, a loose proxy for a person's political commitments, and individual identity groups contain incredibly diverse perspectives. Failure to recognize that fact can result in dangerous consequences: it can lead us to support policies contrary to the best interests of a community simply because of optics, and it can turn us into a "firewall" to lean on, rather than a constituency to be won.

Even worse, *because* the optics are improved, it can actually become harder to combat the harm posed by in-group bad actors: a black-run police force can be just as harmful to a black community as one headed by whites,[53] but the optics of equal representation can obscure the reality of systemic racism. Hillary Clinton was widely accepted as the best candidate for what are considered "women's issues," such as protecting the right to choose and ensuring access to reproductive care, even though Bernie Sanders had a nearly-identical track record.[54] Yet even though Clinton almost automatically received endorsements from Planned Parenthood, NARAL, and other women's organizations, she chose as her Vice Presidential nominee a senator who had historically been a staunch opponent of abortion rights.[55] As governor of Virginia, Tim Kaine had advocated for adoption over abortion, pushed for abstinence-only education, and even supported a law requiring that minors seeking to end their pregnancies get parental approval. This history would ordinarily have caused outrage among reproductive rights advocates, who see abortion as a non-negotiable issue. (Witness the trouble Sanders got into after giving a speech supporting an anti-abortion mayoral candidate in Nebraska.[56]) But Clinton's gender insulated her from scrutiny with respect to women's issues. Those who challenged Clinton's VP choice on the grounds that it demonstrated a lack of commitment to feminist principles were—ironically—dismissed as "bros," regardless of our gender. In short: the interest in *Hillary as a woman candidate* trumped interest in *having the best candidate for women*.

The recent backlash to rumors about Kamala Harris's potential 2020 candidacy shows how this bizarre and cynical version of "identity politics" continues to be used as a weapon to derail progressives whose record of commitment to racial justice, gender equality, and LGBT issues has historically eclipsed that of the Democratic Party itself. Using identity this way is harmful to the interests of progressive politics. Leftists, particularly leftists of color, are invested in ensuring that the Democratic Party learns from its mistakes. To that end, we are committed to helping the party put forward candidates who are less vulnerable to the types of attacks which dogged Hillary – that she was a corporatist, that she was owned by Wall Street, that she could not be trusted. That is why we question candidates like Kamala Harris, Cory Booker, and Deval Patrick–all floated as 2020 possibilities in recent weeks. Though each of them has at least one black parent, it is intellectually dishonest to pretend it is *that* quality, rather than their corporatism, which draws criticism from the left. (And with Nina Turner emerging as the presumptive heiress to Bernie's progressive leadership, it is increasingly difficult to credibly contend otherwise.) It is natural to be skeptical of an out-group member's views about a subject important to members of that group—especially when certain race or gender-based factions have historically been in conflict. But the inquiry into whether to listen to a particular critic cannot stop at that critic's identity.

Of course, identity still matters, and prejudice operates in subtle and pervasive ways. On one level, my instinct is to agree with those who say all Harris's critics are racist: the truth is that everyone *is* racist.[57] But our culture's conscious and unconscious biases won't be resolved before 2020, and until they are, we must rely on something more than mere identity to determine the legitimacy of political criticism. It's fair to ask of a critic: are you able to articulate a reason *why* you are wary of a candidate? Do, they, for instance, cite the candidate's conservative "tough on crime" approach to criminal justice, or do they trade in gendered stereotypes, dog-whistles, or vague statements of "feeling" that suggest an ulterior motive? This analytical step is crucial: a critic should not be impugned on the basis of a candidate's identity, but on the soundness of the critique itself. Nor should a critic be ignored because of their own identity, without anything more. After all: biology is not (political) destiny.

Harris, Booker, Patrick, Biden, Warren: all deserve scrutiny. So does any other potential candidate. That scrutiny should be applied evenly, in proportion to a candidate's likelihood of success and the quality of their record. It's not an act of racism to question whether the Democratic Party should select as its presidential nominee a career prosecutor with a controversial record on misconduct issues. Pretending that these candidates are criticized solely on the basis of race or gender is, in itself, a lesser form of prejudice: it erases their flaws, and flattens their humanity. Treating people as people requires acknowledgment of their imperfections. To err, after all, is human.

RIDING THE HASHTAG

by Yasmin Nair

THE MONTHS FROM DECEMBER TO APRIL ARE, in many households with high-school-age teens, filled with degrees of fear ranging from palpable nervousness to sleeplessness to sheer sweat-inducing terror. Across the United States, young people who should be looking forward to life with excitement instead wait anxiously to hear about their college applications. This is a country that—unlike, say, Denmark—does not think that education should be free and equally available to all, so the stakes of what comes in the envelope are high. These young people's entire lives have been in preparation for this moment, in which they face either humiliation or elation when their preferred schools will inform them if, yes, the years of extra dance classes and soup kitchen duties were not for naught. For millions of teens. the onset of adulthood has been marked by a constant worship of the Unseen Application Gods, an indoctrination process that happens to be an excellent way of easing a person into a lifelong habit of deference toward authority.

These days, as we know, it is not enough to merely be clever. It is not enough to have taken forty AP classes, or excelled on your standardized tests. You must have something extra, something special. Did you think Columbia was going to be impressed by your *grades*? You poor kid. The Ivies reject 9/10 of their applicants. They'll want to see something more than *that*. Oh, you're an intelligent and capable person who would do quite well there and is very nice? Join the queue. What is it they want? Good luck figuring it out.

Since his brief moment of Twitter Fame (a unit of time lasting about half the flap of a hummingbird's wings), Ziad Ahmed has drifted back into the internet ether. But Ahmed had figured out what they wanted. On April 1, the 18-year-old Princeton area native and Muslim-American activist tweeted out that he had been accepted into Stanford. He displayed a picture of the answer he had provided to one of the application questions: "What matters to you and why?" Instead of the more traditional use of "sentences" and "paragraphs," Ahmed had simply written the phrase" #Black Lives Matter" a hundred times. It was bold, it worked, and it got him on NBC News. The predictable reactions flowed from all quarters: Linda Sarsour, a nationally known Muslim American activist, tweeted her support, while on the right there was much grousing about the loss of standards and "identity politics" trumping quality.

Given his youth and his ethnicity, there is no way to write about Ziad Ahmed without being criticized, censured, and called evil. The situation is a bit like defusing a bomb, as we see it in the movies. One crossed wire, the red one cut instead of the yellow, and we blow ourselves to bits. So, one treads carefully. After all Ahmed is eighteen, *eighteen* years old, a mere child, some might argue. And he seems so dreadfully earnest that it seems cruel to be critical of him. What's to hate about a young man who has been photographed holding a sign that lays out his politics that reads: "I stand against racism because it is my responsibility as a human to oppose oppression, dehumanization and systematic detrimental discrimination, which is unfair, moronic, and wrong." It is all of those things, and good for him for standing against them.

But Ahmed is no ordinary activist teen. The son of a hedge fund manager with his own firm, he attended the prestigious Princeton Day School. At the tender age of thirteen, he founded a nonprofit organization called "Redefy," "committed to defying stereotypes, redefining perspectives positively, embracing acceptance and tolerance..." Its exact work and accomplishments are somewhat unclear (it has something to do with hosting workshops about stereotypes), but Ahmed's commitment to redefining perspectives earned him profiles in major media publications and an invitation to the White House, where Barack Obama praised his work. Ahmed didn't stop at Redefy: along with two other teenagers who shared his interest in "business, marketing, and philanthropy" (note which comes first and which comes third), he also created JÜV Consulting, a firm designed to help corporations understand "Generation Z." For $1000 to $5000 per client, JÜV will tell companies "how likely we are to like your brand, follow your social media accounts, or buy your products." Ahmed's consulting and nonprofit work has landed him on MTV's list of the "Top 9 Teens Changing the World" and *Business Insider's* "Top 15 Prodigies." And Stanford wasn't the only college impressed; according to his Twitter page (@ZiadTheActivist), the cover photo of which shows Ahmed performing—what else?—a TED talk. In the fall he'll be joining Yale's class of 2021.

The Twitter handle says it all, really. "Ziad The Activist" is a brand, and a very successful one so far. Activist for what, exactly? For change, of course. The particular type of change can be tailored to suit the client's needs.

Ziad Ahmed can tell us something about both the contemporary elite university and the political worldview that simultaneously creates it and emerges from it. First, Ahmed's story shows how the viciously competitive nature of the admissions process breeds ludicrous acts. When scholastic excellence isn't enough, the children of the wealthy found consulting firms and nonprofits and throw whatever else they possibly can at the Yale admissions committee. None of it actually does much of anything, and most of it will probably be abandoned soon after the start of freshman year, but the dance must be performed. After all, you may be competing against a student with *three* TED talks or *four* nonprofits, so you'd better at least have one of each.

This is perverse, of course: one's teenage years should be a time for simply getting to explore and understand the world. Generally, teenagers probably shouldn't be founding consulting firms, not just because *nobody* should found consulting firms, but because teenagers don't actually know anything yet. That's not a slight against them, any more than it is to point out that newborns don't have teeth or that kittens have trouble playing musical instruments. When you're a teenager, you're still working out your place in the world and how it functions (admittedly a lifetime endeavour for all of us, but the teen years are particularly fraught): it's just in your nature. Demanding that teenagers show world-changing brilliance is, except in the rarest of cases, demanding the impossible. This kind of pressure doesn't cause you to get a slew of applicants with unique moral goodness and historic accomplishment, it causes your existing applicants to puff themselves up as much as possible. In fact, there is a direct incentive *not* to actually try to do something worthwhile: the most successful candidates will be those with the most impressive-looking resumes, not those who have most improved the lives of their fellow human beings, so the rational thing to do is to spend one's time doing nine impressive-sounding but superficial things rather than one less-impressive-sounding but socially helpful thing.

This vicious competitive marketplace now exists at every level of the university. For prospective undergrads, it is a *Hunger Games* scenario— show us how unique you are or you die—that compels kids like Ahmed to come up with ever-new tactics in order to impress. But even PhD-holding candidates looking for tenure-track positions face the dreaded "diversity statement," which, while ostensibly intended to ensure equal opportunity, ends up as a high-pressure demand for applicants to prove that they are not only *good* for the position, but that they are *special* as well.

In a just world, of course, you could simply study and learn and that would be that. If you wanted to go to college, you would enroll in courses that interested you. To the extent that there was an "application" process, it would exist entirely to ensure that you had the basic capability necessary for participating in the program. Teenagers would be encouraged to spend their time both learning and serving the community, but one's life outcomes wouldn't be contingent on having to prove at the age of 17 that one had learned the *most of anyone* and served the community *more than anybody else*. People's performance would be measured against their individual goals and capacities rather than in some brutal death-match against their peers.

But as a college degree becomes more and more necessary for economic success, and the selective schools become ever more selective, that "just world" slips further and further away. We are approaching the point where it seems laughable and utopian to imagine a university as anything other than an anxiety factory, the function of which is to solely to train future workers for the even more anxiety-inducing competitive struggle they will soon face in the labor market.

Ziad Ahmed can tell us about more than just the nature of the university admissions process, however. He's also a parable about how activism itself has changed. Consider the hashtag application: #BlackLivesMatter, 100 times over. We know that words spoken over and over steadily lose their meanings. Here, #BlackLivesMatter is emptied of all substantive content. It no longer has anything to do with black lives. Instead it is simply a chant: "I am good. Admit me. I am good. Admit me." #BlackLivesMatter does not mean that black lives matter, it means that I care about the right things and have allied myself with the correct cause. The phrase "virtue signaling" is often erroneously used by the right to trivialize and dismiss people with sincere and principled beliefs. But it's undoubtedly true that when politics is reduced to the display of a hashtag, when one can be an activist without performing any actual *activity*, slogans can become brands rather than demands.

Perhaps one should blame Barack Obama for this. Ahmed's political worldview seems to be part Obama, part Warren Buffett: vacuous civil rights rhetoric plus vacuous "progressive" corporate rhetoric. Obama was the one who finally sapped the last substantive content from the words "hope" and "change," and who used racial inclusion as a way of justifying the status quo. Obama was politics as image and iconography rather than power and policy, precisely the sensibility that Ahmed has inherited. Obama's realization was the same one that corporate America had about the counterculture: if you incorporated the *images* of radical politics, without any actual threat to the existing power structure, you could produce a version of progressive politics that Wall Street would love. You could feel like a good person and get rich at the same time.

It's interesting that Ahmed finally settled on Yale, of all universities. After all, Yale is the epicenter of American inequality. Situated in high-poverty, mostly black New Haven, it is a gated fortress of the wealthy, funneling the children of the elite into cushy financial jobs. It's also the site of heavy labor conflict, with graduate students recently engaging in a hunger strike amidst a drive for unionization. And it's a place where the legacy of slavery hangs heavy. It took years for Yale to even acknowledge that naming one of its colleges, Calhoun, after an infamous defender of slavery was, in effect, defending his practices and politics (it has recently been renamed). And last year, black Yale janitor Corey Menafee was arrested after smashing a stained glass window depicting happy slaves picking cotton. (Menafee had been fed up with having to look at the window every day while sweeping the floors.)

We might wonder if Ahmed, having entered the belly of the beast, is likely to be radicalized by the sight of all these contradictions. Will he emerge from his four years fighting to bring down the very walls he and his parents spent so many years scaling? I will confess that I gaze upon him with one eyebrow slightly raised. I'm not encouraged by someone who had founded a consulting firm by the age of thirteen, even if the word "activist" is in his Twitter handle and even if MTV is convinced he will change the world. (I am betting the odds are >50% that he will end up working in finance.)

It's hard to blame Ahmed himself, though. He is simply the product of a political logic that has saturated the university. Yes, his use of the hashtag seems exploitative and self-serving. But it's also a product of a type of university that wants the simultaneous demonstration of fealty and individuality, and wants to appear progressive without incurring any possible risk to its existing structure. Yale wants activists, but preferably activists who go to the Aspen Ideas Conference to talk about why black lives matter, rather than activists who actually want to take Yale's money away or disrupt its jobs pipeline. Ahmed is perfect, then: consultant by day, activist by night, friend of Obama, and completely unthreatening. Nobody can accuse the university of backward racial politics: after all, they let in a student who wrote #BlackLivesMatter a hundred times! At the same time, New Haven will still be New Haven and Yale will still be Yale. You might ride the hashtag through the institution's gates, but the question is how to tear them down.

MORE LAWYERS, SAME INJUSTICES

by Oren Nimni

LAST MONTH, IN A GEORGIA COURTROOM, defendant Denver Fenton Allen appeared in front of Judge Bryant Durham, Jr. for a pretrial hearing.[1] Allen was charged with murder, and his trial was scheduled for the next week. As the transcript shows, the hearing quickly became... unusual. By the end of it, the defendant has told the judge dozens of times to "suck my dick," and the enraged judge has replied that the defendant "looks like a queer." The hearing was such a comically vulgar calamity that it has gone viral, and an animated performance of the transcript has been viewed several million times.[2]

It began straightforwardly enough. Allen came before the judge because he wanted to fire his public defender and get a different one. Judge Durham informed Allen that while he was entitled to a lawyer, he was not entitled to have a particular lawyer, and was stuck with the one he had. Allen then explained his reasons for wanting to fire the lawyer. First, he said, the lawyer had made sexual advances on him. Second, the lawyer had sent him against his will to the hospital to have a diagnosis made, presumably of Allen's mental condition. Finally, Allen said, the lawyer had not given Allen access to any discovery documents, including police reports, the autopsy, and the coroner's report.

In response to this, Judge Durham asks Allen's public defender whether he has shared all of his documents with Allen. The lawyer replies that he has. But Allen is insistent. He tells the judge that the only document he has seen is the four-page indictment, explaining the charges against him. The judge tells Allen that perhaps his lawyer doesn't have any other documents.

At this, Allen is becoming angry. "This is a murder case," he says, "and you're telling me the only thing on discovery is a four-page indictment." Allen declares that he refuses to go to trial with the attorney he has been given, to which Judge Durham replies that Allen's only other option is to try the case himself. Durham says that choosing to act as his own attorney would be "the biggest mistake of [Allen's] life." Allen is incredulous: "So you're telling me you're going to find me guilty if I go to trial to try to defend myself?" to which the judge responds "You're probably right. That would be my guess..."

Allen repeats that he will not be tried with the lawyer he has, and says that he will get himself held in contempt if necessary in order to stall the proceedings. At this point in the transcript, the real fireworks begin. Having resolved to be found in contempt of court, Allen intentionally becomes as vulgar as possible:

ALLEN: I'll just hold myself in contempt.

THE COURT: Listen to me—

ALLEN: Fuck you.

THE COURT: Listen to me.

ALLEN: Fuck you.

THE COURT: Listen to me.

ALLEN: Go fuck yourself. [...]

THE COURT: I am—I am finding you in contempt. And I sentence you to twenty days for that. And if you say anything else, I'm going to give you twenty days for everything you say.

ALLEN: Fuck you.

THE COURT: Forty days.

ALLEN: Fuck you again.

THE COURT: Sixty days.

ALLEN: Go fuck yourself.

THE COURT: A year.

ALLEN: Your mama.

THE COURT: Ten years.

Things only get worse from there. Allen repeatedly says he is in a "kanga-roo court," and begins graphically describing the sex acts he intends to per-form on the judge. Durham loses his temper and begins screaming. Allen says he will chop the judge's family into pieces and calls the judge a "horse-ass cracker." The judge says he "bets everyone enjoys sucking your cock." After this continues for many minutes, the judge tries to find his resolve:

THE COURT: We are going to have the trial Monday week.

ALLEN: The fuck we are. I ain't going to trial with this lawyer present.

The obscenities then resume, and the defendant and judge shout at each other for many more minutes before the judge finally declares the hearing over and has Allen escorted from the courtroom.

The hearing lies at the extreme end on the spectrum of judicial dys-function. America's justice system is often called "broken," but even in a highly defective system, it's rare to find judges and defendants liter-ally screaming and bickering like children in a schoolyard. (Judges fre-quently behave like children, but they are sure to cloak their pettiness beneath a veneer of professional decorum.)

But the transcript of the Georgia hearing is not just interesting as an absurd clash between an 'out-of-control defendant' and a lunatic judge. A careful examination reveals important questions that get lost amid the various dick-based taunts.

Why, for example, did the public defender not have an autopsy report when the trial was to be held in a week? The defense of a murder trial requires intensive preparation. Allen's attorney insisted that he had given Allen all of the available discovery documents. Yet in that case, with only days left before the trial, the attorney had failed to get ahold of some of the most crucial documents in the case.

In fact, looking past the headline-grabbing insult-fest, we can see that the real story here is not about the world's filthiest defendant or the world's pettiest judge. In fact, it is about the world's most incompetent public defender. Leave aside Allen's accusation that his lawyer had tried to proposition him sexually, a charge that the judge refused to take seriously. The public defender appears to admit that he has no discovery documents in the case other than a 4-page indictment, and yet somehow intends to try the case within a week. Allen found himself with only one weapon left to delay his trial: getting held in contempt. (It wasn't actually a bad strategy, if Allen's goal was to stall the process for a while.)

The public defender neglects his duty in another way: by standing silently by during the entire exchange, even as his client gets charged with new offenses for threatening the judge. At the time of the hearing, the public defender was still representing Allen, and thus still had an ethical obligation to safeguard Allen's interests. A responsible defense attorney, seeing their client jeopardizing their case, would have made an attempt to intervene, encouraging leniency from the judge, or caution from his client. Of course, given Allen's mood, it's unclear how likely he would have been to heed such advice. But the defense attorney should have done everything possible to interrupt and prevent further damage from being done.

(The judge, too, committed some serious and revealing ethical breaches. Not only was he childish, but he told the defendant he would "probably" find him guilty if he chose to represent himself, even though Allen is supposed to be under a presumption of innocence until the evidence is heard.)

Allen's allegations about his public defender should have been taken much more seriously by the judge. Allen had specifically detailed the various ways in which his lawyer was failing to provide him with a minimal level of constitutional representation. Instead of inquiring into these problems in order to make a determination about their truth or falsity, Judge Durham simply told Allen that his only other option was to be found guilty by representing himself. Allen knew, and stated clearly, that this was no choice at all. But instead of doing what most defendants do, and simply accepting the fact that he was doomed, Allen stood up for his constitutional right to competent counsel.

In the firmness of that refusal, Allen resembles another Southern defendant, one from fifty years earlier. Clarence Earl Gideon was an affable drifter who ended up before a Florida judge on a burglary charge in 1961.[3] Gideon, who was accused of stealing $5 and some beer from a Panama City pool hall, asked the court if he could be represented by counsel. As the transcript shows, when the court told him he was not entitled to an attorney, Gideon stood firm:

THE COURT: Mr. Gideon, I am sorry, but I cannot appoint counsel to represent you in this case. Under the laws of the State of Florida, the only time the court can appoint counsel to represent a defendant is when that person is charged with a capital offense. I am sorry, but I will have to deny your request to appoint counsel to defend you in this case.

GIDEON: The United States Supreme Court says I am entitled to be represented by counsel.

Most lawyers at the time would have said Gideon was wrong. At that point in time, the Supreme Court hadn't decreed that poor defendants had the right to free representation. But he was also prophetic. After being found guilty at trial, Gideon made it to the Supreme Court, which then did establish a right to counsel. Thanks to Gideon's refusal to compromise on what he believed were his constitutional rights, the modern public defender system was born.

Denver Fenton Allen is probably not the next Clarence Earl Gideon. Gideon, after all, did not threaten to cannibalize the judge's family. But

Allen's case is nevertheless instructive, because it reveals what happens in U.S. courtrooms when defendants try to stick up for their constitutional entitlements.

Allen, like so many other defendants, was brushed aside when he tried to complain about a lack of adequate representation. Even though he was facing a murder charge, the court was uninterested in figuring out whether his lawyer was giving Allen a basic adequate level of defense.

That's not especially surprising. While the Supreme Court has guaranteed the right to a lawyer, the Court has an expansive definition of what constitutes "competent" lawyering. Drunk lawyers and sleeping lawyers have been deemed to have adequately represented their clients' interests (even in death penalty cases).[4][5] The country's public defender system is in a very sorry state indeed.[6]

This brings us to an important truth about criminal justice: having a lawyer, in and of itself, does very little to ensure that a person will receive a fair trial. In fact, there are circumstances in which having a lawyer may make a person worse off; some people could have represented themselves better than their inattentive public defender did. We know that many public defender systems are overworked and under-resourced, to the point where they openly admit that they cannot provide a level of representation that meets a minimal constitutional standard.[7]

It's striking, in fact, that the rise of the public defender system has coincided with the rise of mass incarceration. When the Supreme Court decided Gideon v. Wainwright in 1963, the combined federal and state prison population was 217,283.[8] By 2014, it had risen to 1,561,500.[9] That number doesn't include those in local city and county jails, or those under other types of state supervision, including probation, parole, GPS ankle monitoring, community service and alternative court programs. While more people are now represented, far more go to jail.

More lawyers hasn't meant more justice. The introduction of guaranteed representation didn't cause the explosion in America's prison population, but it also didn't prevent it. It's impossible to tell, of course, how much worse the numbers would have been if the Gideon case had never been decided. Presumably, the public defender system has helped a large number of people get better outcomes. But the mere presence of defense lawyers guarantees little, especially if the standards of competence are low.

This is where a "procedural" view of justice falls down. By its nature it overlooks ultimate outcomes. The U.S. Constitution is heavy on procedural rights; you get due process of law and the right to counsel before you're flung in the penitentiary. But people can be given due process on paper without being afforded any actual measure of justice. The Gideon decision looks like a triumph for poor people's rights in U.S. courts, and indeed it was. But in many parts of the country, especially across the South, the public defender system might as well not exist. Where an attorney's job (whether through overwork or ineptitude) is to "meet 'em and plead 'em," defendants often feel as if they'd be better off on their own. Yes, the statistics of indigent clients who now have representation have improved, but to what end. Thinking full representation is synonymous with full justice is like thinking full health care coverage means better health. Quality matters.

In fact, improving procedures can even sanctify perverse outcomes as legitimate. So long as the forms are all filled out correctly, a terrible injustice is deemed acceptable. So long as a death penalty defendant gets the proper number of appeals, they've been given justice. So long as a landlord's eviction papers are properly served upon the tenant, the tenant has no right to complain that their children are being tossed into homelessness.

It's something to bear in mind in discussions over so-called "civil Gideon." Currently, the right to free representation only extends to criminal defendants. But as many have pointed out, certain civil proceedings (such as eviction, employment discrimination, wage theft, and child custody) have stakes nearly as high. Some therefore recommend that the entitlement to a lawyer be expanded to cover a far wider set of cases.

But we should be careful about introducing more procedure, without correspondingly assuring that it leads to more actual justice. Despite having had a vast public defense apparatus for half-a-century, mass incarceration persists. Changing procedures is important to the extent that it affects substance.

As far as Judge Durham was concerned, Denver Fenton Allen had gotten his due. And under the law, he quite probably had. He'd been given a public defender, who had given him access to all of the available documents (i.e. none). The judge saw no problem that could keep the case from going to trial, and Allen appeared to simply be unruly and obstinate. When the case descended into shouts, curses, and threats, the judge probably felt his view of Allen was confirmed. Allen's case is just another trenchant example of what happens when a public defender fails his client. And it should make us skeptical of the usefulness of merely providing lawyers, without ensuring justice.

PRETENDING IT ISN'T THERE
by Nathan J. Robinson

I HAVE LONG HAD AN OBJECTION to the prospect of being blown to smithereens. It is a peculiar fixation of mine. I prefer my life as a fully intact human being, my organs comfortably encased beneath my flesh. I don't wish to be burned to a crisp, splattered onto a wall, or boiled alive. I do not want to be described as "charred beyond recognition." I am strongly opposed to having my limbs, brains, and other components violently extracted from my person and scattered in all directions.

I am therefore somewhat horrified by the prospect of nuclear war. I find it disquieting to realize that the United States possesses about 6,800 warheads, ready to be deployed at any time via submarine, aircraft, and intercontinental ballistic missile (ICBM).[1]

Yet others do not seem to share my horror. Certainly, if they do, they don't talk about it much. The number of nuclear war-related conversations I have overheard or been invited into in the last six months stands at zero. It doesn't seem to come up much.

I suppose it's easy to forget that all the warheads are lying there, ready to vaporize every city on earth in an instant. After all, you rarely see them. Sometimes it's hard to even believe they exist. They don't sit in your front garden waiting to be exploded. They hide deep within secure military installations, often in remote deserts. You don't see many pictures of them, they aren't paraded down the streets. Living under the nuclear threat doesn't *feel* like living with a person permanently pointing a loaded gun at your head.

And yet that's precisely what it is. In fact, it's much, much more terrifying than living with a gun to your head. Because the weapon in question doesn't just threaten you, it threatens *every single thing you love*, every family member, every friend, every colleague, every beautiful and precious thing in your life and the lives of everybody you know.

My God, that makes me sound like some alarmist nutcase. I seem like I'm exaggerating. But I don't think my premises are in any way controversial; it's simply factually true that, in the course of a single day, the world's great powers could end almost all life on earth. We all know this. It's beyond argument. And yet it doesn't really seem *plausible*. It's hard for me to really believe, sitting at my desk in a fuzzy blanket looking out the window at sunshine and trees, that everything could truly be obliterated instantaneously.

But it absolutely could. And by everything, I do truly mean everything. The bombings of Hiroshima and Nagasaki (in which the United States decided to demonstrate its newfound capabilities to the Japanese by detonating atomic weapons in the middle of two cities rather than, as some in the Truman Administration thought would be more reasonable, in an uninhabited area) look like holiday firecrackers next to the explosions we are now capable of producing. A nuclear device 12 feet long could turn every single person in Manhattan into a smudge, and give everyone else within a 100 mile radius both hideous burns and cancer.

I know everybody knows this. I know it's a cliché. But I can't think that everybody really *does* know it, because nobody seems to act as if it's true. Perhaps that's because after a certain amount of repetition, the language and imagery of nuclear war becomes empty of feeling, a set of symbols and signs that don't actually convey much appreciable content. Differing amounts of megatons just seem like numbers, they don't seem real in any substantive way. The word "warhead" becomes innocuous; for decades now it's been a candy with a mushroom cloud logo. The mushroom cloud itself is almost *adorable* or comical. It's still *vaguely* morbid, but if it made us think of Japanese babies without any skin, you wouldn't be able to brand sour candy with it.

Perhaps we've been in a state of relative peace for so long that we've forgotten what war really is. It hasn't been *that* long, of course; there are still World War II veterans and Hiroshima victims alive. And plenty of people on earth *do* have an intimate acquaintance with the realities of large-scale violence. But especially in the United States, it's perfectly possible to go through life with only the fuzziest and most cartoonish understanding of what it means to actually destroy places and people. I've never even seen a very large explosion, let alone had one near me, let alone watched someone I love be torn to bits. How can I possibly contemplate the scale of a nuclear weapon? I can think about it intellectually. But the realities are not just too *horrible*, but too remote from anything in my experiences, for me to be able to seriously conceive of what we are even talking about. Yes, I can affirm that, rationally, I believe a 12-foot long metal object can vaporize everything in the Greater Boston Area. Rationally, I know that there are thousands of hidden underground launching silos, filled with tubes that can fly thousands of miles and turn a million human bodies to ash. I know that the great cities we have spent a dozen generations building are so precarious that Donald Trump could eliminate one within an hour. Yet for these being the *rational* results of inescapable logic, they sounds totally and profoundly *irrational*, because they feel just about as true as the existence of leprechauns or the Great Pumpkin. Really, there are warheads everywhere? I've never seen one. And I can't accept that everything here in Boston, from the Old North Church to the Suffolk Law School to every stop on the Red Line, could cease to exist in a nanosecond.

The good thing about it not seeming like a real threat is that maybe it *isn't* a real threat. Maybe nuclear deterrence really does make us very secure. It certainly seems to have worked for seventy years. Perhaps, despite the counterintuitiveness of the idea, the safest thing for countries to do really is to point the largest possible weapons at one another and depend on the mutual operation of rational self-interest.

I will confess that this does not bring me too much comfort. That's mainly because it only has to fail one time. I actually *do* believe that rational self-interest is a pretty good predictor of much human behavior. Unfortunately, I also believe in the existence of madness. And it only takes one or two nations controlled by the mad or the ambitious in order to plunge humanity into eternal oblivion. To keep nuclear weapons around is to operate on the assumption that there will never again be another Hitler, bent on expansion at all costs and ideologically committed to mass murder. It assumes that a death cult, or a cruel and stupid religious sect like ISIS, will never control the governing apparatus of a major state. And while that may be true in the short term, is it possible that it can be true *forever*? Someday something irrational will happen, and it only needs to happen once.

Maybe that's not the case. Maybe the world *really has* entered a period totally different from every other historical era, in which large-scale war will never again occur. Maybe no government of a major nation will ever again be unhinged and irrational. Or maybe I am a uniquely naïve and pessimistic person, who simply fails to comprehend the way the world works. It's hard not to believe that I am, since everyone else seems so untroubled.

But I just don't know. And it doesn't seem absurd to me to think that some crazed form of religious fundamentalism could have some theory for why the world needed to be destroyed in order to please their god. It doesn't seem a stretch to believe that a chain of small human errors could add up to a very large mistake, one which can never be undone. (As Albert Einstein put it in his warning about the bomb, "So long as there are sovereign nations possessing great power, war is inevitable. [Yet] unless another war is prevented it is likely to bring destruction on a scale never before held possible and even now hardly conceived."[2] Einstein's logic actually leads to the conclusion that the ultimate goal should be the elimination of "sovereign nations possessing great power" altogether.)

I often think of the "Oh, shit" moment that comes along with a catastrophe. This is the moment where someone realizes that everything they thought was true was totally wrong, that what seemed impossible was actually quite possible indeed, and that there is no way to go back and fix the problem. It's the moment where we become fully cognizant of the fact that there was no real logical reason to assume the thing wouldn't happen, that we had just kind of *assumed* it because contemplating it was so unbearable. The last big "Oh, shit" moment was the night of Donald Trump's election. Over the course of the evening, those who were horrified by the prospect of a Trump presidency, but were dead certain that he would lose, realized that they had been conflating desire and reality. They realized that actually, the polls had showed a close race, and the experts' confidence had been completely unwarranted. They realized that the fact that a Trump presidency was *inconceivable* didn't actually affect whether it was *likely*. But by the time that realization came, it was over. There was no way to go back and adjust one's actions accordingly.

My fear is that nuclear war could be similar. It won't seem possible until it becomes inevitable. And once it becomes inevitable, we will have an "Oh, shit" moment. We'll realize that everyone's certainty had been totally groundless, that it had been based entirely on wishful thinking rather than fact. But having the moment of realization doesn't actually let you go back and undo anything. *It's too late.* All you get is those two words. Oh, shit.

I'm not alone in thinking this. William J. Perry, Secretary of Defense under Bill Clinton, has spent the most recent decade or so of his life trying to warn the world of the serious possibility of nuclear catastrophe. In his book *My Journey at the Nuclear Brink*, Perry recounts his experiences with nuclear weaponry from the Cuban Missile Crisis to the present, and issues an urgent call to humanity to wake up and recognize that there is literally no reason to believe that the unthinkable is impossible merely because it is unthinkable. Perry states it plainly: "Today, the danger of some sort of a nuclear catastrophe is greater than it was during the Cold War and most people are blissfully unaware of this danger." Yet during the Cold War, people actually felt the danger. They were afraid. Talk of nuclear war was part of life. (It was even a recurrent theme in pop culture. The six-disc CD box set *Atomic Platters: Cold War Music from the Golden Age of Homeland Security* collects nuclear-themed music from the 40s through 60s, including Muddy Waters playing the "Atomic Bomb Blues" and a gospel number called "Jesus Hits Like An Atom Bomb.")[3]

It's strange, then, that as the destructive capabilities of atomic weapons have only increased, their presence in the public consciousness has diminished. And while during the postwar era, Einstein, Bertrand Russell, and countless other public intellectuals constantly discussed the implications of atomic weaponry for humanity's long-term prospects, today's physicists and philosophers are largely silent on the topic, even as our destructive potential has continued to multiply.

Examining William Perry's work in the *New York Review of Books*, California governor Jerry Brown pondered why nobody was listening:

> *"No one I have known, or have even heard of, has the management experience and the technical knowledge that William Perry brings to the subject of nuclear danger. Few have his wisdom and integrity. So why isn't anyone paying attention to him? Why is fear of a nuclear catastrophe far from the minds of most Americans? And why does almost all of official Washington disagree with him and live in nuclear denial?"*

Brown answers these questions by quoting Perry:

> *"Our chief peril is that the poised nuclear doom, much of it hidden beneath the seas and in remote badlands, is too far out of the global public consciousness. Passivity shows broadly. Perhaps this is a matter of defeatism and its cohort, distraction. Perhaps for some it is largely a most primal human fear of facing the "unthinkable." For others, it might be a welcoming of the illusion that there is or might be an acceptable missile defense against a nuclear attack. And for many it would seem to be the keeping of faith that nuclear deterrence will hold indefinitely—that leaders will always have accurate enough instantaneous knowledge, know the true context of events, and enjoy the good luck to avoid the most tragic of military miscalculations."*[4]

It's reassuring, if that is the right word, to hear Perry confirm this. I keep thinking I must be missing something. But I'm not. Perry knows more about nuclear weapons than anybody, and he says I am right to be shitting myself. The refusal to deal seriously with the nuclear threat can only be based on myths and fallacies, born out of both a desire not to face the unthinkably horrific and a sense that even if one did think about it, it would be impossible to know what to do about it, thus it is better to keep it out of mind.

That type of thinking is suicidal, though. And I am not suicidal. For a person who thinks about the apocalypse as much as I do, I actually believe I am *more* of an optimist than many other people. When I do talk to people about the future of humankind, especially people my age, they often seem to feel resigned to doom. Jokes are made about how the species will be lucky if it survives another fifty years. People do not have much confidence in our ability to solve our problems, to eliminate warfare and the threat we pose to ourselves. Human nature is too flawed, technology advancing too rapidly, militaries too sophisticated, social systems too uncontrollable, for a non-catastrophic future to be possible. We must enjoy what we can while we can, but there's generally very little hope. I find this attitude woefully pessimistic. Yet it's extremely common. I worry, though, that it's a self-fulfilling prophecy and a license to justify inaction through resignation. If you're doomed, why try to fix anything? The courageous and forward-looking thing is to treat human problems and civilizational threats not as our inevitable fate, but as quandaries needing solutions. I may scare people with my talk of nuclear war, with my constant exhortations to people to look at the photos of Hiroshima victims and the numbers on available megatons and ICBM capabilities. But *I* am more scared of those who *refuse* to look at these things, who avoid them and leave them to others, and whose first thoughts about them will come at the "Oh, shit" moment.

I know full well that it's hard. I don't want to think about what happened to the people in Hiroshima. The true horrors are so revolting that if I described or showed them to you fully, you would slam down the lid of your computer. You would be sick to your stomach. And to a certain degree, it is necessary to couch our discussions in morbid jokes, irony, cartoons, because we are ill-equipped to think about what really happens to people when a nuclear weapon is detonated. Actually contemplating it would require us to think of our friends as skeletons, to think of toddlers without skin. I want it so desperately for it to be word, not a physical occurrence in the lives of humans like myself. But it isn't. The bombs are sleeping and waiting, and there's no use thinking they're not.

Let me be clear on what I am trying to argue: I have not advocated immediate nuclear disarmament. My sole contention here is that nuclear wapons need to be *thought about* and understood for what they are, because if their threat isn't taken seriously, it will only be appreciated in hindsight, and in hindsight we will all be dead. I have not taken a position on *how* nuclear war is to be averted, only that it needs to be given the same sober attention that Einstein and Perry have given it.

There are, in fact, good arguments that certain attempts at disarmament could actually make the world less secure. Brad Roberts, in *The Case for U.S. Nuclear Weapons in the 21st Century*, counsels extreme caution in approaches toward reducing U.S. nuclear capability.[5] (Despite a title that makes him sound like Dr. Strangelove, Roberts is sensible and even-handed in his approach.) After all, if the great powers are constantly engaged in a classic "Mexican standoff" situation (the one in films, where the cowboys and banditos are all pointing their guns at each other at once, waiting for one false move), there might be far more risk in trying to get everyone to lower their weapons than in holding things where they are. Roberts, who worked in the Obama administration on nuclear weapons policy, shares a belief that nuclear weapons pose a major threat to humankind, but believes that there are serious perils in trying to disarm quickly. As is often pointed out, if you eliminate nuclear weapons, but countries are still hostile to one another, then instead of being a race to stockpile the most weapons, there will be a race to produce the greatest capacity to reproduce nuclear weapons *quickly* if war were to occur. Thus it may be necessary to focus on reducing *hostility* rather than simply weapons.

I can entertain the intellectual arguments that people like Roberts make, about how from a pragmatic and strategic perspective, campaigns like Global Zero (aiming for the total elimination of nuclear weapons) could increase global instability. However, when reading works on nuclear policy from think tank scholars, I am frequently disturbed by the lack of appreciation shown for the real-world implications of the underlying question. To Roberts, as to many who opine on military strategy, international relations is a policy like any other, to be discussed in precise and technical language. But when we are talking about nuclear weapons, we are fundamentally talking about a set of incredibly violent acts that will be perpetrated upon human beings against their will. It is necessary to appreciate what Hiroshima actually meant to the people it happened to in order to have any kind of sensible discussion about control of nuclear weapons. There is something missing from books like *The Case for Nuclear Weapons in the 21st Century*, which is any sense of what nuclear weapons actually *are*: what they do to people, how they do it, and what the scenarios we are envisaging would really imply. (I feel the same way about the writings of those who defend the Hiroshima/Nagasaki bombings as necessary.[6] I can entertain the *argument* that the bombings were the least worst option. But those making the argument are *never* willing to discuss what the bombings actually did to people. They always wave away these considerations, as Roberts does, with some cursory line about how we all know that nuclear weapons are terrible things that inflict a lot of damage. But *do* we know this? Do we really?) Thus even those who have given the *most* thoughtful consideration of the problems surrounding weapons control still have an insufficient sense of urgency and alarm, and an insufficient appreciation of the true stakes of the issue. When we *do* think about the stakes, we realize in our bones that global nuclear war *cannot be allowed to happen under any circumstances*. However many of these weapons we have, however many we build, we must never, ever fire one. (This makes them, even at their most useful, an incredibly expensive, useless, and inefficient side effect of an unfortunate intercontinental Prisoner's Dilemma.)

Lyndon Johnson's infamous "Daisy" ad is now mostly known as a successful piece of political propaganda, and a milestone in the history of scaremongering.[7] (In it, a little girl picks petals off a daisy before being annihilated in a nuclear explosion; Johnson's voice warns viewers that

"These are the stakes... we must love each other, or we must die." The implication was that one shouldn't vote for Barry Goldwater.) Johnson was criticized for trying to terrify Americans into voting for him.

But the scenario depicted in the ad was perfectly plausible. In fact, we've come close to it several times. Anyone who is insufficiently concerned about arms control should pick up Eric Schlosser's *Command and Control*, which spends 600 pages documenting the United States' long history of very near misses with nuclear bombs.[8] The Johnson ad was absolutely right, and hardly propagandistic, in focusing Americans' attention squarely where it should be: on the issue of which candidate is more likely to end human civilization. Next to this question, everything else is somewhat secondary.

I have a recurring nightmare about nuclear war. In it, I am in a vast cave, deep within a mountain in Colorado or New Mexico. I turn a corner and realize I am in a storage chamber for nuclear warheads. It is totally silent. I cannot believe how peaceful it is. I go up and touch the warheads. They are so still. They seem like they are sleeping. It is difficult to believe that they can even explode, let alone that they can destroy cities. Suddenly, an alert sounds. The usual flashing red lights and sirens. The missiles fire up and launch from the cave. Hundreds of them leave. I know they are heading for cities all over the world. Soon, I am left alone, back in the silence, with the knowledge that in only a few minutes, there will be nothing left of humanity, save for me and the empty cave. I call out, trying to get the missiles to come back. They are gone. I was sitting next to them. But I did not stop them, and now there will be nothing.

The funny thing about this nightmare is that it's not really a nightmare at all. It's the reality we inhabit every day, whether we'd prefer to think about it or not. The missiles are in the caves. They are on submarines, and at air force bases. And if we don't do something while they slumber, there's no calling them back once they've woken up. All you can do is stand at the mouth of the cave, and spend the last few moments thinking about what you did, and what you didn't do.

Oh, shit.

THE SCOURGE OF SELF-FLAGELLATING POLITICS

by Angela Nagle

FROM THE GOSPEL ACCORDING TO LUKE, "For whosoever exalteth himself shall be abased; and he that humbleth himself shall be exalted." If we are to take Luke at his word, then there must be plenty of heavenly exaltation in store for *Jeopardy* contestant turned social justice columnist caricature Arthur Chu, who once tweeted: *"As a dude who cares about feminism sometimes I want to join all men arm-in-arm & then run off a cliff and drag the whole gender into the sea."* Or for those who, on the morning following the election of Donald Trump, took to social media to publicly humble themselves to their followers, expressing their intense inward-turned shame and self-hatred. Typical of the style, *New Statesman* editor Laurie Penny wrote: "I've had white liberal guilt before. Today is the first time I've actually been truly horrified and ashamed to be white." Others expressed their self-disgust at being straight white males and assured followers that while *they* of course did not vote for Trump, merely looking like those who did required some readily self-inflicted penance.[1]

Every time a liberal conducts one of these performances of self-hatred, a predictable reaction cycle is set off. A ragtag army of nasty nihilistic right-wingers (a mixture of quasi-ironic anime-loving Nazis, celibate male separatists, and those who make it their duty to observe and report creeping Cultural Marxism) react with a flurry of anonymous retaliations. To the alt-right, this ritual confession of guilt is further proof of Western civilizational suicide. The self-flagellator is then met with a deluge of racist and/or misogynist abuse, which leaves them even more assured that their own dismal view of the West as white supremacist, misogynist, and essentially evil was correct all along. Online, stuck in an endless loop and unmoored from the cultural mainstream, niche online subcultures from right and left both reinforce their opposed but similarly depressing views of society.

All of which would be a mere curiosity, if it kept itself confined to the darker recesses of the Internet's fetid bowel. However, since the mainstream media is always struggling to keep up with whatever the kids are into, the discourse of white self-criticism has gone somewhat more mainstream. It is now fairly typical to see ritualized confessions of white guilt. As Fredrik deBoer describes it:

> *"[There is] an entire cottage industry devoted to it. Similar arguments calling for white people to own their privilege have been published in places like the Huffington Post and Salon. Popular sites like YouTube and Tumblr play host to hundreds of earnest white people, eagerly disclaiming white privilege and their complicity in white supremacy. White rapper Macklemore recently released his second track concerning his own white privilege."* [2]

Even Donald Sutherland recently felt compelled to describe his feeling "ashamed" for being a "white male." Sutherland apparently had a moment of breakthrough when Helen Mirren, Dame Commander of the Order of the British Empire, informed him "You are the most privileged person on Earth... You are a white male."[3] Damning men for their crimes and defending purest womankind, Michael Moore, author of titles such as *Stupid White Men*, recently observed: "No women ever invented an atomic bomb, built a smoke stack, initiated a Holocaust, melted the polar ice caps or organized a school shooting."[4] (This is false. The Manhattan Project had its unsung female heroes,[5] there are plenty of female oil and gas executives, and female school shooter Brenda Ann Spencer inspired the 1979 Boomtown Rats hit "I Don't Like Mondays." Ironically, Moore erases women's history by neglecting its greatest villains.)

With its obvious channeling of original sin, this style also has parallels in more traditional forms of radical politics than those one might associate with Donald Sutherland and Helen Mirren. One of the stranger incarnations has been the German tendency known as Anti-Deutsch, which has built an entire politics around self-criticism and national collective guilt about the Holocaust. In 1995, to mark the 50th anniversary of the bombing of Dresden, which killed up to an estimated 25,000 people, anti-Germans demonstrated in praise of the bombings on the grounds that it killed people who supported Nazism and was therefore a victory. One year, to mark the event in Dresden, the demonstrators held a sign reading "Bomber Harris, do it again!" in reference to RAF Bomber Command Chief Sir Arthur "Bomber" Harris, who, asked if he felt any guilt at the enormous loss of life, said that he would have destroyed Dresden again.[6] Interestingly, despite its strongest roots being in radical ultra-left politics, the movement's anti-German thinking has led them to support the Israeli state and by extension the United States, especially after 9/11.

In what felt like significant timing, right before Donald Trump's election, the film adaption of Philip Roth's masterpiece *American Pastoral* was released in cinemas. In it, the daughter of the central family who is consumed by hatred for the white America that her ideal bourgeois family exemplifies, bombs the local post office before disappearing into a fictionalized version of the Weather Underground. On her bedroom wall hangs a fictionalized Weatherman motto:

> "*We are against everything that is good and decent in honky America. We will loot and burn and destroy. We are the incubation of your mothers' nightmares.*"

The Weathermen used a style of "criticism-self-criticism" sessions, also called "Weatherfries," which were described by the author of *Bringing the War Home* as "the most harrowing aspect of life within the collective." Based on Maoist struggle sessions, these were used to root out subconscious racism and sexism within their own psyches. Individuals were reportedly hazed for up to twelve hours without a break until the white radicals confessed their deep white supremacism, homophobia and misogyny to their fellow white radicals thus achieving catharsis through their own admission of guilt.

The most famous case of white self-hatred leading to full-scale self-delusion was probably that of Rachel Dolezal, the Africana studies instructor and president of a local branch of the National Association for the Advancement of Colored People (NAACP) who turned out to be a natural blonde white woman in pretty convincing disguise. Dolezal had so successfully persuaded herself that she was black that she seemed unable to understand what she had done, as she struggled to answer interview questions about her motivation. In sympathy with Dolezal, a white female college professor writing for the *Huffington Post*, Ali Michael, later admitted:

"I couldn't have biological children because I didn't want to propagate my privilege biologically." She went on to say: *"...like Dolezal, I wanted to take on Africanness. Living in South Africa during my junior year abroad, I lived with a Black family, wore my hair in head wraps, shaved my head... I didn't want to be White, but if I had to be, I wanted to be White in a way that was different from other White people I knew... But the lesson for me is remembering how deep the pain is, the pain of realizing I'm White... The pain of facing that honestly is blinding."* [7]

Watching the suicidal levels of secularized self-flagellation in the aftermath of Trump made me recall the famous scene in the movie *Malcolm X*, in which a young white woman momentarily blocks Malcolm X's path and asks what she, as a white person, can do to help his cause. He answers with one coldly served word – "Nothing." The scene was based on a real encounter he had with a "little blonde co-ed" after which he wrote, "I'd never seen anyone I ever spoke to before more affected than this little white girl... Her clothes, her carriage, her accent all showed Deep South breeding and money."

"Nothing" could certainly be a succinct one-word summation of what exactly anyone seems to be benefiting from much of the contemporary online performance of self-criticism. But then, Malcolm X went on to regret being contemptuous of the white girl depicted in the scene. Years later, it affected him quite profoundly, and he said:

> *"Well, I've lived to regret that incident. In many parts of the African continent I saw white students helping black people. Something like this kills a lot of argument... I guess a man's entitled to make a fool of himself if he's ready to pay the cost. It cost me twelve years."*[8]

Malcolm came to feel that the strict racial nationalism preached by the Nation of Islam had been fundamentally mistaken. By the end of his life, his political thought was becoming more sophisticated and nuanced, as he thought through the question of how to fight racism without reproducing a crude nationalism.

Could there be a more sympathetic analysis also of today's political self-criticism? The Weathermen were, after all, motivated by the extent to which they despised the racist Vietnam War, and their own culture for enabling it. Spend a little time in Berlin going from grim Holocaust memorial to grim Holocaust museum and you'll soon get a sense of why a tendency like Anti-Deutsch exists, however wacky it may be. In its easily parodied but relatively benign form today, you could interpret the current wave of online self-criticism as youthful emotion and hyperbole with wholly good intentions. In the age of Trump, who is already making boastful threats of unconstitutional punishments for flag burning, perhaps this kind of self-criticism could be an antidote to the excesses of aggressive and unchecked nationalism and the dark forces it has historically whipped up.

Yet, the Weathermen's deeply degenerate and cult-like internal politics didn't do anyone any good. In fact, they seemed far more a product of neurosis and narcissism than of revolutionary strategy–they couldn't stand to be seen as part of the white bourgeois society they came from and so they found entirely negative ways to purge themselves in the presence of other white radicals.

The relatively harmless tweeting of today certainly leaves fewer human casualties behind. But it is still based on a common impulse – the expression of total contempt for one's own society expressed through progressive language. In this internal psychodrama the oppressed appear as purely symbolic, rather than as real people for whom one is trying to generate real material gains. It is difficult to think of any positive political movement past or present that has changed the lives of human beings for the better based on misanthropy and radical performances of self-hatred.

Even the cruelest alt-right critics tend to regard extreme forms of liberal social media self-hatred as simply pathetic, a sign of a lack of self-respect. But in my own more ungenerous moments I wonder if it is something worse. Rather than merely being of benefit to no one, it could be of quite a significant benefit to just one person – the self-flagellator themselves. Publicly declaring your sins makes you appear a better person than those who have not declared them. It is not really a put-down of oneself, but a put-down of others, who are less morally worthy for having been less forthcoming in their confessions.

Online, many liberal commentators and internet personalities have built fame and careers purely through trading in the currency of virtue. As more seek to mimic this, they rely upon the value of this precious currency, even as it is constantly devalued by its own abundance. So the rituals escalate in absurdity. Suddenly denouncing Trump is not enough, he must be "literally Hitler." Soon denouncing all of society as literally Hitler is not enough; one has to turn inward and denounce oneself with the same ferocity. Others climbing the greasy pole of liberal virtue to careers in academia or ideological listicle-writing must seek to outpace and dethrone those taking up their spot in the limited room available at the top.

But beneath the performance of humility and self-criticism may lie something thoroughly self-interested and entirely without real virtue. I'm reminded of the very un-virtuous Nietzsche's scathing inversion of the Christian formulation in Luke's gospel, instead suggesting, "He who humbleth himself *wishes to be* exalted."

AT THE BORDER

by Brianna Rennix

I'M SITTING IN A TRAILER, in a small room furnished with a table and two chairs. There is a woman sitting across the table from me. She has a squirming child held down firmly in her lap. She is telling me why she left Honduras. I half-understand Spanish, so the meaning of her speech is reaching me in a muffled, underwater kind of way. In a few seconds, a telephonic interpreter will translate her words into English for me. The voice from the phone has the polite, neutral cadence of someone who is used to translating business conference calls.

The woman is telling me how a local gang member used to follow her home every day after work. Now the little boy in her lap is chewing on a pen he snatched off the table. His face is covered with small pen-marks. As his mother begins to tell me about the time she was raped, I see the cap of the pen vanish into the boy's mouth. I watch the pointed tip emerge and retract several times threateningly between his lips, like a black bee-stinger. Ah shit, I think, what if this kid accidentally swallows that cap? I don't want to interrupt his mother, who is in the middle of telling me one of the worst things that's ever happened to her. I also don't want her child to choke to death in front of us both.

I've almost mustered up the right combination of Spanish and fran-tic gesticulation to alert the mother to the situation, when the kid suddenly spits out the cap with a wet pop. He grins at me openmouthed, his tongue blue with ink.

I want to smile, so the kid doesn't think I'm angry at him. But this is a bad moment to smile. I don't want the mother to think I'm smiling at what she's telling me. In the end, I have no idea what kind of a face I end up making. Some sort of hideous half-grimace, probably.

As with all of these consultations, I come away thinking of a hundred things I should have done differently. Under other circumstances, I would probably brood over this interaction for hours, replaying it over and over in my mind. But now I simply don't have the time. There are many more women to see.

The inside of the visitors' trailer, and the bits of scenery visible out the various office windows—revealing, what else, more trailers—are the most I ever see of the South Texas Family Residential Center. The Corrections Corporation of America (CCA), the private prison company that manages the center, doesn't allow outsiders to wander around the facilities. Viewed from the front, the optics of this "family residence" aren't too great. There are dozens of floodlights suspended on high poles, and below them, rows upon rows of little trailers, all surrounded by a big fence. It looks like an internment camp. And that, more or less, is what it is.

The South Texas Family Residential Center is the place where we detain many of the mothers and children who approach our southern border without papers. Not all of the women even make it this far. The Border Patrol officers who pick them up will usually attempt to persuade them—sometimes with threats—to sign self-deportation orders. But if a woman tells the officer she's afraid to return to her home country, he may send her and her children to a detention center to await something called a "credible fear interview." The outcome of this interview will determine if she can remain in the United States to formally apply for asylum, or if she'll be deported back to the country she fled.

The vast majority of these women and children are from Guatemala, El Salvador, and Honduras, whose citizens have been fleeing in large numbers since around 2014. In these countries, organized gangs control large territories, and the impunity rate for violent crime, including murder, rape, and domestic violence, is estimated to be as high as 95%. The two biggest gangs in Central America, MS-13 and Barrio 18, were originally founded in Los Angeles, and expanded to Central America when the U.S. deported a large number of gang members in the 1990s. In a region exhausted by decades of conflict (in which U.S. meddling played no small part), with weak civic institutions and high unemployment, the gangs proliferated rapidly. MS-13 and Barrio 18 rely on extortion to sustain themselves, and they exact compliance through terror. For sheer, cinematic horror, their techniques—arson, murder, rape, kidnapping, mutilation, decapitation—rival anything that ISIS has been getting up to on the other side of the Atlantic. A lot of the refugees fleeing the Northern Triangle don't even try to sneak across the border. Rather, they present themselves directly to border patrol officials, hoping they will protect them.

When women and children first began appearing at the border in significant numbers, during Obama's presidency, they were detained and processed in a highly clandestine manner. Women, along with their children, were locked up without access to legal counsel. Exhausted, traumatized, terrified, most of them were rapidly deported without any substantive opportunity to appeal the decision to a judge. The purpose of this high-speed deportation mill was to get people out the country as quickly and unpleasantly as possible, in the hopes that rumors of this poor reception would deter future border-crossers. Then some immigration lawyers got wind of the situation and decided to set up permanent shop right next to the family detention centers. Since the lawyers got involved, rates of positive credible fear determinations have gone up exponentially, indicating that a lot of the people who were deported under the earlier system almost certainly had viable asylum claims.

This legal operation, dubbed the CARA Pro Bono Project, is no small feat, requiring a massive expenditure of private resources: most of the legal assistants on the ground at any given time are out-of-town volunteers who travel to the detention center at their own expense and live out of hotel rooms. The South Texas Family Residential Center is located in Dilley, Texas, a tiny town about an hour's drive from the border, far from the metropolitan centers where lawyers tend to be concentrated. A briefly up-and-coming but now mostly abandoned fracking town, Dilley has a disproportionately large number of gas stations and motels, but not much else. (According to its Wikipedia page, it also has a haunted grain silo, which I regret to say I never visited.) The detainee population inside the detention center, which can house up to 2,400 people, is usually about half as big as the population of the entire town of 3,800.

I first glimpse the women of the detention center sitting in a circle, listening to an orientation speech by a CARA volunteer. I am struck by how small many of them are: seated in their chairs, their dangling feet barely graze the floor. Some of the women are holding babies, or have toddlers playing in front of their chairs. They have all recently traveled approximately 1450 miles across Mexico, partly on foot, a long journey fraught with terrible dangers, from Mexican immigration authorities, from drug cartels, from drifters and fellow-migrants. One woman begins speaking about her time in an hielera: this is a U.S. Border Patrol cell where migrants are held for several days right after they're apprehended. The cells are air-conditioned to uncomfortably frigid temperatures, are continually illuminated all through the night, and usually have no cots or blankets to sleep on. The woman tells a story about how her child wanted a drink of water and the officer wouldn't give her any. My Anglophone brain, trying to parse the Spanish on the fly, catches on a word that I know, that I keep hearing over and over: llorando, llorando, llorando—crying, crying, crying.

One staff member described the CARA Pro Bono Project to me as "a cross between a legal aid office and an emergency room." Every week, new women and children arrive at the detention center. The CARA volunteers' job is to prepare these mothers for their credible fear interviews with the asylum office. In order to pass her interview, the woman must state enough facts to show that she could, potentially, win an asylum case in court. If she can do that, she'll be paroled out of the detention center with a notice to appear before a court on a particular date. But if she doesn't tell the asylum officer the right information, or if the asylum officer doesn't believe her story, she is in immediate danger of deportation. In addition, for the many women who won't be able to afford private lawyers and may not have access to pro bono assistance after they leave the detention center, this consultation with CARA may be the last and only time they get to speak to a legal adviser of any kind.

I talk to women back-to-back for eight or nine hours a day. I hear a lot of stories. The stories are all similar: they all have elements in common, but they are all different: there are always strange details, elaborate side-narratives, that make each story untidy, and thus, somehow, more plausible. "Why did you leave your country?" I ask, and all the women begin their reply, almost without exception, with "Por miedo"—because of fear. Many women talk about the gangs: how the gangs extorted them, attacked them, murdered their family members, threatened to forcibly recruit their young children. Some women fled because they received an anonymous phone call, or a threatening note slipped under their door. It might have come from a gang, it might not: they have no idea. They may have fled because a frightening-looking man stood in front of their house three nights in row, or because a tattooed stranger made an "I'm watching you" gesture at them in the street. In an environment of continuous threat and sudden eruptions of violence, signs of impending lethal danger are often strange, inarticulate, highly contextual.

The other major theme is domestic violence. Abused women who are coming from countries where the police refuse to intervene over "private" family matters, or don't have the resources to control offenders, may have a legally solid asylum case. The precise legal formulation for a successful domestic violence case hinges on whether the woman had the ability to leave her partner without facing retribution, whether her partner considered her to be his personal property. And so you always ask: "Did he ever say you were his property? Did he ever say that because you were a woman, you had to do whatever he said?"

The initial response I get from almost every woman I interview is the same: a sudden, wry smile. What the smile means I can't quite say—I think it's something between gratification that I've guessed correctly, and a kind of amusement that I even had to ask something so obvious.

"Yes," they reply, "he said that all the time."

Many people bring their children into the room with them during consultations. Some mothers are, understandably, reluctant to let their children out of sight. Others are still breastfeeding their infants or toddlers. Consultations are intermittently interrupted by temper tantrums and deferred-naptime meltdowns. One woman has to stop her story of abuse several times as her son barges playfully in and out of the room. "He's old enough to understand," his mother tells me in a nervous voice. Another woman tells me how a gang member tried to run her down in his car, chasing after her while she ran with her child in her arms. "He still has nightmares about the car," she whispers, nodding to her son. The little boy, suddenly frightened, begins grabbing her arms urgently, trying to climb into her lap, saying over and over, "El carro, mamá, el carro." Yet another woman puts her head down on the table and sobs, begging me not to let them send her home, crying that she would rather spend the rest of her life in prison in the United States than go back to her country. Moments earlier, she had described to me how a gang member had threatened to cut up her daughter into four pieces. She had good reason to believe that this was no idle threat: the same gang member had already killed and dismembered her uncle.

In the corner of the office, her daughter is playing with a toy truck. Not long ago, someone, somewhere, was looking at the living body of this child and contemplating cutting her into four pieces.

Like being an EMT, working in asylum law gradually fucks up your normal emotional reactions. You get eerily accustomed to watching near-strangers cry in front of you. You also experience a disturbing sense of relief whenever a client reveals some harrowing detail that will bolster their case. The legal standards in asylum law are, frankly, bizarre. Under the law, you can get asylum if you can show that you have a "well-founded fear" of future persecution, "on account of" a protected ground, at the hands of your government or an actor that your government is "unwilling or unable" to control. Sometimes the hardest thing to prove is the "on account of a protected ground" part: you have to show you were targeted for a specific reason, namely, "race, religion, nationality, membership in a particular social group, or political opinion." If someone in your home country is trying to murder you because he just hates your guts, that's not persecution. If you live in an active conflict zone where everyone is being indiscriminately targeted for violence, that's not persecution. You have to prove that there's something about you, some belief you hold, some "immutable characteristic," that made someone decide to come after you. Tiny details, like the specific insult somebody used when they were threatening you, can become hugely relevant. So a woman comes to you with her story, and its natural points of narrative emphasis: and you must suggest to her different points of emphasis, the ones that are legally relevant, even though no sane person outside our legal system would think these kinds of details mattered a damn, in terms of whether somebody deserves to be sent home to a life of unremitting violence and fear.

In a little office room, it's just you, and this woman you only met a minute ago, talking about some of the worst things that can happen to a human being. It's a strangely intimate experience, having that level of trust suddenly placed in you, even if you know it's borne of desperation, rather than anything you've done to earn it. You want to offer these women some word of encouragement. You want to tell them that they can breathe easy now, that they're in a safe place, that the United States will welcome and protect them after all they've suffered. But of course, you can't promise them anything. So instead, you nudge a box of tissues across the table, and try to think of something you can say. What you can say are mostly platitudes, but they are also true. "You're strong, to have survived so much. You're a brave person, to have come all this way. You did the right thing, to protect your children. You're well-prepared for your interview."

I was a volunteer at Dilley in August 2016. Halfway through my time there, Republican presidential nominee Donald Trump gave his first major immigration policy speech. He announced his intention to build an impenetrable southern border wall, complete with aerial drones and underground sensors. He discussed expanding immigration detention, tripling the number of ICE and Border Patrol officers. He conjured up a terrifying picture of the widespread violence and lawlessness threatening innocent U.S. citizens across the land, all because of lax immigration enforcement.

Listening to Trump's speech, I thought about the dozens of women I had spoken to so far. They had all been, without exception, shockingly gracious, warm, and friendly, greeting me with smiles, laughing indulgently at my bad Spanish, earnestly answering all the terrible and intrusive questions I had to ask them. They were at once ordinary, and also the heroes of unwritten epics. I imagined these women and their children, at the end of their long, perilous journey across the whole length of Mexico, coming up against an impenetrable wall, coming up against a Border Patrol officer who's been implicitly authorized to turn a deaf ear to their pleas. I imagined what the return journey would feel like, heading southwards again, knowing that you were going back to the same hell you had risked so much to leave, knowing that your escape attempt will certainly have been noted, knowing that it will not go unpunished. I felt, viscerally, that a single fingernail or hair follicle of any one of these women was worth more than Donald Trump's entire body.

Now, every one of the talking points from Trump's policy speech has resurfaced in the form of executive orders. Though Trump's "Muslim ban" has received the most national attention, his executive orders on border security and interior enforcement—which include promises to "end the abuse of parole and asylum provisions currently used to prevent the lawful removal of removable aliens"—are the ones that pose the greatest danger to refugees coming from the south. These orders contemplate a relocation of significant enforcement and adjudication resources to the border. They envision the universal detention of all people entering the U.S. without authorization, and a possible halt to the parole system, which has previously allowed people who aren't deemed to pose a security risk—like the mothers at Dilley—to be released from detention centers on bond, or with ankle monitors, during the multiyear adjudication process for their case. It remains to be seen exactly how these orders will be carried out in practice, and whether Congress will appropriate the necessary funds for their most ambitious provisions. But it certainly isn't comforting that all the agencies which deal with immigration matters, including the immigration courts, are part of the executive branch.

The orders, if fulfilled to their maximum extent, would create a system where asylum-seekers are detained in centers near the border until the outcome of their case is resolved, with limited access to attorneys, far from their family members and support networks in the United States. They would not be able to take their cases to, say, California or Massachusetts, where the case law is generally more favorable and asylum grant rates are higher. Instead, more immigration judges would be stationed along the border, where legal aid resources for immigrants are already stretched to the limit.

In these uncertain times, it's far from clear whether CARA and the other legal organizations that work in detention centers will continue to have their present level of access to detainees. The CARA system in Dilley has worked well, in part, because the organization eventually came to enjoy a certain level of respectful cooperation from the private prison authority and from ICE under President Obama. (Indeed, CARA was sometimes annoyingly touted by visiting government officials as an example of how well the family detention system was working; look, we know that detaining toddlers and nursing mothers sounds bad, but hey! We let them have lawyers!). A more hostile tone within ICE could have a huge impact on these arrangements. Small, vindictive policy changes, like reductions in consultation spaces, or banning the volunteers' wireless network, could significantly gum up CARA's operations. Under the Trump administration, ICE might do something even more brazen, like simply refuse to let lawyers see their would-be clients at all. CCA, the private prison authority, has already tried this maneuver at adult detention centers, repeatedly. It's hard to know how far they might now test the boundaries of the law, which already offers far from optimum protection for immigrant detainees.

Inhumane asylum proceedings and unforgiving enforcement policies may well, over time, have a deterrent effect on border-crossings. When those border numbers drop, we can expect to hear the figures cited at press briefings. It will be hailed as a major policy victory. But we mustn't forget what those numbers mean. They mean women trapped in violent homes, in violent cities, with no means of escape. They mean children run down with cars, children chopped into pieces. To plead for the vulnerability of children feels, at times, like a cheap rhetorical trick, or a denial of the deservingness of other kinds of people. But if we can't care about children, we can't care about anyone. And if these children and their parents stop showing up in person to our border, no further hint of their sufferings will even make our morning news.

PECULIARITIES OF THE YANKEE CONFEDERATE

by Alex Nichols

EARLIER THIS YEAR, my rural Massachusetts hometown became unexpectedly embroiled in controversy, after a police officer mounted a Confederate flag at his home in plain view of the 10-year-old African American boy who lived across the street. The boy's parents, raising their son in the age of Tamir Rice, naturally felt somewhat alarmed to discover that local law enforcement harbored Confederate sympathies. The town's Human Rights Commission (we have those here) was promptly alerted and a town meeting was called. There, most attendees condemned the officer's actions and tried to explain the (seemingly) obvious racial subtext.

But plenty of town residents defended the officer. The local newspaper heard from readers insisting that "saying someone is racist by owning a flag" was far more racist than the flag itself. Another encouraged the boy's family to "get over it," lamenting that "if it's not a flag, it's how you say 'happy holidays.' If it's not that, it's a Starbucks cup." And the officer's own response? "The flag has no negative connotations to me."

One can sympathize, for perhaps a second, with those professing themselves baffled by anyone "mad about a flag." But for them, it may be useful to consider how the same response would sound if someone hoisted a "Death to Black People" flag with a picture of a lynching on it. "I can't believe you're mad about a flag; next you'll be mad about a coffee cup" doesn't sound quite so reasonable when we draw out what the Confederacy means to a black audience. (Remember, too, that it was not social justice types but right-wing Christians who threw a fit over the insufficient festiveness of the paper cups at Starbucks.) But the more curious question is: if the flag doesn't have any *negative* connotations, what possible connotations *does* it have, when flown in small-town New England? What causes people born and raised in the North, many of them with no historical or familial connection to the South, to align themselves with a symbol of Southern pride, treason, and slavery?

When challenged, fans of the Stars 'n' Bars have plenty of rehearsed answers. Most often, they will say they appreciate the Confederacy's place in American history and lament the efforts of revisionist historians to erase it from our collective memory. And following up with "Appreciate *what* about it, precisely?" will get one nothing except mumbled clichés about the rebel spirit.

The charge that the left is attempting to wipe away history is a strange one. In reality, it would be nearly impossible to find a left-leaning historian who doesn't want Americans to talk *more* about the Civil War, slavery, and Reconstruction in order to better understand modern institutional racism. Nobody is *less* inclined to erase the Confederacy from American history than the left. When we do see efforts to remove inconvenient facts from the standard curriculum, they usually come from conservatives in the South. It was the Texas Board of Education who refused to allow the fact-checking of history textbooks that used hilariously banal euphemisms to describe chattel slavery, referring to slaves as "immigrants" and "workers." The movement to sanitize and decontextualize Confederate imagery is a far greater crime against the integrity of the historical record than the efforts of leftists to point out that the South did not just stand for "states' rights," but the states' right to *maintain a very particular thing.* It's their own fact-blindness that causes history-challenged conservatives to be genuinely stunned that anyone would want to remove the flag from the South Carolina State House after an avowed neo-Confederate and white supremacist massacred nine black churchgoers.

Understanding the cultural pathology behind Northern use of the Confederate flag is like understanding the rise of Donald Trump as a serious politician. It is inexplicable, essentially unfathomable. Yet one can attempt tentative hypotheses, which involve a nuanced examination of race, class, the rural/urban divide, and the widespread human attraction to nauseating kitsch. Just as one can only hope to approximate the structural causes of our 45th president, one can only guess cautiously at why, in the Berkshires of Connecticut and Massachusetts, the Stars and Stripes and the Stars and Bars can hang from the same flagpole without anyone batting an eye or sensing a paradox.

The entire idea of the flag as an enduring Southern symbol is its own revisionist lie. After all, the Stars and Bars flag was barely used in the Old South, revived only in the mid-20th century by white supremacists who would rather see black children hanged from trees than given equal access to the public school system. The symbols of the Confederacy had largely remained the domain of veterans groups until they were deliberately resurrected as a way to resist the Civil Rights Movement. The rebirth began shortly after World War II, when Truman's decision to integrate the Army increased tensions between Northern and Southern Democrats and inspired Strom Thurmond to run for president as a Dixiecrat. Thurmond, the grandson of a Confederate veteran and a staunch segregationist, employed the battle flag in his campaign as an explicitly racist gesture. In 1956, Georgia creatively incorporated the battle flag design into its state flag to protest *Brown v. Board of Education.*

In 1961, Governor George Wallace raised the battle flag over the Alabama state capitol. Wallace, one of the most passionate defenders of segregation, also espoused a white-centered form of populism. He targeted the federal government not just because it outlawed segregated schools, but because it enriched elites at the expense of the common man. He tailored his message to blue-collar white voters who felt left behind and condescended to by Washington. Wallace had a gift for pandering: "... when the liberals and intellectuals say the people don't have any sense, they talkin' about us people... But hell, you can get good solid information from a man drivin' a truck, you don't need to go to no college professor", he said in 1966. Rather than embracing a truly populist platform like Huey Long in the 1930s, Wallace encouraged his white supporters to direct most of their anger toward newly enfranchised blacks. When he ran as an independent in the 1968 presidential election he won 13.5% of the popular vote, a significant improvement upon Thurmond's 2.4%. Despite being a neoconfederate at heart, he made significant headway outside the South, attracting tens of thousands at rallies above the Mason-Dixon line; his populist rhetoric and outsider image endeared him to blue-collar whites as far north as Wisconsin. Many union members who would have otherwise voted Democratic bought into his warning that integration would destroy the labor movement. (As always, people straddling the line between the lower and middle classes were the easiest prey for fear-based politics.) Through all this, Wallace stood with the Confederate flag behind him, figuratively and literally. Among the many disastrous consequences of the 1968 election was the permanent association of unpolished white populism with Southern pride. From then on, it became a safe bet that whenever lower-middle-class white resentment bubbled to the surface, no matter where in the country, it would come wrapped in the Confederate flag.

Northern whites lack a unified ethnocultural identity. This could be due to the outcome of the Civil War—the victors may write history, but the losers are often awash in fear, resentment, and self-pity. Such forces bind the populace together and can prove very dangerous in the hands of nationalists (think interwar Germany). It may also be due to their relative diversity; in the 19th and 20th centuries America received a massive influx of immigrants from all over Europe and the majority settled in the heavily industrialized Northeast and mid-Atlantic. Maintaining a straightforward regional identity in the face of constant demographic upheaval is difficult if not impossible.

Now, imagine yourself in the rural North in an age where it is mandated that you consciously create a capital-I Identity for yourself. One is supposed to create this "identity" through consumer choices and Facebook cover photos. You are white, as are most of the people you know. You have a high school education and all your employment prospects are either blue collar or low-level white collar. You subscribe to a personal philosophy that emphasizes disciplined physical labor as the bedrock of proper morality, but you also take pride in your lack of city-boy etiquette and frequently engage in lighthearted but legal hedonism. How do you categorize yourself? What do you "identify" as?

Well, fortunately, an identity just for you has been consolidated into a few symbols, hobbies, and character traits, turned into a packaged cultural commodity for your instantaneous adoption and consumption. This identity is The South. The fake, commodified South, that is, not to be confused with the actually existing South, which has a rich cultural history and (unlike the commodified South) has black people in it. This imaginary South is about all-camo outfits and huntin', fishin', and spittin' to spite coastal elites who want to make it illegal to hunt, fish, and spit. The commodified South is *Duck Dynasty*, McDonald's sweet tea, and country songs that have "country" in the title. People seem to really like this stuff, which is why, compared to other regions, the South is overrepresented among Zippo lighter designs and truck decals.

Partially divorced of context, what was once a symbol of an aristocratic slave society becomes, paradoxically, part of a tradition of populist Americana along with John Wayne, Chief Wahoo, and the Pixar version of Route 66. *Fully* divorced of context, the flag becomes a symbol of vague, noncommittal rebellion. It takes its place alongside a series of meaningless but ubiquitous kitschy products including wolf shirts, the pissing Calvin decal, skull-adorned lighters, and overly aggressive Minions memes about what people can and can't do before you've had your coffee.

The small bit of context that the flag *does* retain is used to sinister ends. Among rural whites, a watered-down version of neoconfederate ideology serves as a kind of mutant substitute for class consciousness. This is especially evident in modern country music, where many songs are essentially a bullet point list of stereotypes: big trucks, cheap beer, dirt roads, and physically demanding blue collar work. Take, for example, Lee Brice's 2014 smash hit "Drinking Class":

"I belong to the drinking class / Monday through Friday, man we

bust our backs / If you're one of us, raise your glass / I belong to the drinking class."

The structure of Brice's lyrics shows a keen awareness of socioeconomic class. But this is not the labor movement's conception of class, with its exhortation to social change. The Lee Brice theory of class is empty of meaning. It's hopeless and sad; nothing is left but solipsistic in-group pride and alcoholism. The vice neuters any revolutionary fervor. A member of the Drinking Class isn't interested in social climbing and he would never dream of doing away with class distinctions altogether.

The Drinking Class man knows life is pretty rotten, that you work and drink until you die. But, strongly encouraged by millionaire tribunes of the working poor like the guy from *Dirty Jobs*, the guy from *Duck Dynasty*, and the guy from Larry the Cable Guy (plus fellow reality star Donald J. Trump), he adopts flimsy, prejudiced rationalizations to explain his very real feelings of being forgotten and exploited. He justifies his toil as morally necessary, rather than exploitative. And like a surly teen alienated from his parents and bored with masturbation, he joins a cultural clique and cements his place in it by lashing out at its real or imaginary enemies. To get back at the elites who mocked him for making little sense, he begins to do things that make little sense, such as flying a Confederate flag in Massachusetts. (Half-assed clique membership is often embarrassing, like when homophobic metalheads get tricked into wearing leather daddy outfits.)

We can therefore find explanations, if not justifications, for the peculiar existence of our Yankee Confederate. Some of it is stupid, some of it is racist, and some of it is a misguided response to the need for identity and solidarity. Like depressed teens, alienated rural whites aren't imagining their suffering, and they do have legitimate grievances about the unending despair of the American status quo. But they have reacted in a way that's difficult to defend either rationally or morally.

The solution here is to organize against the policies that created an alienated rural working class in the first place. To the extent that the flag is a product of the search for identity and community, one needs to have a better, less appalling identity to offer people. To the extent that the flag is a product of racism, what is racism itself a product of? Working class whites have often blamed their problems on nonwhites, but this is irrational scapegoating. And *since* it's irrational scapegoating, the left should think seriously about how to give people real explanations for their problems, as well as solutions. The New England Confederate is a bizarre and horrifying sight, but he is not without his structural causes. If we can offer a unifying message to working class people of all races, we may see fewer members of the Drinking Class embrace backward cultural symbols and buy into the South as consumer lifestyle brand. Stars and Bars keychains may create a cheap rush of ersatz proletarian solidarity, but they are no substitute for the real thing.

SUICIDE AND THE AMERICAN DREAM

by Nathan J. Robinson

"THE MILLISECOND MY HANDS LEFT THE RAIL, it was an instant regret," recalled Kevin Hines, a man who attempted suicide from the Golden Gate Bridge in 2000. "My final thought was 'What the hell did I just do? I don't want to die.'"[1] Hines picked the bridge for its "simplicity," it was a four-foot barrier that a person could almost just tumble over. Because the bridge made it so easy to jump, even someone who felt deeply ambivalent, in half a second could impulsively make a choice that they would be unable to undo. You can decide not to jump as many times as you like, but if you decide to jump, it's the last decision you'll make.

Suicide is unforgiving like that. It doesn't matter if one is perfectly content 99% of the time; a single moment of despair will suffice. The majority of suicides are on impulse; studies of people who have survived suicide attempts have found that the time between the decision to kill one's self and the actual attempt is almost always an hour or less. (It is often less than five minutes.) And 90% of survivors will never ultimately kill themselves, suggesting what the *New England Journal of Medicine* calls the "temporary nature and fleeting sway of many suicidal crises."[2] It is disturbing to consider how many people's brief time on Earth ends with that final thought: "What the hell did I just do?"

It's very difficult to write about suicide without appearing dreary, depressing, and morbid. Nobody wants to discuss it, nobody wants to read about it. Online, articles about suicide get about as much readership as exposes of sweatshop labor and cow torture, i.e. not a hell of a lot.

But the moment you appreciate the human implications of the statistics, you realize that silence on suicide is a moral outrage. Suicides in America alone are now at 42,000 per year; the country's suicide rate is the highest it has been in 30 years.[3] That means people, thousands upon thousands of them, made of flesh and deeply sad, are simply popping out of existence one after another. In terms of death toll, it's fourteen 9/11s per year!

And it's largely needless. The impulsive nature of so many suicides means that they are preventable. Reducing the easy availability of means, and supporting people through the brief periods of time during which they are most likely to act, can be the difference between their living a full life and their plunging into eternal oblivion.

It's very difficult to acknowledge the full implications of the evidence. "I'm walking to the bridge, If one person smiles at me on the way, I will not jump," wrote one suicidal man before heading for the Golden Gate.[4] Evidently nobody smiled; he jumped to his death. It might be comforting to believe that a smile wouldn't actually have made a difference, that he would have made the same choice no matter what. But from what we know, that's often not true. Many who contemplate suicide are looking for a way out; most do not want to die. A small act of kindness can nudge people from the ledge. (This is a good argument for remembering to smile at strangers.) That fact should be disquieting; it implies that so many tens of thousands of tragedies have been avoidable. It is heartening, however, insofar as it affirms the possibility of saving countless lives.

That makes the city of San Francisco's longtime indifference toward Golden Gate suicides fairly outrageous. The bridge has been known as a "suicide magnet," and dozens leap from it every year. Yet for decades, the city has been resistant to putting up a suicide net beneath the bridge. This has largely been for aesthetic reasons, as well as out of a reluctance to spend money on a problem that has little political value. After years of pressure from advocacy groups, in 2014 the city finally agreed to put up a barrier,[5] though at the moment it's being held up because the steel for the nets has to be American-made.[6]

It's no surprise that San Francisco dragged its feet, though. Judging from the amount of media attention it gets, suicide is evidently seen as a non-issue in the United States. Partially, the reluctance has been because of that lie we tell ourselves: that people "would have found some other way." That's false, as we know, because the easier it is to do it, the more likely it is to be done. Sometimes it's inevitable, more often it's anything but.

Yet there's also a uniquely American "free choice" aspect to the nation's blasé treatment of suicide. "If people wish to kill themselves, that's up to them" seems to be the dominant unspoken attitude. Nobody is forced to do it, thus nobody is responsible but the person who kills herself. (That's surely one of the reasons that suicide hasn't taken on a larger place in the country's gun control debate. Half of all suicides per year are by firearm, and yet mass shootings—which are far rarer—are treated as the greater tragedy.)[7]

The individualist position, which treats every person's life outcomes as being entirely of their own making, represents both a deep moral callousness and a total indifference to empirical fact. We know that people are irrational, frail, and ambivalent, that they make choices they regret, that their brains lie to them about how much other people love them. Yet the "minding your own business" ethic is a core part of the national ideology. Your choices are your own, and if you don't like the consequences, well, sucks for you. That line of libertarian-ish thinking is common even in cases where people's choices are far less free than suicide; there is little sympathy for those devastated by economic crises, or drowning in medical bills. So it's little surprise that suicide, which appears entirely freely-chosen, should be treated as an entirely private concern.

However, suicide is not some spontaneous product of the will. Like everything else, it's brought about by a combination of a person's internal wiring and their external conditions. Nobody would voluntarily choose to be incredibly, desperately sad all the time. Factors like unemployment and a lack of social support are obvious contributors; joblessness alone is thought to cause 45,000 global suicides annually.[8] Depression alone generally doesn't lead to suicide; on the other hand, depression combined with hopeless life conditions creates the sense of there being "no way out" that can lead a person to feel death is their only available option.

Consider how Gene Sprague felt in the last days of his life. Sprague, a gentle 34-year-old punk rocker, had suffered severe depression since his mother died during his youth. Sprague had often talked about killing himself, and when asked what he wanted to have for breakfast, would sometimes reply "death." Sprague's eventual suicide was therefore not especially surprising, even though it was tragic. But consider, too, what Sprague wrote on his blog in the last entry before his death. Sprague was feeling especially low because he was broke and a job offer hadn't come through:

> *"I have not heard from the future employer, I have not received a plane ticket to fly to Texas to interview for that job (I was supposed to leave tomorrow), I have completely run out of money, I am out of cigarettes, I am completely out of food, my eBay auctions have not been bid on, and I think my ferret is dying."* [9]

Sprague suffered with suicidal depression for decades. But it was only when his material circumstances became unbearable that he actually took his life. In prior times, Sprague had something to cling to. He might have been broke, but at least he had some cigarettes. Or he might have run out of food, but at least his ferret was healthy. It was the "perfect storm" of minor miseries that actually pushed him toward his death. (Even then, Sprague seemed apprehensive, pacing the Golden Gate for 90 minutes before finally standing atop the railing and allowing himself to fall backwards.)

Economic misery can drive people to the brink. The rising suicide rate in America has corresponded with a rising hopelessness among many about their prospects for financial security. At the same time as the suicide rate has risen, there has been a massive rise in death from alcohol and drug use among poor, less educated whites, who have been among those with the bleakest job prospects in the 21st-century global economy.[10][11] And, when it comes to suicide itself, rates have risen fastest in Native American communities, which are serially plagued by material deprivation.[12]

The link between inequality and suicide is important. If a huge swath of people is left without any opportunity for advancement, and told that it is because of their own failure of initiative, can we be surprised at a consequent outbreak of suicides? Just listen to the testimony of one internet commenter, who described how college debt and an impossible job market had turned him fatalistic:

> *"Two B.A.s and I can't find a job making $7.50/hour. Even if I did, what's the point? Spin my wheels and get further into debt because I can't make a wage that covers the costs of life? I got degrees in English and History, graduated Spring of 2008...three months before the economic collapse. Things went from 'you can get $12/ hour with any degree' to 'You will not be able to work if you have a BA and we'd rather hire someone without one.' When I was in high school I was making $1500/week. Now I have $22 in my pocket, no job, and come March 1st my debt to my roommate for rent will reach $1500. That's not including the $30k in student loans I have, or the cost of car insurance...There's no out, there's no way to make it work, that I've found.... I made all A's in 27 hours of class in one semester, I'm god damn motivated. I walked four miles yesterday in Louisiana heat to drop off resumes... I work hard at every fucking thing I do, and I lack no motivation whatsoever. Some people do not get this.... we don't need platitudes and this other bullshit. We need help.... if this shit doesn't get better soon, and some sort of avenue for self-advancement appears, I'm going to be left to assume that people just don't want me here enough, and I'm going to leave... It's either I get an opportunity soon, I step off the mortal coil, or I turn to robbery. If anyone has any better ideas I'm all ears, because fuck if I haven't explored every option I know about."[13]*

At a certain point, if people have to work to live, but do not have any work, they will find that they cannot live. It's hard to know what to tell someone like this; every reassurance is a lie. Is he ever going to pay off his debts while working minimum wage jobs? No. Is he ever going to advance beyond those jobs? Probably not, unless some massive new market for English majors suddenly opens up.

Research on the connections between unemployment and suicide has suggested that the link is strongest in countries that usually have low unemployment, meaning that people who expect to find a job but can't are more likely to kill themselves than people who never had the expectation to begin with. Suicides are therefore partially a product of the frustrated American dream; in a country where one expects that hard work will create success, but hard work yields nothing whatsoever, one is likely to feel like a useless failure.

A serious attempt to address suicide has to start, then, with the actual conditions of people's lives. People are lonely, they are broke, they are desperate, and words of encouragement offer nothing. Usually, attempts to address the suicide problem focus on the lack of adequate mental health care in the country. There are suicide hotlines, but little else to assure people's long-term mental health. Psychiatric counseling is expensive and often inaccessible. Yet it may be necessary to provide more than just increased access to counseling. Giving people support is obviously helpful. But a country with annual 42,000 suicides has a systemic problem, and needs to think about where despair originates.

The ability to counsel someone like Gene Sprague or the unemployed Louisianan may be limited. Certainly, there are things you can try to tell people, theories for why it's better to live than to die. Albert Camus has a nice argument for why we shouldn't kill ourselves; the choice to live is the only way to rebel against the absurdity of our human condition. It's not a helpful argument, exactly, but it's nice. There's always the guilt argument; suicide is a selfish act because it forces other people to feel guilty about stopping you. But as psychiatrist Scott Alexander points out, this amounts to telling the suicidal person that "If you think you're a burden upon others while you're alive, just think how much more of a burden you will be on them if you kill yourself."[14] Perhaps one can shame someone into living, but it's certainly not optimal (besides, the suicidal have a difficult time believing they will be missed... that's half the problem to begin with).

The only real way to eliminate American suicide may be to eliminate the viciousness of American capitalism. If people weren't kept chasing an impossible dream, and were given basic economic security, perhaps they could find the peace and resolve necessary to keep going. At the moment, millions of people face nothing but unendurable bleakness; a less brutally competitive economy means a less brutally unendurable life.

But the first step to addressing a problem is recognizing that we have a problem to begin with. Until America treats every suicide victim as a person, one toward whom we have a responsibility of care, 40,000 people will continue to pop off into the darkness with each passing year. The country must decide whether it cares enough to act, or whether the aesthetic value of our shimmering bridges outweighs the cost of installing a net.

THE CINEMA OF 9/11
by Felix Biederman

EVERYONE HAS A STORY about what they were doing on September 11, 2001. Most of these stories are false. Sure, the fundamentals are correct; where we were, who we were with. But in the retellings, people always seem to have had more profundity and understanding than they actually did. Most people spent 9/11 open-mouthed and baffled, unsure of what to do, though they knew everything was horrible. But when people talk about it, they pretend they understood, that their feelings were deep, their questions wise. Younger people will tell you that they were in social studies, and that after the TV had been wheeled in, they asked the teacher some piercing question, like "Will more people die now?" Older people will tell you about some grave musing, possibly a nearby World War II veteran observing "This is going to be very bad." or will talk about how some interoffice grudge evaporated instantaneously, the aggrieved parties tearfully hugging one another while people were being cooked alive in the World Trade Center. It's not that none of these things happened. It's that their significance is applied retroactively, and the feelings of chaos and shell shock we actually experienced on the day are supplanted by orderly and meaningful narratives.

Only a handful of films have been made about the attacks in the fifteen years since they happened. But the fog that afflicts our collective memories similarly affects the fictionalizations. Just as autobiographies consist of what authors choose to remember, representations of 9/11 display what we wish we had in place of our actual memories. Some precocious youngsters did probably say some profound things. But there were also plenty of people hunkered into their basements with assault rifles because they thought World War III was about to start immediately. And there were others who saw the attacks as an opportunity to commit hate crimes against Sikhs, on the logic that you can upend terror plots by assaulting every stranger in a turban. Not to mention our other post 9/11 indiscretion, when we gave the state free rein to roll back civil liberties while doing to Central Asia and the Middle East precisely what was done unto us in Manhattan (i.e. burning large numbers of people to a crisp).

We look at this behavior now as if recovering from a severe hangover. We speak like a guy apologizing for how he got drunk and did something either racist, horny, or both. That wasn't the real us, we rationalize. The real us was not the still-raging civil war in Iraq, or the ongoing hate crimes against Muslim Americans. It was cute questions to our parents or the hug we gave to a detested coworker.

Our films are here to reassure us that we are right.

The first 9/11 blockbuster was *United 93*, a 2006 drama directed by Englishman and ex-journalist Paul Greengrass (now better known for his contributions to the Bourne franchise). Either despite or because of its proximity to the actual events of 9/11, *United 93* stays impressively far away from saccharine emotionality or crazed bloodlust. It attempts a claustrophobic realism, mostly taking place in the cabin of the Boeing 757 as four terrorists attempt to crash the plane into the U.S. Capitol Building.

The film features no major stars. Even Jeremy Glick (the passenger whose supposed midflight battle cry of "let's roll!" became a slogan for pissed off suburban war dads who wanted to drop Agent Orange on Mecca) is played by the little-known Peter Hermann. The cast of experienced character actors brings competence and gravity to the film, an effect that could easily have been ruined by the addition of the expected maudlin scenery chewing from a top-tier leading man or woman. The creative risks Greengrass took with *United 93* make it a nerve-racking, evocative experience. It uses steadicam to great effect in the tight, panic-inducing spaces of the plane and air traffic control booth. Cinematically, the film is superb, and deserves the acclaim it won from critics.

The film is obviously forced to take some liberties; it is, after all, difficult to reconstruct the precise goings-on of a flight with no survivors. Nevertheless, some story choices are blatant propaganda. A German passenger named Christian Adams (a real victim of the real Flight 93, played by Erich Redman) is portrayed as trying to appease the hijackers, a hyponym for the weak Euros who dared to second-guess us on Iraq. Adams is shown to be simpering and unrealistic in the face of pure evil, even though neither the filmmakers nor anyone else could possibly have known about the real man or events on board.

But in its general tone, the film accurately portrays how people act in situations of crisis. They don't burst into spontaneous displays of unity. They don't understand the geopolitical consequences of the horrors unfolding in front of them. They are alternately confused, terrified, and enraged. The air traffic controllers whom we follow for much of the film are apoplectic, constantly cursing how little they know and making wild guesses as to what could possibly be happening.

The next major movie that directly confronted 9/11 was in many ways *United 93*'s opposite, in that it has zero reluctance to engage in histrionics and melodrama. Mike Binder's 2007 *Reign Over Me* is a confounding treatise on family life, mental illness, and of course, 9/11. Adam Sandler plays Charlie Fineman, a man whose entire family (including the dog) perished that Tuesday morning. Sandler portrays the grieving Fineman as a kind of horror-stricken manchild who responds to reminders of his former family with explosive meltdowns. Putting Adam Sandler in a drama about terrorism and mental illness seems like sketch material to begin with. But even worse, the "angry manchild" persona is precisely the same as Sandler's stock comedy character, and thus we are treated to a bizarre alternate world in which Billy Madison is a devastated 9/11 widower. (One keeps expecting Rob Schneider to show up playing some catchphrase-spewing ethnic stereotype.)

Whenever the film is not pursuing a bizarre subplot about friend Alan Johnson's (Don Cheadle) sexless marriage, it delivers little but over-wrought emotional manipulation, culminating in a final courtroom scene where Sandler in full Billy Madison voice saying things like "my famiwy died that daywuh." After this, it is implied he overcomes his grief and has sex with an insane woman.

Reign Over Me is the most cynical type of tragedy pornography. Yet people love it. To this day, YouTube uploads of the most saccharine scenes are filled with comments about how Sandler is a brilliant dramatic actor and how nuanced the film is. Adam Sandler hollering to Don Cheadle that "my fweakin famiwy died in dah towahs" can be described using many adjectives, but "nuanced" is not among them.

Yet *Reign Over Me* accurately displays the attitude we had right after 9/11. If *United 93* is the horrified confusion in the moment of the attacks, *Reign Over Me* is what we chose to remember. It gives the illusion of profundity to the ridiculous and tragic. It is fake emotion, ascribing depth to every banal and confused word we said in the aftermath of an event that couldn't and shouldn't have been interpreted.

Our most recent cinematic confrontation with 9/11, and the one most representative of our worst impulses, is *Zero Dark Thirty*, Kathryn Bigelow's fictionalized account of the hunt for (and death of) Osama bin Laden.

Zero Dark Thirty, like most defense industry projects, is bloated, over-funded, and barely works. As a viewing experience it is an absolute slog. As a moral narrative it is appalling, an ode to torture, extraordinary renditions, and permanent war as an institution. It is repulsive in its message, and almost courageous in its boringness. It is impossible to invest in any of the characters, who are single minded, expressionless automatons. We first meet them as they torture some guy who apparently might know some piece of important information, and they spend the rest of their time switching between bloodlust and bureaucratic smugness.

I should take a moment to note that I am almost alone in this opinion. The film was a smash hit, received five Academy Award nominations, and appeared on everyone's "top ten" lists for 2012. I saw the film with friends who had "national security" concentrations in college ("national security" being perhaps the most made-up academic discipline besides "economics"). They were thrilled with every interminable scene of people hissing military acronyms at each other in office buildings and doughy CIA contractors torturing people.

Some of that enchantment is understandable—Kathryn Bigelow is in many ways brilliant in a technical sense, and her mastery of shadow and light means that most shots and scenes are beautifully done. But the popularity of *Zero Dark Thirty* is not a product of the viewing public's discerning eye for chiaroscuro. It's the message of *Zero Dark Thirty* that resonates. The film is a security blanket, a boost of confidence. Characters are sleek and stoic. They're doers, not talkers. They're always on the exact right path to catch the people who knocked down the towers.

It is, in other words, a testament to how good it was to put full faith into our political and national security elites right after 9/11. It reassures us that we made the right choice because we put the right people on the job. It tells us that torture is necessary, and that we finally chased all the phantoms out of our head after the final bullet perforated Osama bin Laden, as we see when our hero Maya (Jessica Chastain) bursts into tears at the very end.

Zero Dark Thirty therefore exonerates the dark part of our reaction to 9/11, the part where we were scared so shitless that we tacitly or overtly told our government to do whatever they thought was right, regardless of how many people would die or have electrodes attached to their testicles. No one likes to talk about their insane mixture of rage, confusion, and fear, the way we felt mortal terror while becoming fully erect at the possibility of bloody revenge. It's too shameful to admit that we craved some form of domination, both of ourselves and others.

It's been 15 years since a group of sexually neurotic middle-class Saudis brought down the World Trade Center. The world is smoldering with ruins created as a result of our fear. That fear is the thing we chose to remember least about 9/11. Our films tell us stories about emotional closure, whether it's Adam Sandler finally getting laid or Jessica Chastain weeping cathartically after we killed the big bad guy. Now, nativism rages in the country we declared "united" 15 years ago, and three civil wars take place in the part of the world we said we would democratize. Films will tell you the story you want to hear, but it helps if you've been lying to yourself the whole time, too.

THE GREAT AMERICAN CHEMTRAIL

by Angela Nagle

EARLIER THIS YEAR, after Prince was found dead on the floor of an elevator in his Paisley Park recording studio, some strange headlines appeared through Google News. These included "Did The Chemtrail Flu Kill Prince?"[1] and "Special Report: Was Prince Murdered By Illuminati Record Execs?"[2] These articles suggested that Prince had not been killed by excessive indulgence in opiates, as was the default hypothesis at the time and as the autopsy would eventually confirm. Instead, Prince's death was allegedly related to "chemtrails,"—airborne chemical agents released by planes as part of a global conspiracy.

In fact, the singer himself had been a believer in the sinister influence of "chemtrails." On the Tavis Smiley Show, Prince explained:

> *"You know, when I was a kid I used to see these trails in the sky all the time and 'Oh that's cool—a jet just went over.' And then you started to see whole bunch of them and next thing you know everybody in your neighborhood was fighting and arguing and you didn't know why."*

When Prince died suddenly at the age of 57, some believed the late star was assassinated for speaking out. Others theorized, as swivel-eyed Infowars editor Alex Jones suggested to his two million radio listeners, that he was killed by a "weaponized flu" caused by the trails.

To believers, the "chemtrail" is like any ordinary plane condensation trail (or "contrail") in the sky, but one with suspiciously long-lasting features.[3] Chemtrails, they say, persist for as many as 12 hours, and contain a mixture of ominous particulates such as aluminium, pathogens, and even desiccated blood. To denizens of online chemtrail forums, the trails have all manner of sinister purposes. Believers speculate that the trails may be part of a secret geo-engineering project involving solar radiation management or weather modification. Some on chemtrail forums also insist they have seen changes in the moon's orbit, or claim to possess information that WiFi frequencies could be changing our DNA. They suspect some kind of government attempt at either social manipulation, human population control, or biological/chemical warfare (perhaps even all three). One frequenter of the GeoEngineeringWatch site writes:

> *"They are altering the weather and sunlight to cause a seemingly "natural" global famine to depopulate human beings to numbers of their choosing. They are committing perpetrated democide, depopulating exactly as they said they would do, and they are using "global warming" as their cover story for mass murder."* [4]

Some believe, as Prince evidently did, that the trails are causing illnesses and social problems, part of a plot to spread disease in order to create future markets for powerful pharmaceutical corporations. A few claim to have acquired the symptoms of "Morgellons disease," a delusional non-ailment in which a person believes herself to be infested with insects, parasites or fibers. Chemtrail forum-dwellers call the whole phenomenon a part of "the largest crime against humanity in human history."

It is fair to say that scientists have universally dismissed (and repeatedly, exasperatedly debunked) every single one of the chemtrail theorists' claims. However, this only provides further proof to believers of how deep the conspiracy goes! Believers post photographs depicting the interiors of planes, in which the cabin is stocked with large containers connected by tubes. The photos are accompanied by the exclamation that "This is the spraying equipment!" In fact, the pictures merely show planes filled with ballast barrels, water tanks that are used to simulate passenger loads during the flight testing of new airliner designs. (The tubes allow water to be pumped from tank to tank, simulating passenger motion in the cabin.)

The theory's proponents insist chemtrails are a new phenomenon, but when confronted with photographs of long-lasting condensation trails from as far back as World War II, they refer to the military's long history of weather modification plots. As for so many faiths and cults, every piece of contradictory evidence is seen to further bolster the theory. Moon-landing conspiracies work similarly—every additional photograph of human beings literally standing on the moon is just more evidence that the whole thing was faked.

The allegations of chemtrail theorists are pretty easily dealt with. But the belief has proven impressively persistent. A search for chemtrails brings up 5.5 million Google results and a 2011 study found that 16.6% of a sample of 3105 people in the US, Canada and the UK believed either "entirely" or, more often, "to some extent" in the existence of a conspiracy involving chemtrails.[5] Prince was not the only celebrity to issue expostulations against chemtrail doubters. Aging TV martial artist and right-wing paranoiac Chuck Norris also plugged the theory, insisting that chemtrails regularly appear in the skies over his Texas ranch.[6] Joni Mitchell has publicly claimed to be a sufferer of "Morgellon's disease."[7] Mitchell was among those condemning the CDC for treating the syndrome as imaginary, insisting she had contracted a "weird, incurable disease that seems like it's from outer space" in which "fibers in a variety of colors protrude out of my skin like mushrooms after a rainstorm: they cannot be forensically identified as animal, vegetable or mineral."

The origins of the chemtrail conspiracy narrative can be traced back to the late 1990s when a piece by "investigative journalist" William Thomas suggested that "Contrails spread by fleets of jet aircraft in elaborate cross-hatched patterns are sparking speculation and making people sick across the United States."[8] From there, the idea spread to late-night talk radio, where "UFOlogists" and paranormal investigators have long found a sympathetic ear. But the chemtrails conspiracy also coincided directly with the early rise of the Internet forum as a venue for the sharing of ideas, and it was on exhaustively-compiled, garishly-designed websites that the theory was most successfully promoted.

The success of the chemtrails theory in the online world shows the particular conduciveness of the platform to conspiratorial thinking, though the Internet has also always been the perfect platform for making fun of such thinking. Richard Hofstadter's famous description of the "uncommonly angry minds" that made up the "paranoid style" in American political thought could be a description of just about any contemporary online forum on even the most mundane and uncontroversial of topics.[9] Add to that mix an all encompassing theory of government geo-engineering, population control and a global apocalyptic conspiracy raining down from the sky, throw in Big Oil, Big Pharma and the Jews and Hofstadter's description becomes something of an understatement.

Chemtrail activists frequently attend events and conferences on geo-engineering, and many academics working in the area have been subjected to threats and verbal abuse for their alleged role in the conspiracy. Pilots and weather reporters receive harassment and threats from anti-chemtrails activists. While conspiratorial paranoia may generally be America's harmless national pastime, in the case of chemtrails, online forums are full of justifications and fantasies of violence toward those seen to be involved in the plot. On a generically populist site titled "thepeoplesvoice.org," one writer says, "I can't tell you how many times I've fantasized about firing a missile at the jets laying chemtrails over our skies."[10] Other commenters on chemtrail forums warn, "There's only one answer. Kill them before they kill you" or "Why won't they tell us there [sic] plan and leave us and the world we live in alone." Another wonders, "Am I the only one that is considering picking up a gun and shooting these people dead before they get my mother, my father, my sister, my brother, and even my garden?" (First they came for the begonias, and I said nothing...)

Perhaps needless to say, Jews are often implicated. One believer posted a video on YouTube called "Star of David chemtrails/persistent contrails" in which he films criss-crossing trails in the sky, grimly observing off-camera that "They create the Star of David... speaks for itself."

There is a genteel approach, sometimes found in academic writing, to consider the ill-written and baseless ramblings of conspiracy theory forums as kinds of "counter-knowledges" or as different "ways of knowing." Indeed, such beliefs often do come from seemingly politically disenfranchised people with possible mental health issues.

But the only thing more patronizing than to deride such beliefs would be not to do so. One also has to wonder if such a sympathetic reading would be given if the racial conspiratorial undertones were against any group but the Jews. And in practice it's hard to be patiently open-minded while reading typical communiqués like this on an anti-chemtrails YouTube video:

"MORGELLONS KiLLS!!!!!!! [...] MORGELLONS FROM CHEMTRAiLS
THiS SECRET WAR ON YOU MUST BE STOPPED!!!!
if You don't say no and stop this, we all will suffer and die
THANK YOU FOR STOPPiNG NewWorldOrder/NATO/ Chemtrails/RFiD Powder/Smart Dust!!!!!!!"

The 1990's saw an explosion of conspiracy theory culture in the United States, in the reverberations from decades of the paranoid Cold War years. Beginning in the 1990s, the era-defining TV show *The X-Files* featured Russian nuclear sewer monsters, U.S. government alien cover-ups, secret geo-engineering, population control projects and domestic terrorism (back when the term "terrorism" conjured up nightmare visions of rampaging Southern hillbillies instead of bearded jihadis). And it is worth remembering that many of the conspiratorial domestic terrorists of the 1990's had in fact experienced terrible crimes at the hands of the state. Ted Kaczynski, the Unabomber, was subjected to cruel CIA experiments during his time as a Harvard undergraduate.[11] The so-called

"MK Ultra" research of the '50s and '60s, which used LSD and psychological abuse on unsuspecting subjects, is now a notorious chapter in the agency's history and as horrifying as anything alleged on anti-chemtrails forums.[12] Timothy McVeigh, who carried out the Oklahoma City bombing, killing 168 and injuring around 600, was a veteran who had witnessed the horrific violence of the Gulf War. McVeigh had become fixated on the Clinton Administration's needless massacre at Waco, in which 76 people were shot and burned alive after a siege by the FBI and ATF went horrendously awry.

As in Hofstadter's 1964 analysis, the online world of the chemtrails conspiracy is not recognizably right or left wing. There are elements associated with the fringe of U.S. ultra-conservatism, such as fear of Big Government's statist dastardliness. The overlap between the militia movement and the conspiracy crowd is significant. But there are also elements of the more Romantic-tinged Green left, such as an opposition to the industrial plunder of nature and a fear of being poisoned by sprayed chemicals. There are echoes of ideas also found in the Unabomber's manifesto about the evils of industrial society. Conspiratorial notions also tend to find a sympathetic audience among the socialistically-inclined during times of real political weakness. The Left Forum in New York (a prominent annual gathering attended by what Amber Frost called "bitter old codgers," "Maoist Third World-ists," "sanctimonious Trotskyists," and "adherents of similarly esoteric ideological traditions"[13]) hosts conspiracy theorists on its panels. These include 9/11 "Truthers", who remind the assembled radicals that *jet fuel can't melt steel beams.*

The cultural critic Fredric Jameson argued that conspiracy theories are used as an improvised guide to our overwhelmingly complex social landscape. It is often easier to imagine sinister cabals and physically impossible phenomena than it is to accept the open and known injustices of the world. Who needs the Illuminati when almost the entire British government went to the same schools? One only has to read Yanis Varoufakis' accounts of the internal workings of international financial bodies or look at the dynasties and tiny elites that run the world of government and capital to wonder if the paranoid person is just, as William

Burroughs put it "a person in possession of all the facts." The paranoid impulse is not so much wrong as too often misdirected and it is often not a particularly distant leap from the truth to the fiction. People are right in their intuition that there are dark forces arrayed against them but they're more likely to find the information they seek in the dull finance section of any newspaper than on chemtrails forums that weave more compelling narratives.

In fact, chemtrail believers have a paradoxical mixture of rationalist skepticism and dogmatic faith. They spend their time carefully parsing documents with a scrupulousness worthy of the IRS. Like committed scientists, they quest after "truth," they want to know what's "really" going on. They see unexplained horrors in the world around them, and they are persistent askers of "Why?"

Yet they are fundamentally religious in their outlook, insofar as they believe on faith in something that others cannot see. The online conspiracy world speaks of "sheeple" and issues commands to "wake up." This is one expression of an entire online discourse of waking up, also shared by the "men's rights" online community "RedPill" (a reference to the film *The Matrix*, in which by taking the "red pill," one become aware of the truth about one's fabricated reality.) There is a quasi-spiritual dimension to the born-again experiences people describe when they "woke up" to reality. Although unlike Christians, who awake to something they find beautiful and fulfilling, the online rebirth tends to involve plunging into darkness to see the truth.

Chemtrail conspiracies are, to some extent, just another incarnation of the human search for meaning, albeit one that is irrational and occasionally threatening. Today most of us live at the mercy of unknowably complex and volatile economic forces whose inner financial workings are entirely opaque to all but a few. The all-encompassing chemtrails conspiracy may appeal because it orders a chaotic world. As a replacement for religious traditions and political projects which both contained beautiful and redemptive ideas, individualism as the only surviving ideology has turned out to be thin gruel for some. In the absence of anything else to have faith in and so much to try to understand, why not chemtrails?

THE UNENDURABLE HORRORS OF LEADERSHIP CAMP

by Eric M. Fink

AS A PROFESSOR OF LAW, I am accustomed to leisurely mornings. "There is nothing worth doing," we indolent law professors often say, "that cannot be done better after 11 a.m." Late starts are one of the highlights of a career as a teacher of law (the main lowlight being that you are occasionally forced to teach the law). So I was in a doubly wretched condition when I found myself, in the earliest hours of a Monday morning, arriving at 1 Leadership Place.

1 Leadership Place is home to the Center for Creative Leadership, and I had been dispatched there at my new employer's behest. I was to participate in a five-day "Leadership Development Program" intended to hone my leadership abilities (of which I admittedly have none). This was treated as a great perk of my new job, though given a choice I might have opted to use my time differently (perhaps a week in a Siberian prison camp, or having a series of my organs removed without anesthesia). According to the publicity materials, I would be learning to "think and act systemically," "create buy-in," and "leverage multiple life roles." I did not (and, spoiler, still do not) know what any of these things mean. But I supposed it would be better to be systemic than not systemic, better to leverage the life roles than not leverage them. I therefore insist that I approached the whole thing with an open mind.

As it turns out, sending academics to leadership camp is not an aberration. As the leadership industry has grown over the last three decades, it has roped in all kinds of institutions, convincing them to shell out exorbitant sums for training programs. In a 1993 investigation for *Harper's* entitled "Choice Academic Pork," Benjamin DeMott traces the expansion of leadership education from business to universities:

> *"The current leadership boom has at least one root in an early 1980s pop phenomenon—best-selling business manuals such as Management Secrets of Attila the Hun, The One-Minute Manager, and A Passion for Excellence, by Tom Peters and Nancy K. Austin. Leadership theory then trickled down (or up) into the universities and the public sector."*

DeMott documents how this vast and profitable industry, which resembles a cult in its language and culture, managed to obtain substantial funding from government agencies to conduct endless seminars of dubious value. They have successfully persuaded people in an array of different sectors that leadership training is useful, even necessary. They have, uh, "created buy-in," so to speak.

In the weeks leading up to my internment, I was asked to complete a battery of online "assessment instruments," glorified pop-psych personality tests not unlike the ones people often post on Facebook. There were questions about how I relate to others (badly), how often I embrace new things (seldom to never), my attitude toward work (hate it), and how I solve complex problems (I do not. They fester.)

Many of the questions seemed like they could not possibly yield informative answers, e.g.: "Tradition is valuable. 1. Always 2. Usually 3. Sometimes 4. Rarely 5. Never."

"Surely," I thought, "that would depend on the tradition. Bluegrass music? Noodle kugel? The UNC-Duke rivalry? All valuable traditions. But racism? Gefilte fish? Singing the Star Spangled Banner before every sports event? Not so much.

The tests were ostensibly designed to reveal my leadership style.

Instead they revealed that Leadership Camp was going to be a tedious waste of time and money. A lot of money ($7,000), in fact, which fortunately wasn't my own.

Leadership Place itself turned out to be a driveway leading to a stone-and-glass building set amidst several wooded acres alongside a lake. The triangular building surrounds a courtyard with flowing water, abundant greenery, and several sculptures, resembling discarded bits of plumbing, labeled "Leadership," "Learning," and "Life." The tranquil and tasteful setting could pass for an upscale rehab facility, of the type populated with affluenza-afflicted wayward teens. The company eagerly cultivates an academic aura, and the facility is referred to as its "campus." The campus bookstore sells dozens of business books, of the kind ubiquitous in airport newsstands. Typical selections included The World's Most Powerful Leadership Principle: *How to Become a Servant Leader* (featuring a jacket blurb from the Senior Vice President of Operations for Chik-fil-a) and *Leading with Soul: An Uncommon Journey of Spirit*. Alas, they did not have my favorite managerial tome of all time, *If Harry Potter Ran General Electric: Leadership Wisdom from the World Of Wizards*, which is a genuine, honest-to-God book that you can look up and purchase.

Directed to the meeting room, I took an open seat at a table occupied by what looked like the cast from a community theater production of *The Office*. I soon learned that the group consisted of:

- Don, from an industrial plastics company in Reading, PA.
- Graham, district manager for a retail cosmetics chain.
- Greg, electronic controls
- Derwin, fibre optic cable manufacturer
- Paul, medical devices at Big Pharma Corporation
- John, health insurance
- Tom, dental insurance

I am sure that at some point in human history, a more flavorless collection of white collar bores has been assembled, but I think you would have to search far and wide to find it.

The program began with a PowerPoint intended to provide an overview of the coming week. Even for a PowerPoint presentation on a leadership campus, it was remarkable for its vacuity.

We would receive feedback from executive coaches about our leadership challenges and "gift areas." We were urged to practice active listening. We were given learning journals in which we were to record our "learnings." We would be empowered as change agents armed with best practices for leading change.

The presenter, who was like a whiter Mister Rogers, then had us stand in circles, with each participant offering their definition of leadership, their personal leadership challenge, and three words their friends would use to describe you. The answers were obvious:

1. An ideological construct deployed to legitimize power and domination in the state and the labor process. 2. Avoiding any situation calling for leadership. 3. "Can't stand bullshit."

And bullshit it truly was. Leadership education has its own unique jargon, which is related to, but distinct from, business jargon. "Learnings" is not just a quirk of the Center for Creative Leadership, it's one of the terms of the trade. Leadership studies is a whole field, with leaders categorized as exercising "transactional leadership" or "transformative leadership" (even "toxic leadership" if you screw up). Everything comes with its convoluted diagrams, and its elaborately developed theories, each with "7 Stages" or "5 Types."

The week dragged on through endless further self-reflections, as well as team-building exercises. We stood in opposite rows of three people on a side, attempting to lower a six-foot pole to the ground while keeping it level. I suggested we just count to three and all let go at the same time. There, pole lowered. The others insisted my strategy would be cheating. This, I concluded, was because they were not practicing innovative leadership and creative problem-solving.

We built bridges out of popsicle sticks. Of the available tasks, I opted to hot-glue the sticks together, a job that entailed the least interaction with anyone else. I remain proud of the hot gluing I did there, and of the skillful manner in which I pinned the resulting bridge collapse on Derwin the fiber optics guy. (A true leader, I reasoned, is an expert in foisting responsibility.)

We arranged ourselves in various corners of the room, based on our leadership styles. I found myself all alone in the corner labeled "visionary." The others in my group expressed admiration. "Yep," I said, "that's me. A visionary. Like David Koresh." This did not appear to amuse them. But, I reasoned, a truly visionary leader does not care what does or does not amuse the herd.

Koresh actually isn't a bad parallel, though. Leadership education is distinctly religious in its feel; it's full of recitations and rituals. Dozens of arbitrary dogmas are accepted as revealed truth; God help you if you raise your hand and say that the "9 Stages of Empowered Decision-making" (or whatever) seem like a bunch of opaque redundancies. Of course, that means it's not training for leadership at all; it's training for conformity. "Leadership" just means "being in management," since the sorts of people who actually make leaders don't memorize multi-step diagrams on how to lead.

One of the strange things about the business world is the extent to which its jargon is euphemistic. When we talk about leaders, we're talking about bosses. Yet for some reason bosses don't like to admit what it is they do. That's why employees become "team members," why firing becomes "letting go." In a way, it suggests that people's human instincts are that capitalism is something rotten; the more you describe it with precision, the more horrendous it sounds. At the level of uplifting abstractions, derived from self-help culture, everything can be pleasant and neutral. It's only when you hack through the forest of buzzwords that you can understand what is actually being discussed.

At the end of the week, each participant received a one-on-one "effective coaching" session, which was almost certainly modeled after Maoist self-criticism. I met with my coach in a small room, where I was seated on a stool. It began with the coach offering bits of feedback based on my performance during the week. According to the instructions, I was to regard each comment as a "gift" and accept it by saying only "thank you." "Ok, whatever," I thought. "Thank you," I said.

"During the bridge-building activity, you stuck to hot-gluing sticks together the whole time. The others on your team thought that showed a lacked of engagement."

"Thank you," I said. "Fucking snitches," I thought.

"You made a joke about being like David Koresh. One of your team-mates found that hostile."

"Thank you," I said. "Screw him," I thought.

"You said you 'can't stand bullshit.' This projected negativity to your team."

"Thank you," I said. "Bullshit," I thought.

"I think you would benefit from some executive coaching. We offer follow-up sessions." "Thank you," I said. "Fuck that," I thought.

That evening, there was a group dinner and closing ceremony. Unforgivably, the meal included no alcohol, but did include a series of peppy recitations of our leadership principles by the coaches. If there is a number beyond "umpteenth," it would describe the amount of times I heard the word "paradigm" in a single week. After eating, we had to go around the room (we were always Going Around the Room) so that everyone could "share your learnings from the week." Of course, what I'd learned was that I really can't stand bullshit, and that leadership camp is truly bullshit of the highest order. "What I learned," I said, "is that I am a visionary leader and that I'm very good with a hot-glue gun. Thank you." They seemed satisfied enough.

WHY JOURNALISTS LOVE TWITTER

by Emily Robinson

JOURNALISTS HAVE ALWAYS BEEN LAZY. Anyone who pines for a Golden Age of diligent reportage, when a writer would pound the pavement in search of a good lead, or phone source after source demanding the truth, has never actually picked up an old newspaper or magazine and examined its contents. Then, as now, most writing was swill: thinly-sourced, trivial in subject matter, and slobberingly deferential to power. The *All the President's Men* era of American journalism lasted exactly the duration of the film *All the President's Men*. Do crack investigative reporters exist? Yes. Do they mostly end up fired, or at least in constant conflict with authority? They do. Meanwhile, most of the press remains, as ever, a content mill.[1]

Given that much of the media consists of content-for-the-sake-of-content, the introduction of Twitter came as something of a godsend to journalists. With 500 million new Tweets rolling in every day, and nearly 310 million active monthly users, Twitter offers a sprawling bank of quotable sources.[2] Tweets from all lands are ripe for plucking and republishing,

Hashtags, then, have become something of a goldmine for online publications. Sites like *BuzzFeed* have made a name for themselves in co-opting tweets from teenagers to pad out their pages with such heady articles as "Just 28 Really Real Tweets About Gymnastics"[3] and "19 Tweets Anyone Addicted To Diet Coke Will Completely Relate To."[4] But it's also increasingly common to see tweets quoted as sources in articles from *CNN* or *The New York Times*, who can produce the appearance of doing man-on-the-street reporting even as they sit at their desks trawling through Twitter. With millions of members of the public jabbering at one another at all times, Twitter is a vast ever-refreshing quote bank, an extraordinary tool for the writer in an age of 24-hour demands for fresh content.

There's a basic ethical problem to the *BuzzFeed*-style practice of culling and republishing tweets. This model of article, which simply repackages memes, quips, and observations created by Twitter users, profits from people's writing without compensating them for it (and in many cases, without properly crediting them). This constitutes a kind of low-level theft (somewhat like bullying a nerd to do your math homework, if the nerd was a preteen with 100 Twitter followers and you were a multimillion dollar publishing house), and there's something disquieting about seeing people's wit being resold for profit without their permission.

But Twitter-based journalism is disturbing for reasons that go far beyond questions of intellectual property and attribution. Using Twitter as a prism through which to examine and report the world creates a narrow and distorted impression of reality. And with journalists already prone to clubby insularity, Twitter provides new ways for them to confirm their preexisting worldviews, and further wall themselves off from ordinary experience. As a consequence, the world reported in the press is the world that exists on Twitter, not the world as it actually exists.

Twitter is not a normal place, though its users are ostensibly normal people. Like a Petri dish forgotten in a warm, moist cabinet, it has developed some truly curious cultures. Facilitated by its ease of use and offer of anonymity, Twitter has borne a plethora of unique subgroups with names as terrifying as "ISIS twitter" (self-explanatory), "Woke Twitter" (tweeters who focus on social justice issues, often to the point of self parody),[5] and "Irony Twitter" (tweeters who communicate only in irony and sarcasm).[6] Each of these groups has developed their own vernacular, traditions, and jokes, much like one would expect of high school cliques, or minor league gangs. Far from being some kind of lofty online manifestation of the "public square," Twitter has become the digital equivalent of a stall wall in a public high school bathroom, one in which Neo-Nazis and Communists compete with one another for the most obnoxious Sharpie doodles.

Thus presenting tweets as evidence of some national or global trend (rather than as a trend on a social media platform) is several shades of problematic. Inevitably, if we take trending hashtags for actual trends, we will be dealing with a biased sample: we are looking at what is popular *among people who spend time on Twitter* rather than among people more broadly. Forgetting the Internet's biases creates delusion. We may treat the artisanal cupcake blogs we follow on Tumblr as representative of every cupcake in the world, but frozen, flavor-free grocery-store cupcakes are destined to remain the norm in most of real life.

When it comes to political journalism, treating the Internet as representative of reality can heavily bias coverage. It's because the press gets its worldview from Twitter that it was stunned by the persistence of support for Donald Trump. After all, subsequent to every new vulgar eruption from Trump's mouth during the campaign, a torrent of outrage poured forth on Twitter, leading pundits to repeatedly declare that Trump's campaign was finally dead (*The Onion* captured this kind of wishful insistence nicely with the headline: "'This Will Be The End Of Trump's Campaign,' Says Increasingly Nervous Man For Seventh Time This Year"). Yet Trump maintained support from nearly half the electorate. It was almost as if the online world was a poor representation of the world at large. One is reminded here of Pauline Kael's frequently misconstrued remark on the 1972 election, in which she observed how closed-off her New York social life made her: "I live in a rather special world. I only know one person who voted for Nixon. Where they are I don't know. They're outside my ken." Kael's remark was frequently spun as comically ignorant (it was misquoted as "I don't know how Nixon could have won; nobody I know voted for him"), but it actually showed an impressive self-awareness about the detachment of the media from the public, one that most of today's political pundits couldn't achieve even if they set their best unpaid interns on it.

For writers, Twitter provides a way of deepening one's obliviousness and caressing one's ego. Twitter allows commentators to follow only those whose opinions they wish to consume, and to receive instantaneous praise from their own followers. Thus Twitter provides a streamlined platform from which to shamelessly pimp out your writing to a self-selected group of people who are likely to read it. It's a wonderful place to reaffirm your beliefs, and it's so easy to do so on a platform designed to allow you to tailor the information you receive to what you want to hear, or what you know you'll agree with.

Twitter does have its egalitarian component, however. At its best it is firmly *anti*-elitist, giving a platform to those who would previously have gone unheard. Some of these people (e.g. the neo-Nazis) had been pushed to the fringes for good reason, but others were excluded from mainstream discourse simply because mainstream discourse has a tendency to be snobby, corporate-driven, and exclusive. And where once one would have had to penetrate the Manhattan gala-and-book-talk scene in order to hurl abuse at a *New York Times* opinion columnist, now anyone with an internet connection can politely explain to Nicholas Kristof precisely why he is utterly and completely full of shit (an opportunity that the *Current Affairs* editorial staff takes regular advantage of).[7] The platform thus allows for an unprecedented level of contact between the unwashed public and our patrician overlords.

But one should not overstate the case, and risk painting Twitter as some sort of classless comradely paradise. Pundits can easily filter out dissenting voices from the public, and sometimes take on the appearance of kings and queens holding court before an audience of adoring Followers. And while Twitter amplifies new voices, it does not seem to expand worldviews. For pundits, the general effect seems to be a winnowing down of their informational intake, to the point where it consists almost entirely of the words of other pundits.

To see the consequences of Twitter-centric journalism, one can examine one of the most repeated stories of the Democratic primary: the so-called rise of the "BernieBro." In October of 2015, Robinson Meyer of *The Atlantic* published a brief article titled "Here Comes the Bernie-bro."[8] Meyer, a largely Twitter-dwelling journalist (having 40,100 tweets to his name, plus 41,100 "likes" of other people's tweets)[9], suggested that a new phenomenon had arisen in American politics. The Bernie Sand-ers campaign was attracting a noxious wave of supporters, whom Meyer christened the "BernieBros." This group was "very male, [...] white; well-educated; middle-class (or, delicately, "upper middle-class") and "aware of NPR podcasts and jangly bearded bands." He described these supporters as obstinate and aggressive in their online presence, prone to "performative" appraisals of feminism, and (perhaps worst of all) firm in their belief that Sanders "really could win." Meyer, himself a white man, castigated these white, male Sanders voters for supporting the sins of "free college for all and a $15 minimum wage" and for falling for "Sanders's rhetoric that America is trapped in a number of deep, unprec-edented crises."

But aside from Meyer's bizarre contempt for Sanders voters' idealism, the article suffered from a simple problem: there was no evidence what-soever that some kind of "BernieBro" trend actually existed. The theory that there was something distinctly "bro-ish" about Sanders supporters was in direct conflict with the actual demographic facts (a concession Meyer even made in the article, noting that "Sanders's support skews young, but not particularly male"). Aside from a few dozen isolated tweets, largely by anonymous and unpopular users, nobody could seem to locate the whereabouts of these storied "bros." To be sure, one could find occasional nasty remarks about Hillary Clinton made in comment sections (although when Glenn Greenwald investigated the examples being cited, he found some of the "BernieBros" turned out to be con-servatives or women).[10] People of all stripes are assholes on the internet, though, and no effort was made to answer the real questions, which was how many of these "bros" actually existed.

In a sensible world, then, Meyer's article should not have even been a footnote in the history of the election. It should have been laughed off as shockingly obtuse. Yet somehow, a flimsy story based on a sample of

Robinson Meyer's Facebook newsfeed ended up–miserably–setting the tone for much of the remainder of the online primary. Instead, the political media in residence on Twitter took the specter of Bernie Bros and went hog wild. Soon everyone from Jamil Smith at *The New Republic* to Amanda Marcotte of *Salon* had latched onto the fantasy of an army of evil white men who supported socialist policies as a means of furthering racism and sexism.[11][12] Smith wrote that unless Sanders could somehow contain the "bros," they would damage his political prospects. *The New Yorker* published a cringingly unfunny and cruel "BernieBro Code" containing the "rules" such creatures live by (e.g. "A Bernie Bro is legitimately glad that his uninformed, mainstreamer aunt is part of a generation that is going to be dead soon.")[13] Paul Krugman, dissatisfied with Sanders' economic proposals, went so far as to declare that Bernie himself "is becoming a Bernie Bro."[14] The Sanders campaign was forced to apologize for the BernieBros, despite there being scant evidence of their actual existence.

The explosion of the fake BernieBro trend was both fascinating and appalling. The narrative ruled media Twitter for months, and despite demographic data continually debunking it, pundits clung to it like a safety blanket.[15] It became a convenient way to dismiss all criticisms of Hillary Clinton that didn't come from someone with a byline in a major publication or a degree from an Ivy League school. In fact, Olivia Nuzzi of *The Daily Beast* reported in June that she was skeptical of the BernieBros idea, for the simple reason that the Clinton campaign had tried to pitch her a story about the phenomenon.[16] The BernieBros line proved convenient for the Clinton camp, as it shifted press coverage to questions like "How will Sanders stop the BernieBros?" and away from substantive policy.

The BernieBros story showed how news can be manufactured in an age of Twitter punditry: a writer grabs a few stray tweets and produces an article declaring them a nationwide event. Other writers, sharing both the first writer's political persuasion and constant need to emit content, issue commentaries on the phenomenon, citing the first writer's article as their source. Pundits quote pundits who quote tweets. Then there are more tweets, then additional punditry. At no point is the story checked against the real world: it is solely a dialogue between *The New Yorker*, *The Atlantic*, and Twitter.

Thus there are real-world political consequences to this type of shoddy reporting; we at least know that it can filter into a presidential primary. There's a feedback loop between the media and political elite, and Twitter provides a convenient means of fabricating stories to further particular interests. One can create the news entirely to fit one's agenda and worldview, since there are always Twitter subcommunities where a certain thing is true, even if it is nonexistent in the wider world.

It can be harder to ascertain motive when all of this back-and-forth occurs online. With conventional network political coverage, sycophancy is easily detected. One could simply turn on *Meet The Press*, and witness Chuck Todd's eyeballs morph gruesomely into hearts whenever he was seated across from John McCain or Chuck Schumer. On Twitter, with its veneer of equality, it can be difficult to determine who is doing what for which reasons.

Multiple kinds of journalistic dysfunction are enabled by Twitter. One can draw a distinction between the purely profit-driven lazy journalism of *BuzzFeed* and the brown-nosing and status-driven journalism of *New York* magazine or *The New Republic*. The former is simply unfortunate, in that it gradually turns everyone stupid. The latter, however, is actively pernicious. Through the magic of Twitter, political journalists form incestuous cliques that reaffirm their prejudices, then their own publications treat those cliques as the boundaries of the social world. Twitter helps make politicians our friends, and makes journalists friends with politicians. We have developed an online political culture that is a-okay with calling Dianne Feinstein their "queen" or 83-year-old Supreme Court Justice Ruth Bader Ginsburg their "mom." That is not something a healthy society does.

Perhaps it doesn't matter too much, though. Most of the world happily gets along without ever thinking about what *The Atlantic* has to say about anything. In writing about Twitter punditry, one runs the risk of reinforcing the very problem one is diagnosing, and attributing an outsized real-world significance to inconsequential commentators. But it remains true that political media sets agendas, and if a presidential candidate is forced to spend time responding to empty rubbish spread by pundits, this is time that cannot be spent campaigning. While the inhabitants of Twitter may constitute a comparatively small fraction of the American public, they make a comparatively large fraction of the country's noise. To the extent that it escapes the Internet and poisons us all, their obsession with the insignificant could very well be significant.

YOU SHOULD BE TERRIFIED THAT PEOPLE WHO LIKE "HAMILTON" RUN THIS COUNTRY

by Alex Nichols

IN 2012, CAPTAIN DAN AND HIS SCURVY CREW, a four-man hip-hop ensemble trying to cement "pirate rap" as a tenable subgenre, appeared on *America's Got Talent*.[1] The quartet had clearly put some thought, or at least effort, into the act; their pirate costumes might even have passed historical muster were it not for the leftmost crewmember's Ray-Bans and Dan's meticulously groomed chinstrap beard.

The routine itself went precisely in the direction one might have expected:

> CAPTAIN DAN: *When I say yo, you say ho. Yo!*
> SCURVY CREW: *HO!*
> CAPTAIN DAN: *YO!*
> SCURVY CREW: *HO!*

The group managed to rattle off two-and-a-half stilted lines before the judges began sounding their buzzers. Howard Stern was the last to give them the red "X," preferring to let the audience's boos come to a crescendo before he cut the Scurvy Crew off. Stern seemed to take great pleasure in calling the group "stupid," "moronic," "idiotic," and "pathetic" on a national stage (Captain Dan grimaced through his humiliating dressing-down while his bandmates laughed it off, exposing a gap in emotional investment in the project between captain and crew, one that likely led to some intra-group tension during the post-show commiseration drinks). Howie Mandel: *They have restaurants like this—like Medieval Times—where you go and you get a pirates thing and you get a chicken dinner. We didn't get a chicken dinner with this.*

In 2012, everyone (save for Captain Dan himself, along with people whose tastes range from "music from video games" to "music about video games") was in agreement that performing high-school-history-project rap in Colonial Williamsburg garb was culturally unconscionable. Right?

Wrong. The world in which we live now includes *Hamilton*, a wildly successful "hip-hop musical" about the first Secretary of the Treasury of the United States of America.

Now, perhaps the *America's Got Talent* audience isn't an accurate sample of the American population as a whole. Perhaps they actually thought "when I say yo, you say ho" was clever, but were directed to boo by an off-screen neon sign. Or perhaps something happened in the past four years that made everyone really stupid.

But what if the American public's taste hasn't devolved? What if *Hamilton*'s success is the result of something else altogether? Brian Eno once said that the Velvet Underground's debut album only sold a few thousand copies, but everyone who bought it started a band. The same principle likely applies to *Hamilton*: only a few thousand people could afford to see it, but everyone who did happened to work for a prominent New York/D.C. publication.

The media gushing over Hamilton has been downright torrential. "I am loath to tell people to mortgage their houses and lease their children to acquire tickets to a hit Broadway show," wrote Ben Brantley of the *New York Times*.[2] "But Hamilton... might just about be worth it." The hyperbolic headlines poured forth unceasingly: "Is *Hamilton* the Musical the Most Addicting Album Ever?"[3] "*Hamilton* is the most important musical of our time."[4] "*Hamilton* Haters Are Why We Can't Have Nice Things."[5] The media then got high on their own supply, diagnosing all of America with a harrowing ailment called "Hamilton mania."[6] The work was "astonishing," "sublime," the "cultural event of our time." Clarence

Page of the *Chicago Tribune* said the musical was "even better than the hype."[7] Given the tenor of the hype, one can only imagine the pure, overpowering ecstasy that must comprise the *Hamilton*-viewing experience. The musical even somehow won a Pulitzer Prize this year, alongside Nicholas Kristof and that book by Ta-Nehisi Coates you bought but never read.

One of the publications to enter swooning raptures over *Hamilton* was *BuzzFeed*, which called it the smash musical "that everyone you know has been quoting for months."[8] (Literally nobody has ever quoted *Hamilton* in my presence.) *BuzzFeed*'s workplace obsession with the musical led to the birthing of the phrase "BuzzFeed Hamilton Slack."[9] That three-word monstrosity, incomprehensible to anyone outside the narrowest circle of listicle-churning media elites,[10] describes a room on the corporate messaging platform "Slack" used exclusively by *BuzzFeed* employees to discuss Hamilton. J.R.R. Tolkien said that "cellar door" was the most beautiful phonetic phrase the English language could produce. "BuzzFeed Hamilton Slack," by contrast, may be the most repellent arrangement of words in any tongue.

Those of us unfortunate enough not to work media jobs can never be privy to what goes on in a "BuzzFeed Hamilton Slack." But the Twitter emissions of the Slack's denizens suggest a swamp into which no man should tread. A tellingly ominous and thoroughly representative Tweet:

"When the Buzzfeed #Hamilton slack room has a heated debate about which Hogwarts houses the characters belong to" —@Arielle07[11]

"Nerdcore" music (Wikipedia: "a genre of hip hop music characterized by themes and subject matter considered to be of general interest to nerds") has always had trouble getting off the ground.[12] The "first lady of nerdcore," rapper MC Router (responsible for the song "Trekkie Pride")[13], never achieved the critical success for which she had seemed destined, instead ending up on the Dr. Phil show after an acrimonious dispute with her family over her unexpected conversion to Islam.[14] Similarly, the YouTube series "Epic Rap Battles of History," however numerous its subscribers may have been, has consistently been unjustly robbed of the Pulitzer. Now, finally, nerd rap has apparently found in *Hamil-*

ton its own *Sgt. Pepper*, a lofty, expansive work that wins the hearts and minds of previously skeptical elite critics.

One should have no doubt that "expensively-staged nerdcore" is a perfectly accurate, even generous description of *Hamilton*. Doubters need only examine a brief lyrical snippet. Consider this, from "The Election of 1800":

MADISON: *It's a tie! ...*

JEFFERSON: *It's up to the delegates!...*

JEFF./MAD.:   *It's up to Hamilton!*

HAMILTON: *Yo.*
                The people are asking to hear my voice ..
                For the country is facing a difficult choice.
                And if you were to ask me who I'd promote ...
                Jefferson has my vote.

Perhaps marginally less embarrassing than "when I say yo, you say ho." But only ever so marginally.

One could question the fairness of appraising a musical before putting one's self through its full three-hour theatrical experience. But if nobody could criticize *Hamilton* without having seen it, then nobody could criticize *Hamilton*. One of the strangest aspects of the whole "Hamiltonmania" public relations spectacle is that hardly anyone in the country has actually attended the musical to begin with. The show is exclusive to Broadway and has spent most of its run completely sold out, seemingly playing to an audience comprised entirely of people who write breathless *BuzzFeed* headlines.[15] (Fortunately, when you can get off the waitlist it only costs $1,200 a ticket—so long as you can stand bad seats.) *Hamilton* is the "nationwide sensation" that only .001% of the nation has even witnessed.

There's something revealing in the disjunction between *Hamilton*'s popularity in the world of online media and *Hamilton*'s popularity in the world of actual human persons. After all, here we have a cultural product whose appeal essentially consists of a broad coalition of the worst people in America: *New York Times* writers, 15-year-olds who aspire to answer the phone in Chuck Schumer's office, people who want to get into steampunk but have a copper sensitivity, and "wonks." Yet because a large fraction of these people are elite taste-makers, *Hamilton* becomes a topic of disproportionate interest, discussed at unendurable length in *The New Yorker* and *Slate* and *The New York Times Magazine*, yet totally inaccessible to anyone besides the writers and members of their close social networks.[16] [17] [18] When *The New Yorker* writes about a book that nobody in America wants to read, at least they could theoretically go out and purchase it. But *Hamilton* theatergoing is solely the provenance of *Hamilton* thinkpiece-writers. The endless swirl of online *Hamilton*-buzz shows the comical extreme of cultural insularity in the New York and D.C. media. The "cultural event of our time" is totally unknown to nearly all who actually live in our time.

Given that *Hamilton* is essentially Captain Dan with an American Studies minor, one might wonder how it became so inordinately adored by the blathering class. How did a ten-million-dollar 8th Grade U.S. History skit become "the great work of art of the 21st century" (as the *New Yorker*'s Adam Gopnik says those in his circle have been calling it)?[19]

To judge from the reviews, most of the appeal seems to rest with the forced diversity of its cast and the novelty concept of a "hip-hop musical." Those who write about *Hamilton* often dwell primarily on its "groundbreaking" use of rap and its "bold" choice to cast an assemblage of black, Asian, and Latino actors as the Founding Fathers. Indeed, *Hamilton* exists more as a corporate HR department's wet dream than as a biographical work.

The most obvious historical aberration is the portrayal of Washington and Jefferson as black men, a somewhat audacious choice given that both men are strongly associated with owning, and in the case of the latter, raping and impregnating slaves. Changing the races allows these men to appear far more sympathetic than they would otherwise be. *Hamilton* creator Lin-Manuel Miranda says he did this intentionally, to make the cast "look like America today," and that having black actors play the roles "allow[s] you to leave whatever cultural baggage you have about the founding fathers at the door." ("Cultural baggage" is an odd way of describing "feeling discomfort at warm portrayals of slaveowners.") Thus *Hamilton's* superficial diversity lets its almost entirely white audience feel good about watching it: no guilt for seeing dead white men in a positive light required. Now, *The New York Times* can delight in the novel incongruousness of "a Thomas Jefferson who swaggers like the Time's Morris Day, sings like Cab Calloway and drawls like a Dirty South trap-rapper."[20] Indeed, it does take some getting used to, because the actual Thomas Jefferson *raped slaves.*

"Casting black and Latino actors as the founders effectively writes nonwhite people into the story, in ways that audiences have powerfully responded to," said the *New York Times.*[21] But fixing history makes it seem less objectionable than it actually was. We might call it a kind of, well, "blackwashing," making something that was heinous seem somehow palatable by retroactively injecting diversity into it.

Besides, you don't actually *need* to "write nonwhite people into the story." As historians have pointed out, there were plenty of nonwhite people around at the time, people who already had fully-developed stories and identities. But none of these people appears in the play. As some have quietly noted, the vast majority of African American cast members simply portray nameless dancing founders in breeches and cravats, and "not a single enslaved or free person of color exists as a character in this play." (Although Jefferson's slave and mistress Sally Hemings gets a brief shout-out.)

Slavery is left out of the play almost completely. Historian Lyra Monteiro observes that "Unless one listens carefully to the lyrics—which do mention slavery a handful of times—one could easily assume that slavery did not exist in this world."[22] The foundation of the 18th century economic system, the vicious practice that defined the lives of countless black men and women, is confined to the odd lyrical flourish here and there.

Miranda did consider adding a slavery number. But he cut it from the show, as he explains:

"There was a rap battle about slavery, where it was Hamilton and

Jefferson and Madison knocking it from all sides of the issue. Jeffer-
son being like, 'Hey, I wrote about this, and no one wanted to touch
it!' And Hamilton being very self-righteous, like, 'You're having an
affair with one of your slaves!' And Madison hits him with a 'You
want to talk about affairs?' And in the end, no one does anything.
Which is what happened in reality! So we realized we were bring-
ing our show to a halt on something that none of them really did
enough on."[23]

Miranda found that by trying to write a song about his main characters' attitudes toward slavery, he ran into the inconvenient fact that all
of them willfully tolerated or participated in it. That made it difficult to
square with the upbeat portrayals he was going for, and so slavery had to
go. Besides, dwelling on it could "bring the show to a halt." And as cast
member Christopher Jackson, who plays George Washington, notes:
"The Broadway audience doesn't like to be preached to."[24] Who would
want to spoil the fun?

Instead, *Hamilton*'s Hamilton is what *Slate* called simply "lovable—a
product of the play's humanizing focus on Hamilton's vulnerabilities
and ambitions."[25] The play avoids depicting his unabashed elitism and
more repellent personal characteristics. And in the brief references that
are made to slavery, the play even generously portrays Hamilton as far
more committed to the cause of freedom than he actually was. In this
way, *Hamilton* carefully makes sure its audience is neither challenged
nor discomforted, and can leave the theater without having to confront
any unpleasant truths.

Just as *Hamilton* ducks the question of slavery, much of the actual substance of Alexander Hamilton's politics is ignored, in favor of a story
that stresses his origins as a Horatio Alger immigrant and his rivalry
with Aaron Burr. But while Hamilton may have favored opening America's doors to immigration, he also proposed a degree of economic pro-
tectionism that would terrify today's free market establishment.

Hamilton believed that free trade was never equal, and worried about
the ability of European manufacturers (who got a head start on the

Industrial Revolution) to sell goods at lower prices than their American counterparts. In Hamilton's 1791 *Report on Manufactures*, he spoke of the harms to American industry that came with our reliance on products from overseas. The *Report* sheds light on many of the concerns Americans in the 21st century have about outsourcing, sweatshops, and the increasing trade deficit, albeit in a different context. Hamilton said that for the U.S., "constant and increasing necessity, on their part, for the commodities of Europe, and only a partial and occasional demand for their own, in return, could not but expose them to a state of impoverishment, compared with the opulence to which their political and natural advantages authorise them to aspire." For Hamilton, the solution was high tariffs on imports of manufactured goods, and intensive government intervention in the economy. The prohibitive importation costs imposed by tariffs would allow newer American manufacturers to undersell Europe's established industrial framework, leading to an increase in non-agricultural employment. As he wrote: "all the duties imposed on imported articles... wear a beneficent aspect towards the manufacturers of the country."

Does any of this sound familiar? It certainly went unmentioned at the White House, where a custom performance of *Hamilton* was held for the Obamas. The livestreamed presidential *Hamilton* spectacular at one point featured Obama and Miranda performing historically-themed freestyle rap in the Rose Garden.

The Obamas have been supporters of *Hamilton* since its embryonic days as the "Hamilton Mixtape song cycle." By the time the fully-fledged musical arrived in Washington, Michelle Obama called it the "best piece of art in any form that I have ever seen in my life,"[26] raising disquieting questions about the level of cultural exposure offered in the Princeton undergraduate curriculum.

In introducing the White House performance, Barack Obama gave an effusive speech worthy of the BuzzFeed Hamilton Slack:

> *[Miranda] identified a quintessentially American story in the*
> *character of Hamilton — a striving immigrant who escaped pov-*

erty, made his way to the New World, climbed to the top by sheer force of will and pluck and determination... And in the Hamilton that Lin-Manuel and his incredible cast and crew bring to life—a man who is "just like his country, young, scrappy, and hungry"—we recognize the improbable story of America, and the spirit that has sustained our nation for over 240 years... In this telling, rap is the language of revolution. Hip-hop is the backbeat. ... And with a cast as diverse as America itself, including the outstandingly talented women—(applause)—the show reminds us that this nation was built by more than just a few great men—and that it is an inheritance that belongs to all of us.[27]

Strangely enough, President Obama failed to mention anything Alexander Hamilton actually did during his long career in American politics, perhaps because the Obama Administration's unwavering support of free trade and the tariff-easing Trans-Pacific Partnership goes against everything Hamilton believed. Instead, Obama's *Hamilton* speech stresses just two takeaways from the musical: that America is a place where the poor (through "sheer force of will" and little else) can rise to prominence, and that *Hamilton* has diversity in it. (Plus it contains hip-hop, an edgy, up-and-coming genre with only 37 years of mainstream exposure.)

The Obamas were not the only members of the political establishment to come down with a ghastly case of Hamiltonmania. Nearly every figure in D.C. has apparently been to see the show, in many cases being invited for a warm backstage schmooze with Miranda. Biden saw it.[28] Mitt Romney saw it.[29] The Bush daughters saw it. Rahm Emanuel saw it the day after the Chicago teachers' strike over budget cuts and school closures.[30] Hillary Clinton went to see the musical in the evening after having been interviewed by the FBI in the morning. The Clinton campaign has also been fundraising by hawking *Hamilton* tickets; for $100,000 you can watch a performance alongside Clinton herself.[31]

Unsurprisingly, the *New York Times* reports that "conservatives were particularly smitten" with *Hamilton*.[32] "Fabulous show," tweeted Rupert

Murdoch, calling it "historically accurate."[33] Obama concluded that "I'm pretty sure this is the only thing that Dick Cheney and I have agreed on—during my entire political career."[34] (That is, of course, false. Other points of agreement include drone strikes, Guantanamo, the NSA, and mass deportation.)

The conservative-liberal D.C. consensus on *Hamilton* makes perfect sense. The musical flatters both right and left sensibilities. Conservatives get to see their beloved Founding Fathers exonerated for their horrendous crimes, and liberals get to have nationalism packaged in a feel-good multicultural form. The more troubling questions about the country's origins are instantly vanished, as an era built on racist forced labor is transformed into a colorful, culturally progressive, and politically unobjectionable extravaganza.

As the director of the *Hamilton* theater said, "It has liberated a lot of people who might feel ambivalent about the American experiment to feel patriotic."[35] "Ambivalence," here, means being bothered by the country's collective idol-worship of men who participated in the slave trade, one of the greatest crimes in human history. To be "liberated" from this means never having to think about it.

In that respect, *Hamilton* probably *is* the "musical of the Obama era," as *The New Yorker* called it.[36] Contemporary progressivism has come to mean papering over material inequality with representational diversity. The president will continue to expand the national security state at the same rate as his predecessor, but at least he will be black. Predatory lending will drain the wealth from African American communities, but the board of Goldman Sachs will have several black members. Inequality will be rampant and worsening, but the 1% will at least "look like America." The actual racial injustices of our time will continue unabated, but the power structure will be diversified so that nobody feels quite so bad about it. *Hamilton* is simply this tendency's cultural-historical equivalent; instead of worrying ourselves about the brutal origins of the American state, and the lasting economic effects of those early inequities, we can simply turn the Founding Fathers black and enjoy the show.

Kings George I and II of England could barely speak intelligible

English and spent more time dealing with their own failsons than ruling the Empire—but they gave patronage to Handel. Ludwig II of Bavaria was believed to be insane and went into debt compulsively building castles—but he gave patronage to Wagner. Barack Obama deported more immigrants than any other president and expanded the drone program in order to kill almost 3,500 people—but he gave patronage to a neoliberal nerdcore musical. God bless this great land.

AGAINST DOMESTICITY

by Amber A'Lee Frost

RECENTLY I SOLICITED TWITTER for the best Tom Kha Gai in New York City. The slightly spicy chicken coconut soup is a standard menu item in most Thai restaurants, but although it's often served as an entrée in Thailand, here in New York it's generally ordered as an appetizer. Appetizers are unlikely to be the dish that creates buzz around an eatery, so the quality often varies wildly from restaurant to restaurant, and a lot of places bullshit their way through a Tom Kha Gai. I'm ideologically and aesthetically opposed to reading Yelp reviews, and as a result, I have consumed a lot of very phoned in Tom Kha Gai. However, I'm also opposed to *leaving* Yelp reviews, so I won't name names. It's true that half-assing such a glorious soup is an ignoble disservice to the dish, but that's a sin that's better left between the chef and their god.

I should never have asked Twitter for a restaurant recommendation of course, because when one asks any large group of people for a restaurant recommendation, one will inevitably get the *opposite* of a restaurant recommendation: a recipe. "It's actually really easy to make!" they chirp. "All you need is…"—this is the point at which I slam my laptop in indignation, not because the crowd has responded to my inquiry with information I have not requested, but because they have responded with treachery and lies.

It is *not* easy to make Tom Kha Gai. That is simply empirically untrue.

Unless you live near a market with a Thai section, the ingredients are expensive and difficult to source. It's a fairly time-consuming and labor-intensive dish, and honestly the process is quite fraught; is difficult to get the flavor out of lemongrass, coconut milk burns easily, and if you overdo it even a little bit on the fish sauce, the entire batch will taste like low tide.

Of course Tom Kha Gai is hard. Cooking is often highly skilled labor (a fact that usually goes overlooked, especially when women or immigrants are the ones feeding people, as they usually are). But nowadays there is absolutely no dish, no matter how time-consuming or elaborate, that cooking enthusiasts won't describe as "actually really easy to make!!!". This is because they are delusional, unsympathetic people, who want nothing more than to draw you into their anachronistic cult of domesticity.

To clarify, it is not that I think people *should not* cook, or clean, or launder or garden. I like restaurants, and delivery, and I adore the odd fast food indulgence, but I understand that various aspects of keeping a home are enjoyable—even soothing—to some people. I can only assume a propensity toward housework of any kind can well be attributed to nature as well as nurture. A friend once claimed to me that his Italian Catholic upbringing inscribed upon him an almost spiritual pleasure in the ritualistic cleansing of his floors. Meanwhile his Jewish girlfriend, raised by a lesbian feminist, was happy to encourage his pious compulsions.

As a bohemian layabout made nervous by industriousness, I don't even like when someone cleans *on my behalf*. I would prefer robots to clean my house, and maintain that dining programs must be integrated into any socialist vision (hardly a radical proposition; seize the hot bar at Whole Foods and you've got yourself a ready-made Soviet-style cafeteria). Anyway, home-cooked meals are nice, but they're hardly necessary for a healthy and delicious diet. For example, I usually eat as if I were at a party—nibbling on charcuterie all day.

I understand that everyone has their strange little kinks—but as drudgery is not my personal fetish, I'm simply saying I'd rather press my hand on the burner than actually spend any measurable amount of time sweating over a hot stove. But obviously housework is a valid and nec-essary perversion—my issue is that a contemporary cult of neo-domes-ticity appears intent on undermining the difficulty and complexity of traditionally feminine labor by insisting upon the myth of effortlessness.

And it didn't use to be this way. Take for example, the late great Julia Child, a radiant soul if ever there was one.

Child *loved* cooking, but she also loved the challenge of it, and never denied that it was complex work, and allowed viewers to witness her frustrations and defeats. "Cooking," she proclaimed, "well, lots of it, is one failure after another, and that's how you finally learn." Once, after a botched attempt to flip a potato pancake, she scooped up the spilled and splattered bits of latke and mashed them back into the pan, giving the viewer permission to do the same, remaining cavalier in her trade-mark sing-song voice, "if you're alone in the kitchen, who is to see?" She would chuck broken or inadequate cookware into the garbage can like lovers that had outworn their use. She had strong aesthetic principles, and abhorred abstemious health and weight loss trends, once saying during a show, "I'm going to put some light cream in, or you can put in some more milk… if you're on one of those hideous diets."

As a true sensualist, she paired entrées not only with wine, but with beer, and often recommended bubbly with dessert. "You could serve this with coffee or tea, but we're going to serve it with champagne." (Yes Julia, yes we are.) She had good taste, but she was never pretentious or snobby, and when asked what her favorite wine was, she would shrug and laugh and say "gin." Numerous interviews asked her for her favorite meal, and without fail she would reply "red meat and gin." She had a natural élan, an easy laugh, and a contagious bravery.

Compare that to one of the most prevalent genres of cooking instruc-tion now: the time-lapse tutorial. You've probably seen them on Face-book, as *BuzzFeed*'s Tasty vertical has over 82.5 million followers. The videos are comparable to POV porn, which is shot from the perspective of the party receiving sexual attention (usually orally); correspondingly, the cook's face is not visible in Tasty videos. You don't hear their voice, you see only a pair of hands doing the work in a rapid fast-forward that belies the actual amount of work necessary for the dish. Most prep work is never shown—ingredients are pre-portioned and measured. Repetitious tasks are shown only once. No mess or dirty dishes are ever visible, and the twee instrumental music that plays (they love ukulele) seems to imply a breezy, mess-free little craft project, rather than the toil of dicing onions. The food itself is almost always some Guy Fieri nightmare of inelegant American gluttony, but look! It only takes two minutes to make macaroni and cheese breadsticks! And of course, sometimes the videos are sponsored, though often in confusing ways. Philadelphia cream cheese makes sense for the cream cheese stuffed monkey bread, but I'm not quite sure why this Garlic Citrus Chicken and Veggies video is brought to you by Bank of America.

Tasty videos aren't just sterile lies, they're a social media servants' entrance, where you're the servant, and all the unsightly or dull work that you're being invited to perform has been hidden away. They edit the prosaic labor of cooking into an effortless leisure pursuit. Every time I see another one on Facebook I have to resist the urge to denounce the person who posted it as a closet reactionary and possible misogynist. The most generous assumption I can make is that they're a hopeless philistine suffering from a pathological compulsion. If you eat cheeseburger onion rings at the State Fair, you're an American. If you're fantasizing about actually *making* them, *in your own home*, you are in need of treatment.

And it *is* a fantasy. That's why those videos are primarily shot from the perspective of the cook. They're hardcore domestic pornography, so they don't have to be real, they just have to be graphic. The people who circulate Tasty's content almost never actually make that terrible, nearly poisonous food, but they like to imagine themselves as the sort of person who could, the sort of person who has the time to learn and try new indulgent recipes. Tasty tutorials edit and accelerate cooking into a carefree blur of alienation because we don't have the time to do anything at a regular pace, and these sedative little videos (dare I call them "opiates?") offer a little bit of escapism.

The frantic bleakness of neoliberal efficiency does make a retreat to the home sound appealing, but the idyllic warmth of the hearth actually comes with a lot of maintenance—home is another workplace. Nonetheless *The New Yorker* declared 2016 "the year of *hygge*"—a Danish term that everyone insists has no translation but appears to mean little more than "coziness." The lifestyle craze imagines a home replete with "candles, nubby woolens, shearling slippers, woven textiles, pastries, blond wood, sheepskin rugs, lattes with milk-foam hearts, and a warm fireplace." Being aspirationally cozy sure sounds expensive and time-consuming. And collecting all the accoutrements of relaxation sounds pretty stressful; in fact it sounds a lot like a job, specifically the sort of job worked mostly by women.

What's worse, these lifeless, cutesy interiors, with all their bland affectations of comfort, have become the aesthetic of choice for so-called "creatives." What was once the boho dirtbag pad is now clean white walls, décor artfully curated to look "rustic," and perhaps an austere but lovely potted succulent. (In my own experience, real bohemians can't even keep a cactus alive.)

There is a feminine energy to the entire domestic lifestyle endeavor, but nowadays even men love making a house into a home, reveling in anachronistic skills that they inevitably get an absurd amount of credit for. (Cooking is one of those things that people are always shocked that men are capable of. Parenting is similar; they wipe one ass and they're father of the year.)

Of course there's a lot of brilliant feminist thought on housework, but one of my favorites is literally quite elementary. *Free to Be You and Me* was a 1974 progressive children's entertainment project created by actress Marlo Thomas, and co-produced by The Ms. Foundation for Women. The book was popular, but the album and television special were a legitimate phenomenon. My favorite segment was from the record, but it was so mired in controversy that they decided not to include it in the TV special. In the poem "Housework," the glamorous and ebullient Carol Channing gives the kids a dose of reality:

> *Remember, nobody smiles doing housework but those ladies you see on TV.*
> *Your mommy hates housework,*

Your daddy hates housework,
I hate housework too.
And when you grow up, so will you.
Because even if the soap or cleanser or cleaner or powder or paste or
*   wax or bleach*
That you use is the very best one,
Housework is just no fun.
Children, when you have a house of your own,
Make sure, when there's housework to do,
That you don't have to do it alone.
Little boys, little girls, when you're big husbands and wives,
If you want all the days of your lives
To seem sunny as summer weather,
Make sure, when there's housework to do,
That you do it together!

In her review for *The New York Times*, Deborah Jowitt managed to take the poem personally, saying, "The skit, unintentionally, I'm sure, demeans those who accept the clean-up chores without fuss, and makes those who take pleasure in such chores sound like real suckers." *Ms* actually received letters from upset parents as well, one of whom felt uncomfortable hearing the track in the presence of their maid, saying "It seemed too demeaning and insensitive to this woman, who does derive a sense of satisfaction and accomplishment from her work." Now it's very possible this woman enjoyed her job cleaning up for wealthier people than herself, but I think the fact that her cleaning was wage labor and not a hobby may have been lost on her employer.

Personally I am only domestic to be social. Aside from wage labor, I never cook or clean for anyone that I do not love. (If I have ever so much as made you a cup of tea, it is likely that you are very dear to me.) I avoid the broom and spray bottle until I have a guest that I don't want to disgust. When I actually get an urge to cook for myself, I almost immediately regret the commitment, seething with boredom and dreading the clean-up (handy tip: if you have a friend suffering from depression, finger foods, disposable plates, bowls and cutlery make a merciful gift). And I like home-cooked food, but there is nothing social or intimate or culturally resonant for me about a pot of stew for one. I learned to cook from my grandmother, from whom I inherited an ancient cast iron skillet that I almost never use. The most delicious cuisine from where she's from in rural Kentucky is labor-intensive, and evolved from the batch production necessary to feed large families. Talk about anachronistic labor—tending to a pot on simmer for six hours probably isn't so bad when you have nine children thanking you for the meal (of course, Jesus always gets thanked first, feminine labor slighted yet again).

As for even more ambitious domesticity, like say, gardening, I am unable to even discuss it without sputtering in incoherent anger. If my grandparents knew that they left their bleak cabins and precarious agrarian lives in Appalachia only to see their granddaughter raise chickens in Brooklyn, they'd assume I had cracked, or perhaps fallen on hard times.

It used to be that domesticity was the province of conservatives, but progressives now adore a cultivated domestic lifestyle and frankly I find the fetish insidious. On the other hand, I think Rosa Luxemburg missed the mark in her 1914 barnburner, "The Proletarian Woman," when she said that domesticity is a reliable way to keep women complicit and complacent, saying:

> "The bourgeois woman has no real interest in political rights, because she exercises no economic function in society, because she enjoys the finished fruits of class rule. The demand for equal women's rights is, where it arises with bourgeois women, the pure ideology of weak groups of individuals, without material roots, a phantom of the contrast between woman and man, a quirk. Thence the farcical character of the suffragette movement."

It's not an exaggeration to say that petit bourgeois domesticity has driven many a woman to literal suicide, and that anxiety of crushing boredom has historically been pretty fertile ground for radicalization. (Also, call me a bourgeois reformist, but women's suffrage was a Good

Thing.) What Rosa got right in that essay though, was the gilded cage of capitalist *hygge* patriarchy:

> *"For the propertied bourgeois woman her house is the world. For the proletarian woman the whole world is her house, the world with its sorrow and its joy, with its cold cruelty and its brutal size."*

It's not only a poetic insight, but a liberating truth to we feminists of the lazy, louche and carousing variety; one cannot roam the world and keep it clean and cozy at the same time. Feminism once championed a salient skepticism of domesticity's so-called "comforts," and I think that labor critique (and intellectual tradition) is due for a comeback. At this point it would be ideal for me to leave you with a thought from *Revolution at Point Zero: Housework, Reproduction, and Feminist Struggle*, by Sylvia Federici, but honestly I'm on deadline, and I can't seem to find the book. I think it's under some dirty laundry.

HOW LIBERALS FELL IN LOVE WITH THE WEST WING

by Luke Savage

IN THE HISTORY OF PRESTIGE TV, few dramas have had quite the cultural staying power of Aaron Sorkin's *The West Wing*.

Set during the two terms of fictional Democratic President and Nobel Laureate in Economics Josiah "Jed" Bartlet (Martin Sheen) the show depicts the inner workings of a sympathetic liberal administration grappling with the daily exigencies of governing. Every procedure and protocol, every piece of political brokerage—from State of the Union addresses to legislative tugs of war to Supreme Court appointments—is recreated with an aesthetic authenticity enabled by ample production values (a single episode reportedly cost almost $3 million to produce) and rendered with a dramatic flair that stylizes all the bureaucratic banality of modern governance.

Nearly the same, of course, might be said for other glossy political dramas such as Netflix's *House of Cards* or *Scandal*. But *The West Wing* aspires to more than simply visual verisimilitude. Breaking with the cynicism or amoralism characteristic of many dramas about politics, it offers a vision of political institutions which is ultimately affirmative and approving. What we see throughout its seven seasons are Democrats governing as Democrats imagine they govern, with the Bartlet Administration standing in for liberalism as liberalism understands itself.

More than simply a fictional account of an idealized liberal presidency, then, *The West Wing* is an elaborate fantasia founded upon the shibboleths that sustain Beltway liberalism and the milieu that produced them.

> *"Ginger, get the popcorn*
> *The filibuster is in*
> *I'm Toby Ziegler with The Drop In*
> *What Kind of Day Has It Been?*
> *It's Lin, speaking the truth*
> —Lin-Manuel Miranda, "What's Next?"[1]

During its run from 1999 to 2006, *The West Wing* garnered immense popularity and attention, capturing three Golden Globe Awards and 26 Emmys and building a devout fanbase among Democratic partisans, Beltway acolytes, and people of the liberal-ish persuasion the world over. Since its finale more than a decade ago, it has become an essential part of the liberal cultural ecosystem, its importance arguably on par with *The Daily Show, Last Week Tonight,* and the rap musical about the founding fathers people like for some reason.

If anything, its fandom has only continued to grow with age: In the summer of 2016, a weekly podcast hosted by seasons 4-7 star Joshua Malina, launched with the intent of running through all 154 episodes (at a rate of one per week), almost immediately garnered millions of downloads[2]; an elaborate fan wiki with almost 2000 distinct entries is maintained and regularly updated, magisterially documenting every mundane detail of the *West Wing* cosmos save the characters' bowel movements; and, in definitive proof of the silence of God, superfan Lin-Manuel Miranda has recently recorded a rap named for one of the show's most popular catchphrases ("What's next?").

While certainly appealing to a general audience thanks to its expensive sheen and distinctive writing, *The West Wing*'s greatest zealots have proven to be those who professionally inhabit the very milieu it depicts: Washington political staffers, media types, centrist cognoscenti, and various others drawn from the ranks of people who tweet "Big, if true" in earnest and think a lanyard is a talisman that grants wishes and wards off evil.

The West Wing "took something that was for the most part considered dry and nerdy—especially to people in high school and college—and sexed it up," former David Axelrod advisor Eric Lesser told *Vanity Fair* in a longform 2012 feature about the "Sorkinization of politics" (Axelrod himself having at one point advised *West Wing* writer Eli Attie).[3] It "very much served as inspiration", said Micah Lasher, a staffer who then worked for Michael Bloomberg.

Thanks to its endless depiction of procedure and policy, the show naturally gibed with the wonkish libidos of future Voxsplainers Matt Yglesias and Ezra Klein. "There's a cultural meme or cultural suggestion that Washington is boring, that policy is boring, but it's important stuff," said Klein, adding that the show dramatized "the immediacy and urgency and concern that people in this town feel about the issues they're working on." "I was interested in politics before the show started," added Yglesias. "But a friend of mine from college moved to D.C. at the same time as me, after graduation, and we definitely plotted our proposed domination of the capital in explicitly *West Wing* terms: Who was more like Toby? Who was more like Josh?"[4]

Far from the Kafkaesque banality which so often characterizes the real life equivalent, the mundane business of technocratic governance is made to look exciting, intellectually stimulating, and, above all, honorable. The bureaucratic drudgery of both White House management and governance, from speechwriting, to press conference logistics, to policy creation, are front and center across all seven seasons. A typical episode script is chock full of dweebish phraseology — "farm subsidies", "recess appointments", "census bureau", "congressional consultation" — usually uttered by swift-tongued, Ivy League-educated staffers darting purposefully through labyrinthine corridors during the infamous "walk-and-talk" sequences. By recreating the look and feel of political processes to the tee, while garnishing them with a romantic veneer, the show gifts the Beltway's most spiritually-devoted adherents with a vision of how many would probably like to see themselves.

172 THE CURRENT AFFAIRS MINDSET

In serving up this optimistic simulacrum of modern US politics, Sorkin's universe has repeatedly intersected with real-life US politics. Following the first season, and in the midst of the 2000 presidential election contest, *Salon*'s Joyce Millman wrote: "Al Gore could clinch the election right now by staging as many photo-ops with the cast of *The West Wing* as possible."[5] A poll published during the same election found that most voters preferred Martin Sheen's President Bartlet to Bush or Gore. A 2008 *New York Times* article predicted an Obama victory on the basis of the show's season 6-7 plot arc. The same election year, the paper published a fictionalized exchange between Bartlet and Barack Obama penned by Sorkin himself. 2016 proved no exception, with the *New Statesman*'s Helen Lewis reacting to Donald Trump's victory by saying: "I'm going to hug my *West Wing* boxset a little closer tonight, that's for sure."[6]

Appropriately, many of the show's cast members, leveraging their on-screen personas, have participated or intervened in real Democratic Party politics. During the 2016 campaign, star Bradley Whitford—who portrays frenetically wily strategist Josh Lyman—was invited to "reveal" who his [fictional] boss would endorse:

> *"There's no doubt in my mind that Hillary would be President Bartlet's choice. She's—nobody is more prepared to take that position on day one. I know this may be controversial. But yes, on behalf of Jed Bartlet, I want to endorse Hillary Clinton."*[7]

Six leading members of the cast, including Whitford, were even dispatched to Ohio to stump for Clinton (inexplicably failing to swing the crucial state in her favor).

During the Democratic primary season Rob Lowe (who appeared from 1999-2003 before leaving in protest at the ostensible stinginess of his $75,000/episode salary) even deployed a clip from the show and paraphrased his own character's lines during an attack on Bernie Sanders' tax plan: *"Watching Bernie Sanders. He's hectoring and yelling at me WHILE he's saying he's going to raise our taxes. Interesting way to com-*

municate." In Season 2 episode "The Fall's Gonna Kill You", Lowe's character Sam Seaborn angrily lectures a team of speechwriters:

> *"Every time your boss got on the stump and said, 'It's time for the rich to pay their fair share,' I hid under a couch and changed my name...The top one percent of wage earners in this country pay for twenty-two percent of this country. Let's not call them names while they're doing it, is all I'm saying."*

What is the actual ideology of *The West Wing*? Just like the real American liberalism it represents, the show proved to be something of a political weather vane throughout its seven seasons on the air.

Debuting during the twilight of the Clinton presidency and spanning much of Bush II's, it predictably vacillated somewhat in response to events while remaining grounded in a general liberal ethos. Having writing credits for all but one episode in *The West Wing*'s first four seasons, Sorkin left in 2003, with Executive Producer John Wells characterizing the subsequent direction as more balanced and bipartisan. The Bartlet administration's actual politics—just like those of the real Democratic Party and its base—therefore run the gamut from the stuff of Elizabeth Warren-esque populism to the neoliberal bilge you might expect to come from a Beltway think tank having its white papers greased by dollars from Goldman Sachs.

But promoting or endorsing any specific policy orientation is not the show's true *raison d'être*. At the conclusion of its seven seasons it remains unclear if the Bartlet administration has succeeded at all in fundamentally altering the contours of American life. In fact, after two terms in the White House, Bartlet's gang of hyper-educated, hyper-competent politicos do not seem to have any transformational policy achievements whatsoever. Even in their most unconstrained and idealized political fantasies, liberals manage to accomplish nothing.

The lack of any serious attempts to change anything reflect a certain *apolitical* tendency in this type of politics, one that defines itself by its manner and attitude rather than a vision of the change it wishes to see in the world. Insofar as there is an identifiable ideology, it isn't one definitively wedded to a particular program of reform, but instead to a particular aesthetic of political institutions. The business of leveraging democracy for any specific purpose comes second to how its institutional liturgy and processes look and, more importantly, how they make us feel—virtue being attached more to posture and affect than to any particular goal. Echoing Sorkin's 1995 film *The American President* (in many ways the progenitor of *The West Wing*) it delights in invoking "seriousness" and the supposedly hard-headed pragmatism of grownups.

Consider a scene from Season 2's "The War at Home", in which Toby Ziegler confronts a rogue Democratic Senator over his objections to Social Security cuts prospectively to be made in collaboration with a Republican Congress. The episode's protagonist certainly isn't the latter, who tries to draw a line in the sand over the "compromising of basic Democratic values" and threatens to run a third party presidential campaign, only to be admonished acerbically by Ziegler:

> *"If you think demonizing people who are trying to govern responsibly is the way to protect our liberal base, then speaking as a liberal... go to bed, would you please?...Come at us from the left, and I'm gonna own your ass."*

The administration and its staff are invariably depicted as tribunes of the serious and the mature, their ideological malleability taken to signify their virtue more than any fealty to specific liberal principles.

Even when the show ventures to criticize the institutions of American democracy, it never retreats from a foundational reverence for their supposed enlightenment and the essential nobility of most of the people who administer them. As such, the presidency's basic function is to appear presidential and, more than anything, Jed Bartlet's patrician aura and respectable disposition make him the perfect avatar for the *West Wing* universe's often maudlin deference to the liturgy of "the office." "Seriousness," then— the superlative quality in the Sorkin taxonomy of virtues—implies presiding over the political consensus, tinkering here and there, and looking stylish in the process by way of soaring oratory and white-collar chic.

"Make this election about smart, and not. Make it about engaged, and not. Qualified, and not. Make it about a heavyweight. You're a heavyweight. And you've been holding me up for too many rounds."
—Toby Ziegler, Hartsfield's Landing (Season 3, Episode 14)

Despite its relatively thin ideological commitments, there is a general tenor to the *West Wing* universe that cannot be called anything other than smug.

It's a smugness born of the view that politics is less a terrain of clashing values and interests than a perpetual pitting of the clever against the ignorant and obtuse. The clever wield facts and reason, while the foolish cling to effortlessly-exposed fictions and the braying prejudices of provincial rubes. In emphasizing intelligence over ideology, what follows is a fetishization of "elevated discourse" regardless of its actual outcomes or conclusions. The greatest political victories involve semantically dismantling an opponent's argument or exposing its hypocrisy, usually by way of some grand rhetorical gesture. Categories like left and right become less significant, provided that the competing interlocutors are deemed respectably smart and practice the designated etiquette. The Discourse becomes a category of its own, to be protected and nourished by Serious People conversing respectfully while shutting down the stupid with heavy-handed moral sanctimony.

In Toby Ziegler's "smart and not," "qualified and not" formulation, we can see a preview of the (disastrous) rhetorical strategy that Hillary Clinton would ultimately adopt against Donald Trump. Don't make it about vision, make it about qualification. Don't make it about your plans for how to make people's lives better, make it about your superior moral character. Fundamentally, make it about how smart and good and serious you are, and how bad and dumb and unserious they are.

In this respect, *The West Wing*'s foundational serious/unserious binary falls squarely within the tradition that has since evolved into the "epic own/evisceration" genre characteristic of social media and late night TV, in which the aim is to ruthlessly use one's intellect to expose the idiocy and hypocrisy of the other side. In a famous scene from Season 4's "Game On", Bartlet debates his Republican rival Governor Robert Ritchie (James Brolin). Their exchange, prompted by a question about the role of the federal government, is the stuff of a John Oliver wet dream:

> RICHIE: *"My view of this is simple. We don't need a federal Department of Education telling us our children have to learn Esperanto, they have to learn Eskimo poetry. Let the states decide, let the communities decide on health care and education, on lower taxes, not higher taxes. Now he's going to throw a big word at you — 'unfunded mandate', he's going to say if Washington lets the states do it, it's an unfunded mandate. But what he doesn't like is the federal government losing power. I call it the ingenuity of the American people."*
>
> BARTLET: *"Well first of all let's clear up a couple of things: unfunded mandate is two words, not one big word. There are times when we are 50 states and there are times when we're one country and have national needs. And the way I know this is that Florida didn't fight Germany in World War Two or establish civil rights. You think states should do the governing wall-to-wall, now that's a perfectly valid opinion. But your state of Florida got 12.6 billion dollars in federal money last year from Nebraskans and Virginia's and New Yorkers and Alaskans, with their Eskimo poetry — 12.6 out of the state budget of 50 billion. I'm supposed to be using this time for a question so here it is: Can we have it back please?"*

In an even more famous scene from Season 2 episode "The Midterms", Bartlet humiliates homophobic talk radio host Jenna Jacobs by quoting scripture from memory, destroying her by her *very own logic*.

If Richie and Jacobs are the obtuse yokels to be epically taken down with facts and reason, the show also elevates several conservative characters to reinforce its postpartisan celebration of The Discourse. Republicans come in two types: slack-jawed caricatures, and people whose high-mindedness and mutual enthusiasm for Putting Differences Aside make them the Bartlet Administration's natural allies or friends regardless of whatever conflicts of values they may ostensibly have. Foremost among the latter is Vinick: a moderate, pro-choice Republican who resembles John McCain (at least the imaginary "maverick" John McCain that liberals continue to pretend exists) and is appointed by Bartlet's Democratic successor Matthew Santos to be Secretary of State. (In reality, there is no such thing as a "moderate" Republican, only a polite one. The upright and genial Paul Ryan, whom President Bartlet would have loved, is on a lifelong quest to dismantle every part of America's feeble social safety net.)

Thus Bartlet Democrats do not see Republicans as the "enemy," except to the extent that they are rude or insufficiently respectful of the rules of political decorum. In one Season 5 plot, the administration opts to install a Ruth Bader Ginsburg clone (Glenn Close) as Chief Justice of the Supreme Court. The price it pays—willingly, as it turns out—is giving the other vacancy to an ultra-conservative justice, for the sole reason that Bartlet's staff find their amiable squabbling stimulating. Anyone with substantively progressive political values would be horrified by a liberal president's appointment of an Antonin Scalia-style textualist to the Supreme Court. But if your values are procedural, based more on the manner in which people conduct themselves rather than the consequences they actually bring about, it's easy to chuckle along with a hard-right conservative, so long as they are personally charming (Ziegler: "I hate him, but he's brilliant. And the two of them together are fighting like cats and dogs ... but it works.")

Through its idealized rendering of American politics and its institutions, The West Wing offers a comforting avenue of escape from the grim and often dystopian reality of the present. If the show, despite its age, has continued to find favor and relevance among liberals, Democrats, and assorted Beltway acolytes alike, it is because it reflects and affirms their worldview with greater fidelity and catharsis than any of its contemporaries.

But if anything gives that worldview pause, it should be the events of the past eight years. Liberals got a real life Josiah Bartlet in the figure of Barack Obama, a charismatic and stylish politician elected on a populist wave. But Obama's soaring speeches, quintessentially *presidential* affect, and deference to procedure did little to fundamentally improve the country or prevent his Republican rivals from storming the Congressional barricades at their first opportunity. Confronted by a mercurial TV personality bent on transgressing every norm and truism of Beltway thinking, Democrats responded by exhaustively informing voters of his indecency and hypocrisy, attempting to destroy him countless times with his own logic, but ultimately leaving him completely intact. They smugly taxonomized as "smart" and "dumb" the very electorate they needed to win over, and retreated into an ideological fever dream in which political success doesn't come from organizing and building power, but from having the most polished arguments and the most detailed policy statements. If you can just *crush* Trump in the debates, as Bartlet did to Richie, then you've won. (That's not an exaggeration of the worldview. Ezra Klein published an article entitled "Hillary Clinton's 3 debate performances left the Trump campaign in ruins," which entirely eliminated the distinction between what happens in *debates* and what happens in *campaigns*.[8] The belief that politics is about argument rather than power is likely a symptom of a Democratic politics increasingly incubated in the Ivy League rather than the labor movement.)

Now, facing defeat and political crisis, the overwhelming liberal instinct has not been self-reflection but a further retreat into fantasy and orthodoxy. Like viewers at the climax of *The West Wing*'s original run, they sit waiting for the decisive gestures and gratifying crescendos of a series finale, only to find their favorite plotlines and characters meandering without resolution. Shockingly, life is not a television program, and Aaron Sorkin doesn't get to write the ending.

The West Wing is many things: a uniquely popular and lavish effort in prestige TV; an often crisply-written drama; a fictionalized paean to Beltway liberalism's foundational precepts; a wonkish celebration of institutions and processes; an exquisitely-tailored piece of political fanfiction.

But, in 2017, it is foremost a series of glittering illusions to be abandoned.

MIKE CERNOVICH:
HOW TO BECOME THE
GORILLA MAN OF YOUR DREAMS

by Brianna Rennix & Nathan J. Robinson

MAKING MONEY OFF SAPS has always been the real American Dream, and by this measure Mike Cernovich is doing his best to truly live out our great national aspiration. One not might have thought the presidential candidacy of Donald Trump would make compelling raw material for a self-help franchise, but in *MAGA Mindset: Making YOU and America Great Again*, Cernovich manages to meld the nationalist rhetoric of the "alt-right" with the affirmational platitudes of *The Secret*.[1]

Over the course of the presidential campaign, Cernovich built up a reputation as the man too toxically right-wing for even FOX News. When the network invited him on, a *RedState* blogger exclaimed, "They're giving this motherfucker legitimacy? Oh my god!"[2] Cernovich, after all, is a Pizzagate truther known for sending tweets about how date rape doesn't exist. He regularly uses the word "bitch" in describing women, and has called the Syrian refugee crisis a media-created "hoax." Yet Cernovich has built up a considerable platform on (where else?) Twitter, where he preaches to a swarm of over one hundred and fifty thousand followers.

In his conspiratorial and misogynistic pronouncements, Cernovich is a run-of-the-mill creature of the online alt-right. He nevertheless makes for an interesting subspecimen, as one of the only fixtures of the movement to parlay his politics into a self-help brand. Cernovich's blog and books are not just Trumpist propaganda. They sell a lifestyle, a package of inspirational macho clichés to help weedy, socially inept men become their ultimate selves. Cernovich takes Trump's sales pitch one step further: Make America Great Again is not just a political program. It is a whole new you.

Cernovich himself is a classic rags-to-riches story: the inspiring metamorphosis of a poor, fat kid from the Midwest into a fully-fledged asshole in Venice Beach, California. During this remarkable journey, Cernovich learned martial arts, went to law school, was accused of rape, self-published three entire books on juicing, married a highly successful Silicon Valley patent attorney, was divorced by a highly successful Silicon Valley patent attorney, got a seven-figure alimony payout, rose to internet prominence by savaging a bunch of female gamers on Twitter, and finally became a thought-leader in the world of tinhat fake news (e.g.: "The Orlando Shooter Did Not Act Alone").[3] Also, his podcast has more followers than James Altucher's. (We have no idea who James Altucher is either, but Mike Cernovich mentions this fact in every single one of his books, so we must assume it is one of Cernovich's more significant achievements.)

Cernovich's internet writings include such thinkpieces as "How to Choke a Woman During Sex"[4] and, entirely unrelatedly, "How to Avoid a False Rape Case." (Cernovich's professional advice is that you should secretly film the woman during sex.) Given this provocative online oeuvre, the surprising thing about Cernovich's first self-help book, *Gorilla Mindset* (other than how little it actually discusses gorillas), is just how milquetoast and prototypical Cernovich's advice is.[5] Confronting your challenges, reaching your goals, maintaining your focus. For a masculinist tract, parts of it have a surprisingly *Chicken Soup for the Soul* vibe.

The gorilla conceit itself goes unexplained. Why gorillas? Presumably because they are muscly and do not suffer from self-doubt. (They are also, however, not known for being especially sophisticated political thinkers, a fact one may wish to bear in mind when assessing how much credence to give Cernovich's theory of an international war on whites.) The gorilla mindset seems to have something to do with unleashing an inner animal. But what gorillas have to offer, other than large chests and a constrained capacity for higher-order reasoning, one is never told.

We do learn one characteristic of people with gorilla mindsets, which is that they are very organized. "When stepping outside of my door and before closing the door," Cernovich reveals, "I stop. I feel for my wallet, cell phone, and keys. Because of this Gorilla Mindset habit, I have never locked myself out of my apartment." A real gorilla never forgets his keys! Mike Cernovich is laying down all the hard truths those effeminate left-wing nature documentaries will never tell you. Later on, in a list of Gorilla Focus habits, we are told that gorillas "do not eat in front of the television." A real gorilla knows this will only make him lose track of his calorie intake! The discoveries continue to pile on. A real gorilla pees eight times a day, clear urine! A real gorilla always registers as self-employed on his tax returns! A real gorilla COOKS WITH A CROCKPOT!

Cernovich's next book, *Danger & Play*, continues the themes of *Gorilla Mindset* in a more aggressive style.[6] The content is edgier, the formatting is far worse, and Mike Cernovich wants you to know that he is *done coddling you*. Straight away, he lays down the central traits of Masculine Men. Masculine men are aggressive. Masculine men move with purpose. But above all else, masculine men are hard. Do you have what it takes to be hard, Cernovich taunts his eunuch readers, or are you a coward? "Are you afraid of drinking a green juice?" he asks, "and instead look for your milk and cookies?"

Cernovich's writing on dating and relationships is predictably full of bad advice. "Acting like a narcissist will make people like you," he says. (This is not the case.) There's the usual stuff from "pick-up artist" culture about being mean to women to make them like you, and about how it's a good idea to bite a woman on the neck if you're not totally sure she wants you to kiss her. (Though you'd better make sure you film it, lest you be brought up on a false vampirism charge.) His declarations often have the interesting quality, in common with virgins writing letters to *Penthouse*, of leading the reader to emit a long "Suuuuuuuure." "My first marriage was ruined by feminist indoctrination," he insists. (Suuure it was.) "I was friends with a lot of girls who had crushes on me, but I was too polite to fuck them." (Suuuuure they did.) Not all of the claims he makes are implausible, though. A long list of "what I juiced this week" (including recipes for cabbage carrot juice, kale lemonade, and a celery refresher) is too exhaustively-documented to be fictionalized.

One can glimpse the fruits of Cernovich's gender philosophy in a *New Yorker* profile of him, which portrays his current marriage as wracked by tension and nervous laughter on the part of his indulgent wife.[7] ("Never marry for love," Cernovich advised his readers in a December 2016 blog post, published just two days after his wife gave birth to their child.) Cernovich's principled commitment to being an asshole to women seems to have, shockingly enough, caused its share of tearful rifts in the home:

> *"Early in Shauna's relationship with Mike, she read Danger and Play, including such posts as 'How to Cheat on Your Girlfriend.' She said, 'I would come home from work crying—'How can you write such rude things?' He'd go, 'You don't understand, babe, this is just how guys talk.' (Advice from the blog: 'Always call your girl "babe,"' to avoid mixing up names.) Shauna, who has stopped working, continued, "I was still upset, though, and he eventually deleted some older posts.' 'I rewrote some of the wording,' Mike insisted. 'I never disavow things I've said.'"*

Though Cernovich may draw a principled distinction between disavowing and deleting the things he's said in the past, he certainly has no aversion to simply lying. His championing of Donald Trump, for example, began as a cynical ploy to sell e-books. In a 2015 Twitter exchange with a follower, who remarked that Cernovich "took a damn sharp turn to the right," Cernovich replied: "My real views are far more moderate, but now is the time to win. Arguing over details is reserved for the winners."

MAGA Mindset, Cernovich's Trump-themed book, is 75% alt-right screed against the evils of feminism and the ethnic adulteration of the United States, and 25% of the usual warmed-over gorilla feces sandwiched between Trump block quotes. Cernovich is eager, in this book, to cast himself as a defender of white working-class folk against the diabolical coastal elites who say that such people "deserve to die." This is a fascinating evolution from Cernovich's pre-election view, which was that the people from his own small Midwestern town were human garbage. "My brother is a loser who just got out of prison for shooting his meth dealer," he writes in *Danger and Play*. "I haven't talked to him in more than a decade. Why would I associate with such a scumbag? Because he's family?" If Cernovich himself hadn't moved to California, he added, "I'd be stuck working a shit job in a shit downtown, married to some shit cow and raising some shit kids." Instead, he's now living the dream in Orange County, alternating between making his wife cry and blogging about liberal media conspiracies. He is truly a populist in the Donald Trump mold.

Reading Cernovich, one gets the distinct impression that he is urgently trying to prove something. The *New Yorker* profile provides one possible explanation of this might be:

> *"After law school, his wife became a successful attorney in Silicon Valley. But Cernovich was not admitted to the California bar until nine years after getting his law degree. In the meantime, he says, he got by with 'freelance legal research' and 'appellate stuff.' Cernovich's wife earned millions of dollars in stock from an I.P.O.; he told me that he received 'seven figures' in the divorce settlement. This seems to have been, and might still be, his primary source of funds. (He insists that book sales provide his main income.)"*

Thus Cernovich, who wishes to restore American masculinity, is a parasite on his much more successful ex-wife. (It is this, presumably, to which he is referring when he says that feminism killed his first marriage.) The amusing thing, when delving into the Cernovich's writings, is realizing just how contrived and desperate the masculine posturing seems. Margaret Pless, a blogger who has made it her gleeful mission to catalogue Cernovich's many egregious fibs and hypocrisies, has described Cernovich as a "Potemkin Alpha Male," whose online persona is cobbled together from a whole host of unlikely claims.[8] Though

Cernovich boasts of his lawyerly credentials—and routinely threatens lawsuits against his opponents during online feuds—he has apparently never served as counsel in a single state or federal court case. Though he's publicly mocked other men for accepting alimony, he's also repeatedly contradicted his own claims that his media products have been the source of his financial success, and seems content to stealthily subsist on the drippings of his high-powered ex-wife's IPO. His pickup game includes such medically dubious advice as "the best condom a man has is the skin on his dick," and even his 10,000 juicing books contain lengthy legal disclaimers against foolish readers who expect any kind of health benefit from his recipes. "Although Michael claims to be a self-made man, he trolls more well-known men, drafting off their fame to get attention," Pless writes. "His tales of sexual conquest are just that, and Michael's legal career is a similarly trumped-up story with little to no basis in fact."

One could be amused by Cernovich's constant attempts to puff himself into the gorilla he knows he isn't. After all, if this is masculinity, then masculinity is pitiable. And it's a shame that Mike Cernovich and his followers feel the need to become these ghastly creatures, who call women bitches and never leave the gym, just so they don't feel like failures. It says something dispiriting about the way boys are raised. Cernovich himself writes of a childhood plagued by bullies, which led him to adopt the following life philosophy: "I hurt anyone who wrongs me and hold lifetime grudges." One feels for the boy Cernovich, the pudgy kid with the speech impediment, who still spends every day trying to prove himself to his imagined tormentors.

Yet as much pity as one may have for men destroyed by the impossible quest to eliminate personal failure and weakness, the Cernovich mentality is still disturbing. By finding a way to fuse Trumpism with self-esteem building, Cernovich offers a tempting ideological framework for today's angry white man. One of the ways that Cernovich distinguishes himself from other conservatives is that his brand of right-wing politics openly embraces power rather than logic. Cernovich does not want to have a debate. He wants to achieve dominance. One hesitates to use the word fascist, because of its emptiness. But Cernovich, like Trump, seems a dash like Mussolini by way of Norman Vincent Peale.

Not that Cernovich's books themselves are especially threatening. The reader feels more likely to die of tedium than at the hands of right-wing terror squads. Your reviewers had a very difficult time getting through them (the Cernovich assignment required two reporters, as the boredom was too much to justify inflicting on one). They are not very slickly made. The paperback version of Cernovich's blog posts includes hyperlinks that do not work because they are, well, on paper. For *MAGA Mindset*, someone has evidently forgotten to include the page numbers (even though there is a table of contents). They are produced by a tiny publishing house whose other offerings include *There Will Be War, Vol I-X* and a guide to "extreme composting." (None of the usual weak, girly composting here. You must compost like a man.)

Under different circumstances, one might be inclined to simply give Cernovich a gentle pat on the head and coo "There, there," perhaps also passing him a recommendation for a good therapist, who could help him work through some of his lingering complexes about his childhood. But unfortunately, Trump is president, and the cruel, self-aggrandizing philosophy that could usually be met with ostracism and disdain now threatens us all. Mike Cernovich's philosophy of vanity, bombast, and sexual assault has become national policy.

None of that changes the underlying facts, though. A gorilla may be strong enough to mash you into the pavement, but that doesn't mean he knows anything. A man may get a lot of people to buy his books, but that doesn't mean they are good. And an insecure, narcissistic rape apologist may look in the mirror and fancy himself a great and powerful beast, but he's still Mike Cernovich.

GEORGE W. BUSH:
I DON'T CARE HOW GOOD HIS PAINTINGS ARE, HE STILL BELONGS IN PRISON

by Nathan J. Robinson

CRITICS FROM THE *New Yorker* and the *New York Times* agree: George W. Bush may have been an inept head of state, but he is a more than capable artist. In his review of Bush's new book *Portraits of Courage: A Commander in Chief's Tribute to America's Warriors* (Crown, $35.00)[1], *New Yorker* art critic Peter Schjeldahl says Bush's paintings are of "astonishingly high" quality, and his "honestly observed" portraits of wounded veterans are "surprisingly likable."[2] Jonathan Alter, in a review titled "Bush Nostalgia Is Overrated, but His Book of Paintings Is Not," agrees: Bush is "an evocative and surprisingly adept artist."[3] Alter says that while he used to think the Iraq War was "the right war with the wrong commander in chief," he now thinks that it was the "wrong war" but with "the right commander in chief, at least for the noble if narrow purpose of creatively honoring veterans through art."

Alter and Schjeldahl have roughly the same take on Bush: he is a decent person who made some dreadful mistakes. Schjeldahl says that while Bush "made, or haplessly fronted for, some execrable decisions... hating him took conscious effort." Alter says that while the Iraq War was a "colossal error" and Bush "has little to show for his dream of democratizing the Middle East," there is a certain appeal to Bush's "charming family, warm relationship with the Obamas, and welcome defense of the press," and his paintings of veterans constitute a "message of love" and a "step toward bridging the civilian-military divide." Alter and Schjeldahl both see the new book as a form of atonement. Schjeldahl says that with his "never-doubted sincerity and humility," Bush "obliviously made murderous errors [and] now obliviously atones for them." Alter says that Bush is "doing penance," and that the book testifies to "our genuine, bipartisan determination to do it better this time—to support healing in all of its forms."

This view of Bush as a "likable and sincere man who blundered cata-strophically" seems to be increasingly popular among some American liberals. They are horrified by Donald Trump, and Bush is beginning to seem vastly preferable by comparison. If we must have Republicans, let them be Bushes, since Bush at least seems *good at heart* while Trump is a sexual predator.[4] Jonathan Alter insists he is not becoming nostalgic, but his gauzy tributes to Bush's "love" and "warmth" fully endorse the idea of Bush's essential goodness. Now that Bush spends his time painting puppies and soldiers, having mishaps with ponchos and joking about it on *Ellen*, more and more people may be tempted to wonder why anyone could ever have hated the guy.[5][6]

Nostalgia takes root easily, because history is easy to forget. But in Bush's case, the history is straightforwardly accessible and extremely well-docu-mented. George W. Bush did not make a simple miscalculation or error. He deliberately perpetrated a war crime, intentionally misleading the public in order to do so, and showed callous indifference to the suffering that would obviously result. His government oversaw a regime of brutal torture and indefinite detention, violating every conceivable standard for the humane treatment of prisoners. And far from trying to "atone," Bush has consistently misrepresented history, reacting angrily and defensively to those who confront him with the truth. In a just world, he would be painting from a prison cell. And through Alter and Schjeldahl's effort to impute to Bush a repentance and sensitivity that he does not actually pos-sess, they fabricate history and erase the sufferings of Bush's victims.

First, it's important to be clear what Bush actually did. There is a key number missing from both Alter and Schjeldahl's reviews: 500,000, the sum total of Iraqi civilians who perished as a result of the U.S. war there.[7] (That's a conservative estimate, and stops in 2011.) Nearly 200,000 are confirmed to have died violently, blown to pieces by coalition air strikes or suicide bombers, shot by soldiers or insurgents.[8] Others died as a result of the disappearance of medical care,[9] with doctors fleeing the country by the score as their colleagues were killed or abducted.[10] Childhood mortality and infant mortality shot up, as well as malnutrition and starvation,[11] and toxins introduced by American bombardment led to "congenital malformations, sterility, and infertility."[12] There was mass displacement, by the millions.[13] An entire "generation of orphans" was created, with hundreds of thousands of children losing parents and wandering the streets homeless.[14] The country's core infrastructure collapsed, and centuries-old cultural institutions were destroyed, with libraries and museums looted, and the university system "decimated" as professors were assassinated.[15] For years and years, suicide bombings became a regular feature of life in Baghdad, and for every violent death, scores more people were left injured or traumatized for life. (Yet in the entire country, there were less than 200 social workers and psychiatrists put together to tend to people's psychological issues.)[16] Parts of Iraq became a hell on earth: in 2007 the Red Cross said that there were "mothers appealing for someone to pick up the bodies on the street so their children will be spared the horror of looking at them on their way to school."[17] The amount of death, misery, suffering, and trauma is almost inconceivable.

These were the human consequences of the Iraq War for the country's population. They generally go unmentioned in the sympathetic reviews of George W. Bush's artwork. Perhaps that's because, if we dwell on them, it becomes somewhat harder to appreciate Bush's impressive use of line, color, and shape. If you begin to think about Iraq as a physical place full of actual people, many of whom have watched their children die in front of them, Bush's art begins to seem ghoulish and perverse rather than sensitive and accomplished. There is a reason Schjeldahl and Alter do not spend even a moment discussing the war's consequences for Iraqis. Doing so requires taking stock of an unimaginable series of horrors, one that makes Bush's colorful brushwork and daytime-TV bantering seem more sickening than endearing.

But perhaps, we might say, it is unfair to linger on the subject of the war's human toll. All war, after all, is hell. We must base our judgment of Bush's character not on the ultimate consequences of his decisions, but on the nature of the decisions themselves. After all, Schjeldahl and Alter do not deny that the Iraq War was calamitous, with Alter calling it one of "the greatest disasters in American history," a "historic folly" with "horrific consequences," and Schjeldahl using that curious phrase "murderous error." It's true that both obscure reality by using vague descriptors like "disaster" rather than acknowledging what the invasion meant for the people on whom it was inflicted. But their point is that Bush *meant well*, even though he may have accidentally ended up causing the birth of ISIS and plunging the people of Iraq into an unending nightmare.

Viewing Bush as inept rather than malicious means rejecting the view that he "lied us into war." If we accept Jonathan Alter's perspective, it was not that Bush told the American people that Iraq had weapons of mass destruction when he knew that it did not. Rather, Bush misjudged the situation, relying too hastily and carelessly on poor intelligence, and planning the war incompetently. The war was a "folly," a bad idea poorly executed, but not an intentional act of deceit or criminality.

This view is persuasive because it's partially correct. Bush did not "lie that there were weapons of mass destruction," and it's unfortunate that anti-war activists have often suggested that this was the case. Bush claims, quite plausibly, that he believed that Iraq possessed WMDs, and there is no evidence to suggest that he didn't believe this. That supports the "mistake" view, because a lie is an intentional false statement, and Bush may have believed he was making a true statement, thus being mistaken rather than lying.

But the debate over whether Bush lied about WMDs misstates what the actual lie was. It was not when Bush said "the Iraq regime continues to possess and conceal some of the most lethal weapons ever devised" that he lied to the American people.[18] Rather, it was when he said Iraq posed a "threat" and that by invading it the United States was "assuring its own national security." Bush could not have reasonably believed that the creaking, isolated Saddam regime posed the kind of threat to the United States that he said it did. *WMDs or not*, there was nothing credible to suggest this. He therefore lied to the American people, insisting that they were under a threat that they were not actually under. He did so in order to create a pretext for a war he had long been intent on waging.

This is not to say that Bush's insistence that Saddam Hussein had WMDs was sincere. It may or may not have been. The point is not that Bush knew there *weren't* WMDs in Iraq, but that he didn't *care* whether there were or not. This is the difference between a lie and bullshit: a lie is saying something you know to be untrue, bullshit is saying something without caring to find out if it's true.[19] The former highest-ranking CIA officer in Europe told *60 Minutes* that the Bush White House intentionally ignored evidence contradicting the idea that Saddam had WMDs.[20] According to the officer, when intelligence was provided that contradicted the WMD story, the White House told the officer that "this isn't about intel anymore. This is about regime change," from which he concluded that "the war in Iraq was coming and they were looking for intelligence to fit into the policy." It's not, then, that Bush knew there were no WMDs. It's that he kept himself from finding out whether there were WMDs, because he was determined to go to war.

The idea that Saddam posed a threat to the United States was laughable from the start. The WMDs that he supposedly possessed were not nuclear weapons, but chemical and biological ones.[21] WMD is a catch-all category, but the distinction is important; mustard gas is horrific, but it is not a "suitcase nuke." Bashar al-Assad, for example, possesses chemical weapons, but does not pose a threat to the U.S. mainland. (To Syrians, yes. To New Yorkers, no.) In fact, according to former Saddam aide Tariq Aziz, "Saddam did not consider the United States a natural adversary, as he did Iran and Israel, and he hoped that Iraq might again enjoy improved relations with the United States."[22] Furthermore, by the time of the U.S. invasion, Saddam "had turned over the day-to-day running of the Iraqi government to his aides and was spending most of his time writing a novel."[23] There was no credible reason to believe, even if

Saddam possessed certain categories of weapons prohibited by international treaty, that he was an active threat to the people of the United States. Bush's pre-war speeches used terrifying rhetoric to leap from the premise that Saddam was a monstrous dictator to the conclusion that Americans needed to be scared. That was simple deceit.

In fact, Bush had long been committed to removing Saddam, and was searching for a plausible justification. Just "hours after the 9/11 attacks," Donald Rumsfeld and the Vice Chairman of the Joint Chiefs of Staff were pondering whether they could "hit Saddam at the same time" as Osama bin Laden as part of a strategy to "move swiftly, go massive."[24] In November of 2001, Rumsfeld and Tommy Franks began plotting the "decapitation" of the Iraqi government, pondering various pretexts for "how [to] start" the war.[25] Possibilities included "US discovers Saddam connection to Sept. 11 attack or to anthrax attacks?" and "Dispute over WMD inspections?" Worried that they wouldn't find any hard evidence against Saddam, Bush even thought of painting a reconnaissance aircraft in U.N. colors and flying it over Iraqi airspace, goading Saddam into shooting it down and thereby justifying a war.[26] Bush "made it clear" to Tony Blair that "the U.S. intended to invade... even if UN inspectors found no evidence of a banned Iraqi weapons program."[27]

Thus Bush's lie was not that there were weapons of mass destruction. The lie was that the war was *about* weapons of mass destruction. The war was about removing Saddam Hussein from power, and asserting American dominance in the Middle East and the world. Yes, that was partially to do with oil ("People say we're not fighting for oil. Of course we are... We're not there for figs," said former Defense Secretary Chuck Hagel,[28] while Bush CENTCOM commander John Abizaid admitted "Of course it's about oil, we can't really deny that").[29] But the key point is that Bush detested Saddam and was determined to show he could get rid of him; according to those who attended National Security Council meetings, the administration wanted to "make an example of Hussein" to teach a lesson to those who would "flout the authority of the United States."[30] "Regime change" was the goal from the start, with "weapons of mass destruction" and "bringing democracy" just convenient pieces of rhetoric.

Nor was the war about the well-being of the people of Iraq. Jonathan Alter says that Bush had a "dream of democratizing the Middle East" but simply botched it; Bush's story is almost that of a romantic utopian and tragic hero, undone by his hubris in just wanting to share democracy too much. In reality, the Bush White House showed zero interest in the welfare of Iraqis. Bush had been warned that invading the country would lead to a bloodbath; he ignored the warning, because he didn't care.[31] The typical line is that the occupation was "mishandled," but this implies that Bush tried to handle it well. In fact, as Patrick Cockburn's *The Occupation* and Rajiv Chandrasekaran's *Imperial Life in The Emerald City* show, American officials were proudly ignorant of the Iraqi people's needs and desires.[32] [33] Decisions were made in accordance with U.S. domestic political considerations rather than concern for the safety and prosperity of Iraq. Bush appointed totally inexperienced Republican Party ideologues to oversee the rebuilding effort, rather than actual experts, because the administration was more committed to maintaining neoconservative orthodoxies than actually trying to figure out how to keep the country from self-destructing. When Bush gave Paul Bremer his criteria for who should be the next Iraqi leader, he was emphatic that he wanted someone who would "stand up and thank the American people for their sacrifice in liberating Iraq."[34]

As the situation in Iraq deteriorated into exactly the kind of sectarian violence that the White House had been warned it would, the Bush administration tried to hide the scale of the disaster. Patrick Cockburn reported that while Bush told Congress that fourteen out of eighteen Iraqi provinces "are completely safe," this was "entirely untrue" and anyone who had gone to these provinces to try and prove it would have immediately been kidnapped or killed. In tallies of body counts, "U.S. officials excluded scores of people killed in car bombings and mortar attacks from tabulations measuring the results of a drive to reduce violence in Baghdad."[35] Furthermore, according to the *Guardian* "U.S. authorities failed to investigate hundreds of reports of abuse, torture, rape and even murder by Iraqi police and soldiers" because they had "a formal policy of ignoring such allegations."[36] And the Bush administration silently presided over atrocities committed by both U.S. troops (who killed almost 700 civilians for coming too close to checkpoints, including pregnant women and the mentally ill)[37] and hired contractors (in 2005 an American military unit observed as Blackwater mercenaries "shot up a civilian vehicle" killing a father and wounding his wife and daughter).[38]

Then, of course, there was the torture and indefinite detention, both of which were authorized at the highest levels. Bush's CIA disappeared countless people to "black sites" to be tortured,[39] and while the Bush administration duplicitously portrayed the horrific abuses at Abu Ghraib as isolated incidents, the administration was actually deliberately crafting its interrogation practices around torture and attempting to find legal loopholes to justify it.[40] Philippe Sands reported that the White House tried to pin responsibility for torture on "interrogators on the ground," a "false" explanation that ignored the "actions taken at the very highest levels of the administration" approving 18 new "enhanced interrogation" techniques, "all of which went against long-standing U.S. military practice as presented in the Army Field Manual."[41] Notes from 20-hour interrogations reveal the unimaginable psychological distress undergone by detainees:

> "Detainee began to cry. Visibly shaken. Very emotional. Detainee cried. Disturbed. Detainee began to cry. Detainee bit the IV tube completely in two. Started moaning. Uncomfortable. Moaning. Began crying hard spontaneously. Crying and praying. Very agitated. Yelled. Agitated and violent. Detainee spat. Detainee proclaimed his innocence. Whining. Dizzy. Forgetting things. Angry. Upset. Yelled for Allah. Urinated on himself. Began to cry. Asked God for forgiveness. Cried. Cried. Became violent. Began to cry. Broke down and cried. Began to pray and openly cried. Cried out to Allah several times. Trembled uncontrollably."

Indeed, the U.S. Senate Select Intelligence Committee's report on CIA interrogation tactics concluded that they were "brutal and far worse than the CIA represented to policymakers."[42] They included "slamming detainees into walls," "telling detainees they would never leave alive," "Threats to harm the children of a detainee, threats to sexually abuse the mother of a detainee, threats to cut a detainee's mother's throat," water-boardings that sometimes "evolved into a series of near drownings," and the terrifyingly clench-inducing "involuntary rectal feedings."[43] Some-times they would deprive detainees of all heat (which "likely contrib-uted to the death of a detainee") or perform what was known as a "rough takedown," a procedure by which "five CIA officers would scream at a detainee, drag him outside of his cell, cut his clothes off, and secure him with Mylar tape. The detainee would then be hooded and dragged up and down a long corridor while being slapped and punched."[44] All of that is separate from the outrage of indefinite detention in itself, which kept people in cages for years upon years without ever being able to con-test the charges against them. At Guantanamo Bay, detainees became "so depressed, so despondent, that they had no longer had an appetite and stopped eating to the point where they had to be force-fed with a tube that is inserted through their nose." Their mental and emotional conditions would deteriorate until they were reduced to a childlike bab-bling, and they frequently attempted self-harm and suicide. The Bush administration even arrested the Muslim chaplain at Guantanamo Bay, U.S. Army Captain James Yee, throwing him in leg irons, threatening him with death, and keeping him in solitary confinement for 76 days after he criticized military practices.[45] [46]

Thus President Bush was not a good-hearted dreamer. He was a rabid ideologue who would spew any amount of lies or B.S. in order to achieve his favored goal of deposing Saddam Hussein, and who oversaw serious human rights violations without displaying an ounce of compunction or ambivalence. There was no "mistake." Bush didn't "oops-a-daisy" his way into Iraq. He had a goal, and he fulfilled it, without consideration for those who would suffer as a result.

It should be mentioned that most of this was not just immoral. It was illegal. The Bush Doctrine explicitly claimed the right to launch a pre-emptive war against a party that had not actually attacked the United

States, a violation of the core Nuremberg principle that "to initiate a war of aggression...is not only an international crime; it is the supreme international crime, differing only from other war crimes in that it contains within itself the accumulated evil of the whole."[47] Multiple independent inquiries have criticized the flimsy legal justifications for the war.[48] [49] Former U.N. Secretary General Kofi Annan openly declared the war illegal,[50] and even Tony Blair's former Deputy Prime Minister concurred.[51] In fact, it's hard to see how the Iraq War could be anything *but* criminal, since no country—even if it gathers a "coalition of the willing"—is permitted to simply depose a head of state at will. The Iraq War made the Nuremberg Laws even more empty and selective than they have always been, and Bush's escape from international justice delegitimizes all other war crimes prosecutions. A core aspect of the rule of law is that it applies equally to all, and if the United States is free to do as it pleases regardless of its international legal obligations, it is unclear what respect anybody should hold for the law.

George W. Bush may therefore be a fine painter. But he is a criminal. And when media figures try to redeem him, or portray him as lovable-but-flawed, they ignore the actual record. In fact, Bush has not even made any suggestion that he is trying to "atone" for a great crime, as liberal pundits have suggested he is. On the contrary, he has consistently defended his decision-making, and the illegal doctrine he espoused. He even wrote an entire book of self-justifications.[52] Bush is not a haunted man. And since any good person, if he had Bush's record, *would* be haunted, Bush is not a good person. Kanye West had Bush completely right.[53] He simply does not think very much about the lives of people darker than himself. That sounds like an extreme judgment, but it's true. If he cared about them, he wouldn't have put them in cages. George W. Bush may love his grandchildren, he may paint with verve and soul. But he does not care about black or brown people.

It's therefore exasperating to see liberals like Alter and Schjeldahl offer glowing assessments of Bush's book of art, and portray him as warm and caring. Schjeldahl says that Bush is so likable that hating him "takes conscious effort." But it only takes conscious effort if you don't think about the lives of Iraqis. If you do think about the lives of Iraqis, then hating him not only does not take conscious effort, but it is automatic. Anyone who truly appreciates the scale of what Bush inflicted on the world will feel rage course through their body whenever they hear his voice, or see him holding up a paintbrush, with that perpetual simpering grin on his face.

Alter and Schjeldahl are not alone in being captivated by Bush the *artiste*. The *Washington Post*'s art critic concluded that "the former president is more humble and curious than the Swaggering President Bush he enacted while in office [and] his curiosity about art is not only genuine but relatively sophisticated."[54] This may be the beginning of a critical consensus. But it says something disturbing about our media that a man can cause 500,000 deaths and then have his paintings flatteringly profiled, with the deaths unmentioned. George W. Bush intentionally offered false justifications for a war, destroyed an entire country, and committed an international crime. He tortured people, sometimes to death.[55]

But would you look at those *brushstrokes*? And have you seen the little doggies?

ARIANNA HUFFINGTON:
KILLING YOU SOFTLY
WITH HER DREAMS
by Yasmin Nair

ARIANNA HUFFINGTON WANTS TO PUT YOU TO SLEEP.

In her new book, *The Sleep Revolution: Transforming Your Life, One Night at a Time,* Huffington dramatically announces that we are in the middle of an unacknowledged *sleep crisis.* There is a problem in our society, Huffington tells us: we have forgotten how to sleep. Fortunately, sleepless readers need not fear: Huffington's handy little book is here to show you how to combat sleeplessness.

Sleep Revolution is written in classic Huffington style: part Deepak Chopra, part Oprah, and strung together with quotes from everyone from Persian poet Rumi to art critic Jonathan Crary to even (bafflingly for a self-described progressive), the anti-immigrant, Brexit-enabling, racist former Mayor of London, Boris Johnson.

The writing, it should go without saying, is bad. A chapter begins: "From the beginning of time, people have struggled with sleep." In fact, from the beginning of time, sophomore English teachers have been taking red pen to any essay that starts with "from the beginning of time." Her phrasing is often corny and uses too many exclamation points.

Sleep Revolution is less a book than a business plan, a typical product of the can-do inspiration industry made popular by the likes of Andrew Weil and Suze Orman, the snake oil salespeople of the 21st century.

202 THE CURRENT AFFAIRS MINDSET

Like them, Huffington first tells you that you have a problem, one you were unaware you had. She then generously reveals the many products that can help alleviate your symptoms, suggesting plenty of expensive solutions. Huffington has learnt her trade from the best hucksters. She absorbs the techniques of assorted rich people's gurus, like cult leaders Bhagwan Rajneesh and John-Roger, combining new age verbiage with sly admonitions to give up one's material wealth (into their outstretched hands, of course).

Huffington undoubtedly possesses a kind of brilliance. It lies not in the quality of her thought or writing, but in her ability to understand and exploit the zeitgeist. The ideas in *Sleep Revolution,* such as they are, are mostly bits and pieces about sleep deprivation and the problems thereof cribbed and culled from a range of sources (likely the product of several intensive hours of Googling). To be sure, they are banal. And yet Huffington's book is perfect for our moment in time: it arrives just as capitalism is making many of us more sleepless than ever.

Huffington is never so impolite as to mention that capitalism, which has done well by her and made her a multimillionaire, may be to blame for keeping people working long, sleepless hours. She prefers proposing solutions to diagnosing causes. She tells you to leave your smartphone outside your bedroom, to have warm baths, to disengage. Don't tackle work emails after a certain time.

Her solutions have the convenient consequence of making you a better worker for your employers, without actually raising your material standard of living. After all, she writes, "it would actually be better for business if employees called in tired, got a little more sleep, and then came in a bit late, rather than call in sick a few days later or, worse, show up sick, dragging themselves through the day while infecting others." Her advice to her fellow bosses is purely expedient: if the worker drones rest, more labor can be wrung out of them.

This approach to sleep is common in the discourse of "self-care," in which people are constantly admonished to heal themselves with candles, self-affirmation, and long baths but not told that they can actually revolt against the systems that create their exhaustion in the first place.

According to a massive amount of sleep literature, the worst thing we do is not sleep enough, yet that same literature never bothers to wonder what might be keeping us up at night.

Yet many people know full well why they can't sleep. Many of us juggle multiple jobs to cobble together our livings, and the problem of sleeplessness cuts across class barriers. While those with little or no money battle exhaustion as they travel from job to job, even wealthier people are frequently like hamsters in their wheels, constantly working against the clock to hold on to and add to their fortunes. No matter who you are, under competitive capitalism the rule is the same: you sleep, you lose. Marx once pointed out that capital is vampire-like and feeds on dead labor. But that's somewhat unfair to vampires. After all, unlike vampires, capital never sleeps.

Capitalism has never slept much, and has always relied on the lack of sleep of millions of workers to be as efficient as possible. In fact, until the invention of the eight-hour day and the weekend (both startlingly new ideas, for which workers had to fight hard) "work" as such simply carried on day by draining day. Even the idea of a legally mandated lunch break is astonishingly recent.

Among all of the Huffingtonian pro-sleep, self-help guidance, there is no discussion of the fact that people are *compelled* to walk around like zombies, without sleep. Take, for instance, the website *Everyday Health* which poses the question: "Why Don't Americans Sleep Enough?" The answer: "Reasons why we're not getting enough sleep abound, but one of the biggest changes behind the sleep decline is the availability of electricity and technological advances that allow us to work and play 24/7." Note the phrasing: *allow* us to work 24/7! Yet most people don't actually have a choice.

Consider that even something as simple as the lack of good transit systems can effectively ruin your chances of a good night's sleep. In Chicago, where I live, and where the city's segregation is enforced through its transit system, it can take two hours or more to get from the mostly white north side to the mostly black and brown south and west sides, and the trip usually involves multiple buses and trains. That's a commute performed daily by many poorly-paid workers.

And that's Chicago, a place with relatively good infrastructure. The situation is much worse for those living in cities and towns with little or no public transit (which is most of the United States). Researchers point to the economic consequences of rough commutes, but there are also substantial health costs involved when people spend so much of their lives traveling to and from their jobs and have little energy or time left to recharge or fully rest before the next day's work. The sheer stress of getting to work can, in the long run, literally kill you. But work we must if we are to survive, and those on the bottom rungs run themselves ragged even before they start their workday.

Huffington is willfully oblivious to all of this, evading questions about workplace conditions even when they are most obvious. She writes that a "2015 Stanford University study of Chinese workers found that those who worked from home saw their productivity go up by 13 percent." Only Arianna Huffington could so blithely use the words "Chinese workers" and "productivity" together and not even offer the slightest hint that, perhaps, the rise in productivity is due to factors like the grinding exploitation they are likely to experience. Examples of such obtuseness about the exploitation of capitalism abound in the book, including her glowing praise for Goldman Sachs banning summer interns from staying overnight. *Quartz*'s sarcastic response to the news puts it best: "A rule that may be obvious to those of us in normal people jobs, this apparently was not clear enough to the aspiring bankers entering the intense Wall Street working environment for the first time." Praise for such global and rapacious corporations makes it clear that success for Huffington is defined at astronomical levels; it's not at all about ordinary workers, whose only job is to buy the products she and her friends sell.

Instead of discussing the larger context surrounding sleeplessness, Huffington wants, instead, to remind you of different consequences. Wrinkles, for instance. She cites a UK experiment that showed that a lack of sleep resulted in a 45 percent increase in fine lines and wrinkles in women, and a rise in blemishes by 13 percent. She is also concerned that sleeplessness can cause "bad decisions," and explains away Bill Clinton's most indefensible presidential decisions as a possible result of a lack of sleep, for example "his inept handling of the issues of gays in the military — now widely considered to be one of the low points of his two-term presidency." Here, as everywhere in the book, she simply ignores political ideology in favor of a diagnosis that locates acts and consequences entirely on the plane of personal problems.

Huffington is an inveterate name-dropper, and that's no surprise given that her biggest project so far, *Huffington Post*, relies on the appearance of many of her celebrity "friends" to supply free labor. "My friend Nora Ephron" makes an appearance, and she describes how "at a lunch for Jennifer Aniston, her manager took me aside," and the time "when I interviewed [the Dalai Lama]," Oh, and we must not forget the time when "for my Thrive e-course on Oprah.com, I invited basketball great Kobe Bryant..." (That last one is a small masterpiece of economy, rolling her business enterprise, the planet's most famous woman after the Queen of England, and a sports legend all into the same sentence.) Huffington's desire to suck up (there is no elegant way to put this) to powerful and famous people requires her to be spectacularly clueless at times. Following up on the wrinkles theme, she writes effusively that "Jane Fonda credits her age-defying looks to sleep." In fact, Fonda has gone on record as having had plastic surgery, a fact confirmed by no fewer than three aggregated stories on the *Huffington Post* itself.

Ultimately, *Sleep Revolution* tells us very little about what we need to know to get more sleep. Huffington's slender thesis ("Sleep more so you can make more money") is covered fully in her 4-minute TED talk on the subject, and solutions to sleeplessness are available in innumerable resources on the internet. The book is less important for what it says and more for what it reveals about Huffington's place in enabling a particularly rapacious form of capitalism, one which first deprives people of sleep and then sells them the methods by which they might regain some of it.

Arianna Huffington likes to tell her life story as follows: once, a middle-class 16-year-old Greek girl saw a picture of Cambridge University and decided to study there. Against all odds, and with the help of a determined mother, she entered the august institution and quickly made a name for herself, even becoming only the third female president of the 200-year-old Cambridge Union. She became a well-known conservative author and public figure in England, and eventually left for America where she gained spectacular amounts of both wealth and fame.

But the story's reality is somewhat more complex, and reflects her alliances with two particular powerful men. At the age of 21, Huffington, whose maiden name was Stassinopoulos, met the famed and influential British intellectual Bernard Levin, 22 years her senior, on a game show. Huffington wrote books in which she insisted that feminism could only appeal to "women with strong lesbian tendencies."

Not surprisingly, it was in England, still replete with class snobbery, that she earned her most infamous put-downs, being labeled "the most upwardly mobile Greek since Icarus," as well as "the Edmund Hillary of social climbing." They're good lines, though they're also sexist. No one calls Bill Gates a social climber, and women seem to be the only ones subjected to such snide comments as they make their way upwards. That said, it's true that large parts of Huffington's social and financial capital have come about because she was the consort of two powerful men, and she does make much of her immense network of famous friends.

Huffington remained with Levin till she was 30, and then embarked on the next step of her journey, to New York. Only six years after her arrival in America, having ensconced herself in a social circle that included Barbara Walters and Henry Kissinger, she married the oil billionaire Michael Huffington. Levin had given her access to enormous intellectual and cultural capital; Huffington provided her with massive amounts of financial capital.

They divorced in 1997, when their two daughters were eight and six. She would go on to tell an interviewer that she doesn't believe in marriage, just very good divorces. (Her settlement reportedly gained her $25 million.) Soon after, Michael Huffington came out as bisexual, and Arianna turned into a blazing liberal (whether or not those two facts are connected were the subject of speculation). She began working with Al Franken on Air America. (Remember Air America?) Explaining her sudden right-left shift, Huffington insists that she had always been socially liberal, and simply saw the light. A different hypothesis can be found in a friend's observation that in famously liberal Los Angeles, to which Huffington returned after her divorce, her conservatism "would not have gotten [her] invited to a lot of parties."

Huffington's rapid geographic and ideological shape-shifting also meant additional scrutiny of the contradiction between her politics and her lifestyle. In 2003, the same year she ran unsuccessfully against Arnold Schwarzenegger in a gubernatorial campaign, she launched an incendiary ad campaign linking SUV owners to terrorists, despite having driven a Lincoln Navigator until the previous year. Huffington has complained about big money corroding democracy, but was a pivotal part of her husband's unsuccessful campaign against Dianne Feinstein, in which he spent a then-unprecedented $30 million of his personal wealth. Whenever she has been challenged on these inconsistencies, Huffington has simply claimed to have subsequently seen the light.

In a 1995 *Mother Jones* piece designed as a Guide to Republicans, the comedian Paula Poundstone wrote, "It's hard to pin down Arianna's species. If only her ears drooped forward." It's a sharp assessment of Huffington's innate tendency to switch positions. Poundstone also described what was then the celebrity's fourth book, *The Fourth Instinct*: "[S]he says we should be nice. She says it in 248 pages, using her own nice thoughts as a standard toward which we all should strive." Clearly, the ability to expand a few scant phrases into hundreds of pages has not left Huffington.

But when it comes to discerning what species of political animal Huffington represents, the most striking and truthful description may come from an anonymous source, quoted by the *Washington Post*, speaking about her then-husband's disastrous second campaign:

> "[O]ne person who knows the couple makes a particularly unflattering analogy. It is to the movie a while ago in which a creature would suddenly spring out of a human's chest.
> 'I think of that thing in John Hurt in "Alien,"' he says, 'but with better hair.'
> 'In Michael,' he says, 'she's found a host.'

In the mythology of the *Alien* films, the central figure (the aforementioned "thing") is a vicious space species that exists purely to breed and take over every terrain it encounters, whether a ship or an entire planet. Its method of self-propagation, enabled by a gigantic queen, is to implant eggs in any available host. The egg eventually and quickly gestates and finally emerges as a fast-developing creature, mutating in the process and eventually becoming more human-like. By the fourth film in the series, *Alien: Resurrection,* the creature has developed a womb and gives live birth to its progeny, which proceeds to eat its mother alive.

In the films, alongside the titular, rapacious and monstrous being, there exists another equally deadly force: the ubiquitous Weyland Corporation. All through the series, it becomes clear that Weyland is, if not the only one left, at least one of the biggest corporations in the known universe. Its interests extend from the petty junk-harvesting of space debris and old ships to dreams of universal domination. Its intense desire to harness the Alien itself comes from the corporation's ambition to use the creature as the ultimate biological weapon. The alien is a perfect killing machine, with acid for blood, blood so toxic it can melt thick steel and spurts out at even the slightest injury, causing massive harm to its adversaries. In the first film, the robot Ash describes the creature with admiration as a "[p]erfect organism. Its structural perfection is matched only by its hostility....I admire its purity. A survivor... unclouded by conscience, remorse, or delusions of morality."

It is no wonder, then, that the *Washington Post's* source should be reminded of the *Alien* franchise when asked to analyze Huffington. Yet the *Alien* comparisons are striking not only for their insight into Huffington personally, but as a means by which to understand her enterprise and the larger formations of capitalism that she has helped to create and cement.

In August 2016, Huffington announced that she was leaving the *Huffington Post* to focus on her new startup, Thrive Global. The venture, according to the *Wall Street Journal,* will "work with companies to improve the well-being of their employees." Set to launch in November, Thrive describes itself as a "corporate and consumer well-being and productivity platform." At Thriveglobal.com, the visitor is led to understand that "By reducing stress and exhaustion, we can improve people's health and increase productivity for both companies and individuals around the world," and that "Thrive Global is a corporate and consumer well-being and productivity platform."

The point of such an enterprise, wrapped in such transparently vacuous new age verbiage, remains a mystery. For all their pretense otherwise, it's clear that Huffington and her commercial partners care very little about the effects of sleeplessness on those who are not their target audience. In April 2016 a sleep-deprived Uber driver, too tired to continue driving, asked his passenger to take over, and woke up to find the car embroiled in a high-speech chase with police. A *Huffington Post* reporter, Sarah DiGiulio, was prevented from "writing" about the story. (At the *HuffPo*, "writing" means "linking to.") *Post* senior editor Gregory Beyer told DiGiulio that they wouldn't be linking to it because *Huffington Post* was currently "partnering with Uber on our drowsy driving campaign." In other words, Huffington's policy was to ignore or actively censor any story that actually proved that sleeplessness is a function of capitalism, and to protect her financial partner from being implicated in any resulting damage. In response to the story, Uber suspended the driver, then issued a statement about the dangers of sleeplessness (which predictably cited the company's link up with the *HuffPo* and Toyota "to raise awareness of the issue and help save lives.")

> "I cried to dream again,"
> —Caliban, *The Tempest*

The great irony of Huffington's new enterprises, which promise both sleep and thriving, is that the *Huffington Post* itself feeds off the sleeplessness of its writers, people who are compelled to stay up all night in order to read and repost pieces about how sleeplessness is ruining their lives. The *Huffington Post* is notorious for paying *not a single cent* for most of its contributions, paying writers solely in illusory "publicity." By building a hugely popular website on unpaid labor, *HuffPo* played a major role in establishing the pitiful compensation structure currently faced by online writers. If writers can't sleep, it's because they make *HuffPo* rates, i.e. nothing.

The Sleep Revolution is therefore a work of extraordinary gall. There is no consideration of the structural problems with sleeplessness, no critique of the systems which drive people from their beds toward jobs where they nod off to sleep in exhaustion. Arianna Huffington did not invent the web, but she is among those who created the news that never sleeps, in turn created by aggregators working around the clock, so that you might wake up at midnight or three or four in the morning, entertained by yet another set of links about Kate Middleton in a red dress or a hammock for your head so you can sleep on the train on the way to work.

In the *Alien* films, the Weyland Corporation sends its workers across the universe, millions of light years away in search of material and profits. But travel across the cosmos is time-consuming; workers would inevitably age along the journey, dulling their efficiency. Weyland's solution is simple: Sleep pods that hold the bodies in suspended animation. Here all natural bodily functions cease, and the workers are reduced to nothing more than bodies. Once at their destination, the ship, a machine that possesses complete control over them, wakes them up and they continue their work. Everyone is a freelancer; everyone is put to sleep till their next gig. In the first film, when Captain Dallas hacks into the ship's computer to discover the mission's operating mandate, he discovers a chilling command stating that capturing the alien is the first and only priority. "Crew expendable," it reads.

On her Twitter feed, Huffington retweets yet another famous billionaire, Melinda Gates, wife of Bill Gates: "Make sure to be gentle to yourself. Take time for yourself. Make sure that you're taking care of yourself in order to be the best person and do your best job." Ultimately, that's all that matters to Huffington and her ilk, that the workers remain at their most fit, churning out content when awake, then suspended in pods until their labor is next required. And should these freelancers prove too costly, well, "crew expendable." In space, no one can hear you cry in your dreams.

RUTH BADER GINSBURG:
RISE OF THE R.B.G. CULT

by David Kinder

THE PAST TWO YEARS HAVE SEEN AN EXPLOSION of pop culture affection for 82-year-old Supreme Court Justice Ruth Bader Ginsburg, much of it under the moniker "Notorious RBG." The name is a riff on "Notorious BIG," one of the most celebrated rappers of all time, and now adorns t-shirts, hoodies, and a popular Tumblr page. A fiery Ginsburg caricature has been played on *Saturday Night Live*, an opera has been written about her, and Warholian screen prints depict her regal visage complete with crown and jabot. After spending several decades quietly inhabiting the minor limelight afforded to high-ranking American jurists, Ginsburg has suddenly found herself an icon.

Now Irin Carmon and Shana Knizhnik have written an entire book, *Notorious RBG: The Life and Times of Ruth Bader Ginsburg* (Dey Street Books, $19.99), based on the "Notorious RBG" sobriquet, a curious collection of biography, excerpts from Supreme Court opinions, cartoons, and a recipe for pork loin from the Justice's late husband.[1] The book does not attempt to grapple with *why* this surge of Ginsburg-mania has come about—it is thoroughly an example of the phenomenon rather than an attempt to analyze it. But as the most fully-realized embodiment of the trend, *Notorious RBG* is a helpful window into Ruth Bader Ginsburg's journey from Supreme Court Justice to viral meme.

Calling the book a hagiography could hardly offend its authors—most biographies don't conclude their introduction with "We are frankly in awe of what we've learned about her, and we're pretty excited to share it with you." Adoration oozes from the page with every tidbit and factoid the authors giddily present. So we learn that Justice Ginsburg began smoking because she was brave. When she argued before a case before an unusually quiet Supreme Court, the authors infer that she stunned the nine Justices into silence.

This incessant lionizing can border on the embarrassing, even in its most lighthearted and transparent form. The authors tell the (possibly apocryphal) story of Justice Ginsberg rejecting an applicant for a clerkship who had included an error in his application with a personal letter telling him to "note the typo." Carmon and Knizhnik see this as a charming example of Ginsburg's attention to detail. Readers may not find it quite so endearing to see one of the country's most powerful people going out of her way to pointlessly humiliate a young job applicant.

The desire to keep the book reverential forces the authors into some contradictory postures, as *Notorious RBG* alternates between referring to the Justice, admiringly, as a radical with referring to her, also admiringly, as a center-left pragmatist. Ginsburg must be faultless, thus she is both stubborn and diplomatic, both activist and restrained, both moderate and audacious.

But when you get down to it, the fundamental premise of the pop culture adulation for Ginsburg is that she is a headstrong liberal firebrand. Of course, much of the ordinary work of a Supreme Court justice consists of painstakingly adjudicating mundane interpretive questions, such as deciding what standard of review to apply in evaluating administrative determinations of the definition of "U.S. waters." (see *United States Army Corps of Engineers v. Hawkes Co., Inc.*)[2] But such matters leave little room for gutsy feminist ass-kicking, and elucidating the federal procedure controversies of the day does not earn one's face on Amy Schumer's tank top.

Making an activist hero out of an administrative functionary like a Supreme Court Justice was therefore always going to require a bit of distortion. Yet a reader of *Notorious RBG* (even after using the book to prepare a delicious pork loin) might be left wondering whether the characterization of Ginsburg as a fearless champion of progressive principles can be defended, even by the relaxed standards necessary for evaluating Justices.

The task of glorifying Ginsburg is made easier if one conflates her early career as a litigator with her later tenure as a justice. For despite *Notorious RBG*'s portrayal of Ginsburg's life and work as a unified package, there are distinctly different phases, and it's difficult to appreciate Ginsburg's complexity and evolution without separating the 30-something feminist dynamo from the 70-something robed bureaucrat.

In her early years, Ruth Bader Ginsburg was a spectacular law student in the face of rampant sexism and personal challenges. She became a formidable civil rights lawyer, dedicating her career to eradicating laws that discriminated on the basis of gender. Her use of male plaintiffs to demonstrate how sex-based classifications harmed men and women alike was shrewd strategy and smart politics. If you were a young, fiery liberal looking for a role model, you could do worse than Ruth Bader Ginsburg, *civil rights lawyer*.

Yet the recent outpouring of ardor has celebrated not just this period, but her time the court as well, and *Justice* Ginsburg is a different story. Empirical measurements of ideology confirm the eye test: Ginsburg is a center-left Justice roughly in line with President Obama's two appointees and Stephen Breyer. This gang is less liberal than the recently retired John Paul Stevens (appointed by Republican President Gerald Ford) and miles to the right of recent justices Thurgood Marshall and William Brennan. Of course, in today's court, which contains four of the most conservative justices of the last century, that still makes them the left flank. But even measured against her decidedly non-radical judicial peers, Ginsburg is a cautious centrist. Thus while she might maintain broadly progressive sympathies, she is equally willing to allow the government to threaten the withdrawl of funding in order to punish universities that ban discriminatory job recruitment by the military (*Rumsfeld v. Forum for Academic & Institutional Rights, Inc.*)[3] or to rule against paying overtime to Amazon warehouse workers (as in *Integrity Staffing Solutions v. Busk*).[4]

Ginsburg's liberal supporters—whose raves fill *Notorious RBG*—portray her record differently. Forced to accept that her voting pattern is nothing like that of Thurgood Marshall or legendary radical William O. Douglas (who fashioned a constitutional right to birth control out of thin air, and famously argued that trees had the right to be represented in court), they treat her moderation as cunning. The law, after all, requires five votes to change, not one. What looks on an empiricist's scatterplot like a fainthearted liberal, they argue, is instead a practical coalition builder. Ginsburg is merely being strategic.

This argument is too clever by half. One does not need to be meek and compromising to advance one's legal views. Justice Scalia, Ginsburg's best friend on the court, has not let his successful coalition building prevent him from being an outspoken, even crude conservative. Scalia has stated that he writes his dissents for the law students, and over the course of his tenure the Court has gradually slid rightward to join him on several important issues. The ability of Supreme Court justices to set agendas through nonbinding rhetoric is one of their most potent.

Ruth Bader Ginsburg undoubtedly understands this, and has given her fair share of blistering dissents. But on the issues where she is silent, her abstention from controversy can be difficult to defend. Where criminal justice is concerned, for example, she has trailed her colleagues in recognizing the stakes, and may have done real harm to large numbers of vulnerable people through her refusal to engage.

Prolonged solitary confinement, the practice of locking one or two people in a small area without meaningful social contact for over twenty-two hours per day for long periods of time, is a widespread practice in American prisons. This starvation of social contact is devastating to the mental and physical health of people in solitary. For decades, psychologists have considered the practice so damaging as to constitute torture.

In 2009, the American cultural elite caught on to the practice's horrors in the typical way: *The New Yorker* published a thorough, clinical condemnation of solitary confinement by its resident medical explainer Atul Gawande.[5] If the scientific consensus that the practice constituted torture was not enough to end the practice, one might imagine the burst of outrage the article provoked to have finished it off. Even a basic syllogism seems like it should have led the courts to eradicate long-term solitary confinement for good: the practice is torture; torturing people violates the Constitution; the practice violates the Constitution.

Not so. Although a handful of lower court cases in recent years have found solitary confinement unconstitutional when applied to certain particularly vulnerable groups such as the seriously mentally ill, the law has lagged behind the science by not mandating the practice's abolition.

Last term, in the mostly unrelated case of *Davis v. Ayala*, Justice Anthony Kennedy wrote a lengthy concurrence condemning solitary confinement.[6] He described the new and growing awareness that solitary confinement caused massive harm and closed by inviting a challenge to the practice: "In a case that presented the issue, the judiciary may be required, within its proper jurisdiction and authority, to determine whether workable alternative systems for long-term confinement exist, and, if so, whether a correctional system should be required to adopt them." Most notably, Justice Kennedy made no reference to any particularly vulnerable group, instead suggesting that long-term solitary confinement may be unconstitutional for all. Justice Ginsburg did not join the concurrence.

The reaction to Justice Kennedy was significant. *The New York Times* dedicated an editorial to the concurrence and the *Los Angeles Times* wrote a story on it.[7][8] Lower courts have already begun quoting Justice Kennedy's language when discussing cases on solitary confinement. When long-term solitary confinement is abolished, Justice Kennedy's concurrence will appear in the history.

The example, in which Ginsburg sat out an opportunity to condemn the brutal and illegal conditions of America's most marginalized people, is not trivial. Mass incarceration and the reluctance of the federal judiciary to check it are major stories of our time. The number of people we send to prison, the length of time they serve there, and the conditions in which they live are collectively among the country's biggest civil rights disasters. They're also among the few social problems that the Court is actually well-positioned to do something about. Constitutional litigating is gen-

erally a feeble means of repairing disastrous public policies, but it should
be perfectly designed to prohibit government officials from shooting children in public parks, raping adults in American jails, and torturing people
in prison through the use of long-term solitary confinement.

Alas, the Supreme Court has not seen fit to give the Constitution such
a reading, and Justice Ginsburg has been as much a bystander as many of
her peers on the Court. Take just the last few terms. In *Heien v. North Carolina*, the court held that the police may justifiably pull over cars if they
believe they are violating the law even if the police are misunderstand-
ing the law, so long as the mistake was reasonable.[9] In *Taylor v. Barkes*,
the Court held that the family of a suicidal man who was jailed and then
killed himself could not sue the jail for failing to implement anti-suicide
measures.[10] In *Plumhoff v. Rickard*, the court held that the family of two
men could not sue the police after they had shot and killed them for fleeing a police stop.[11] Ginsburg joined the opinion in every case.

In fact, she has gone so far as to join the conservatives on criminal justice,
even when all of her fellow liberals have sided with a criminal defendant.
In *Samson v. California*, the Court decided the issue of whether police
could conduct warrantless searches of parolees merely because they were
on parole.[12] Instead of joining the liberal dissenters, Ginsburg signed onto
Clarence Thomas's majority opinion in favor of the police.

In January, the Court issued its opinion in the case of *Kansas v. Carr*.[13]
The Kansas Supreme Court had overturned a pair of death sentences,
on the grounds that the defendants' Eighth Amendment rights had
been violated in the instructions given to the jury. The U.S. Supremes
swooped in, informing Kansas that it had made a mistake; nobody's
Eighth Amendment rights had been violated, thus the defendants
ought to have continued unimpeded along the path toward execution.
The Court's decision was 8-1, the lone dissenter being Sonia Sotomayor.
Ginsburg put her name on Justice Scalia's majority opinion instead.

It was no random chance that made Justice Sotomayor the particular
dissenter. Since her appointment in 2009, Sotomayor has emerged as a
strong opponent of the more egregiously inhumane aspects of American
criminal justice. She has repeatedly taken on all eight of her colleagues;

last year she lambasted them for shielding a police officer from legal liability for shooting a man during a high-speed chase. Sotomayor wrote that by "sanctioning a 'shoot first, think later' approach to policing, the Court renders the protections of the Fourth Amendment hollow." The other justices, including Ginsburg, felt the case so unimportant that they dispensed of it with a brief, unsigned opinion.

During her time on the court, Sotomayor has been recognized as making a conscious effort to educate her fellow justices and the American public about issues of race and criminal justice. Writing in *The New Republic*, David Fontana has said that Sotomayor's spirited fight against racism makes her a "national treasure," and that "Sotomayor, uniquely among recent liberal justices, has used her public appearances to effectively communicate her liberal perspective on the constitution to regular members of the public, in addition to legal and academic elites."[14] Importantly, Sotomayor also sees herself as an "outsider," uncomfortable with the pomp and affectation of her eight judicial brethren.

In *Slate*, Mark Joseph Stern contrasted Sotomayor's perceptiveness about police and prisons issues with Ginsburg's indifference: "When it comes to understanding the systemic flaws and violent behavior of America's criminal justice system, there's no one quite like Justice Sonia Sotomayor...Sorry, Notorious R.B.G. groupies, but [Ruth Bader Ginsburg] has a bit of a law-and-order streak."[15] (This despite Sotomayor being an ex-prosecutor, while Ginsburg worked for the ACLU.)

Carmon and Knizhnik discuss none of this, instead treating as an implicit assumption that Ginsburg's aggressive battle for justice extends from gender equality to fighting racism. Of course, *Notorious RBG* is not obligated to interrogate every facet of her career, and Ginsburg need not be perfect to be worthy of admiration. But the assumption that she is a role model on racial inequality is not an ancillary question. Racial inequality is a defining feature of American life and a national disgrace. Racial animus is also the bedrock of mass incarceration, which erupted partially on Ginsburg's watch and which she has expressed little interest in attempting to eliminate.

Carmon and Knizhnik must surely be aware of this. After all, the very opening scene of *Notorious RBG* depicts Ginsburg reading her fiery dissent in *Shelby County v. Holder*, an important voting rights case in which the court implied that Black voters in the South no longer needed Congress's protection from their states' efforts at disenfranchising them.[16] (The intervening years have proved the Court wrong, if there was ever any question.) The Court, *Notorious RBG* notes, was "threatening the progress for which she had fought so hard." As for Ginsburg, "when the work is justice, she has every intention to see it to the end. RBG has always been about doing the work." In the lengthy discussion of her career to follow, one might therefore expect to read about Ginsburg fighting so hard for progress in the eradication of racism; doing the work; seeing it to the end.

Notorious RBG barely mentions race again. The authors seem to believe that because of Ginsburg's many accomplishments fighting for women's rights, we can safely assume that she was a force for good in the fight against racism without considering the evidence.

In fact, one of *Notorious RBG*'s few mentions of race is particularly strange. In the book's discussion of *Bush v. Gore*, the contentious decision that decided the 2000 presidential election, the authors mention that Ginsburg's draft of her dissent had a footnote alluding to the possible suppression of Black voters in Florida.[17] Justice Scalia purportedly responded to this draft by flying into a rage, telling Ginsburg that she was using "Al Sharpton tactics." Ginsburg removed the footnote before it saw the light of day.

This anecdote's inclusion in the book is baffling. *Notorious RBG* unrepentantly fawns over Ginsburg as a civil rights hero. Yet in this story, Ginsburg contemplates calling attention to straightforward, anti-Black racism in the most facile of ways. But when her friend Justice Scalia plucks an argument straight from right-wing talk radio to shame her out of doing so, Ginsburg instantly capitulates. Some commitment to racial equality.

Ginsburg's legendary chumminess with the late Justice Scalia should be another red flag in itself. Here was a man openly (and brashly) against every value Ginsburg supposedly holds. He suggested that affirmative action may be keeping African Americans from attending the "slow-er-tracked" schools where they belong. He would have seen *Roe v. Wade* overturned, and the reproductive rights Ginsburg fought for completely stripped. He called the Voting Rights Act a "racial entitlement" and consistently defended the legitimacy of anti-gay prejudice.[18] Not the sort of character one would expect Ginsburg to attend the opera with.

Yet somehow these two opposites managed to get along and maintain mutual respect and good humor, and a legendary extrajudicial friendship. How? On the one hand, it seems a charming parable about the setting aside of differences and the embracing of common ground. But it's also odd that anyone who takes their values seriously could simply "set aside" the fact that, by their own metric, their friend was one of the most powerful enforcers of systematized bigotry and repression in the country. (What can you say? "Oh, that was just his day job"?) Now, perhaps Ginsburg would reject that description of Scalia's position. But if you think the rights of black and gay people are of major moral consequence, and you think Scalia's work profoundly undermined those rights, it's difficult to escape the conclusion that this was not someone you ought to regularly be taking to dinner.

The perverse Scalia/Ginsburg friendship speaks to a disturbing trait shared by both the Court itself and the specific *Notorious RBG* approach to understanding it. This is the tendency to become wrapped up in the genteel, sober, ritualized world of the Court's chambers, and forget the human consequences of the work that is done there. A torture victim would not so easily be able to compartmentalize Scalia's repeated defenses of torture. A gay or trans person might have had a difficult time going out and watching Scalia eat risotto and tell jokes, knowing the world he would build for them if he could. During Scalia and Ginsburg's occasional public appearances together, Scalia usually cracked his line "What's not to like [about her]? ...Except her views on the law."[19] Well hah, hah. Yet "her views on law" embody her fundamental conception of justice and morality (at least ostensibly). Only in the detached and rarified world of the Court could someone accept such a remark as a gentle joke among colleagues rather than a nasty dismissal of everything one holds dear, including the basic rights of women.

In 2011, several public figures, including Harvard Law Professor Randall Kennedy, urged Justice Ginsburg retire while she could be sure that President Obama could pick her successor.[20] Ginsburg was seventy-eight and had survived cancer twice. (Kennedy also called for the retirement of the only slightly-younger Stephen Breyer.) Ginsburg refused to pay any heed to the suggestion, and appears determined to remain on the Court until it pleases her to depart. (With Republicans now firmly committed to judicial obstructionism, it may even be too late fo her to change her mind and assure an Obama-nominated successor.) *Notorious RBG* addresses this controversy in its introduction, and the response is worth considering in full:

> *"Historically, one way women have lost power is by being nudged out the door to make room for someone else. Not long before pop culture discovered RBG, liberal law professors and commentators began telling her the best thing she could do for what she cared about was to quit, so that President Barack Obama could appoint a successor. RBG, ardently devoted to her job, has mostly brushed that dirt off her shoulder. Her refusal to meekly shuffle off the stage has been another public, high-stakes act of defiance."*

It should first be noted that "women" as a whole would are unlikely to lose any power by Ginsburg's retirement; it is widely assumed that any selection Obama would make to replace Ginsburg would be a woman. But other contemporaneous responses to the call to retire made more sophisticated claims that they whiffed of sexism. Emily Bazelon wrote in *Slate* that since Ginsburg is "a small, slender woman who speaks in low tones and looks like a bird... people tend to assume she is frail when in fact she is anything but."[21] This point is important. Even those of us who find excellent, logical reasons to urge Ginsburg to retire should concede that research on implicit bias makes those excellent, logical reasons inherently suspect. When they happen to coincide with the outcome that traditional gender norms or racial animus would suggest—such as urging a slight woman to step down from her powerful position because she is too frail—alarm bells should go off.

Yet the main argument falls to bits upon a gentle prodding. First, the charge of sexism is hard to maintain so long as one equally favors the retirement of the similarly senescent Justice Breyer. (Ageism may be another matter, though it should hardly be unduly discriminatory to point out that the elderly have a noticeable tendency to suddenly expire.) Second, it's very strange indeed to defend against the sexism experienced by Ginsburg without weighing it against the sexism experienced by the 162 million other women who live in the United States and have to live with the Supreme Court's rulings. The authors of *Notorious RBG* must find important the actual work the Supreme Court does—they wrote a whole book about a Supreme Court justice! Yet they do not even engage with the argument that Justice Ginsburg is actually putting the rights of people at risk by entering her mid-eighties on a Supreme Court with four pathologically conservative justices, all salivating at the prospect of recruiting a fifth and restoring the toxic ideological configuration of the Scalia years. Justice Ginsburg's "public, high-stakes act of defiance" may be gratifying and symbolically powerful, but if the end result is the reversal of *Roe*, can a victory for feminism truly be claimed? (In fact, replacing Ginsburg might actually help women's rights, at least the rights of women prisoners, if someone more Sotomayor-ish were given the post.)

One of the authors' favored metaphors can explain how they so blithely dismissed the merits of allowing President Obama to pick Ginsburg's successor: that of the court as "stage." Ginsburg refused "to meekly shuffle off the stage." It's a word commonly used in descriptions of Supreme Court proceedings. Indeed, *Notorious RBG* on its opening page notes that "What happens inside the hushed chamber is pure theater." *No, it is not.* It may be *theatrical*, but very few of your ordinary community stage productions retain the power to impose or revoke the death penalty.

A less glib reply to the pro-retirement argument came from ex-*New York Times* court-watcher Linda Greenhouse. Greenhouse explained Ginsburg's intransigence thusly:

"I think from her perspective she is taking a long view of history, not a case by case one, or a term by term one...I think she feels that it belittles and diminishes the court to have retirements so obviously timed for political reasons." [22]

There, in a nutshell, is the difference between Ginsburg and the people her work affects: she and her followers can afford to take the long view, to see political fights as important without seeing them as an end-all, be-all struggle. From the tables of the Supreme Court cafeteria or the leather chairs of one's chambers, lofty abstractions like "the preservation of judicial dignity" can appear to carry equal weight to questions of actual human consequences. One's fellow justices can be droll and amiable drinking companions, even if they wouldn't bat an eyelid at seeing homosexuals put in prison. And "political reasons" can appear as something tawdry and unbecoming, even though they refer to matters like "keeping children from being put in solitary confinement" and "making sure colleges don't exclude black people." What a luxury it surely is to be able to relax and take "the long view" of these questions, a luxury unshared by the victims of the Court's judgments.

So one must adopt a somewhat cynical hypothesis as to why this middle-of-the-road Justice is the object of the cartoons, the hoodies, and this coffee table ode: the readers of *Notorious RBG* spend as little time thinking about the people abused in American prisons and jails as the Notorious RBG herself does. Elsewhere, people in America's worst prisons, their families, and their advocates have to hope that either a Democrat will win the 2016 presidential election or that Justice Ginsburg will make it to 87 in good health. If neither come to pass, thousands of additional people may be assaulted, raped, or killed in American prisons and jails, and it's likely that most of the people wearing "Notorious RBG" paraphernalia will never know their names.

BARACK OBAMA:
WHO HE REALLY IS

by Luke Savage & Nathan J. Robinson

THE BEST THING ABOUT BEING an ex-president is that you can do whatever you want. Do you want to retire to the countryside to build henhouses and tootle around in your amphibious car?[1][2] You can do that. Do you want to teach Sunday school and build houses for poor people, and maybe broker an occasional international peace agreement?[3][4][5] You can do that also. Do you want to spend your days painting pictures of your dogs, your feet, and the soldiers you caused to be maimed?[6][7][8] It's an option! The retirement activities of presidents offer useful insights into their natures, because they are finally freed of all political constraints on their action. At liberty to pursue activities of their choosing, we get a sense for what they *actually* enjoy, and who they *actually* are.

During his two terms in office, Barack Obama's most zealous devotees tended to explain away apparent failures or complacencies by referring to the constraints high office places on anyone who ascends to it. Even some critics on the left may have suspected that the deeds of Obama's administration were out of sync with his natural instincts, that Obama was a man of high conscience weighed down or blunted by Washington's leviathan bureaucracy, or frustrated by the exigencies of an unstable world.

Obama's retirement should therefore finally give us meaningful insight into who he really is or, to put it another way, who he has been all along.

The albatross of office finally lifted from his neck, America's 44th president is now free to do anything and everything he desires without impediment. He can be the person he has always wanted to be, the person whom he has had to keep hidden away. Who, then, is the real Obama?

Well, it turns out the real Obama is quite like the one we knew already. And what he most wants to do is nestle himself cozily within the bosom of the global elite, and earn millions from behind a thinly-veiled philanthropic facade.

In January, Obama launched his post-presidential foundation with a board that consists of private equity executives, lobbyists, and an Uber advisor,[9] tasking it to implement the world's most meaningless mandate ("to inspire people globally to show up for the most important office in any democracy, that of citizen").[10] Able to choose his friends from out of anyone in the world, Obama has been seen kitesurfing with venture capital magnate Richard Branson (worth more than $5 billion)[11] and brunching with Bono.[12] (You can usually judge a person pretty well by their friends, and nobody who voluntarily spends his free time with Bono should be trusted.)

Obama's recent forays into politics have also confirmed him as a friend to the elite. He used his last weeks in office to personally help derail the candidacy of left-wing congressman Keith Ellison for DNC chair. After Ellison became an early favorite in the race, Obama used his influence to recruit and boost the more centrist and less controversial Tom Perez, who won after a series of vile smears were launched against Ellison by influential party donors.[13]

Obama also extended his influence overseas. Ahead of the first round of voting, he effectively endorsed French presidential candidate Emmanuel Macron, a former investment banker who "wants to roll back state intervention in the economy, cut public-sector jobs, and reduce taxes on business and the ultra-rich."[14] [15] (Macron also once responded to a union worker who needled him over his fancy suits by declaring that fancy suits accrue to those who work the hardest, an assertion that is manifestly false.)[16] [17]

Then there were the speeches. In December, conservative commentator Andrew Sullivan, asked what Obama should do with his post-presidency, had jokingly pleaded: "No speeches at Goldman Sachs, please."[18] After all, Hillary Clinton's Wall Street speeches had become the ultimate symbol of Democratic hypocrisy, a clear demonstration of how those who profess to oppose inequality will happily reap financial benefits from it. For Sullivan, it was laughable to think that a man like Obama, who maintained a public image characterized by modesty and personal integrity, would instantly lapse into the tawdry and unscrupulous Clinton practice of cashing in.

But then Obama cashed in. Mere weeks after leaving 1600 Pennsylvania Avenue he signed on with the Harry Walker Agency (the very same outfit through which the Clintons have jointly pocketed a virtually incomprehensible $158 million on the speaker's circuit).[19] It was then revealed that he had been paid a whopping $400,000 fee by Cantor Fitzgerald — a bond firm which deals in credit default swaps, the inscrutable instruments of financial alchemy that helped cause the 2008 financial meltdown.[20] (After that came news of *another* $400,000 speaking fee.)

At the first sign of backlash against Obama's pursuit of riches, media and political elites unleashed a torrent of toadyism in his defense. After expressing faint concern about Obama's speaking fees, Amanda Marcotte chastised "people who've never had money worries" for casting judgement on "those who have," elsewhere complaining: "The obsession with speaking fees is politics version of begrudging athlete salaries while ignoring owner profits" (an analogy that only holds up if Obama literally works for Wall Street).[21] *The Boston Globe*'s Michael Cohen added: "If someone wants to pay Barack Obama $400,000 to give a speech I can't think of a single reason why he shouldn't take it...Obama is not doing anything wrong. He's giving a speech. Nothing to apologize for."[22] It seemed that American liberalism's eight year journey from "Change We Can Believe In" to "Everybody Grifts..." was finally complete. (There is a fun game one can play with ideologically-committed Democrats that we might call "Rationalize That Injustice." See if there are any right-wing policies that they won't justify if told that Obama did them.)

Certain defenses of Obama opted for an explicitly racial framework.

The Daily Show's Trevor Noah exclaimed "So the first black president must also be the first one to not take money afterwards? Fuck that, and fuck you!" April Reign, creator of the viral hashtag #OscarsSoWhite, equated Obama's critics with defenders of the slave trade.[23] Attorney Imani Gandy, who litigated foreclosure cases on behalf of J.P. Morgan before becoming a prominent social justice activist on Twitter,[24] seized upon the controversy to call antipathy towards Wall Street "the whitest shit I've ever heard." This particular line of argumentation almost defied credulity, especially since critics of Obama's speaking fees were simply extending a criticism originally applied to Bill and Hillary Clinton.

But while certain rationalizations of Obama's conduct have ventured into burlesque satire, it is worth taking Michael Cohen's question seriously: what's so wrong with Obama doing a speech for money? He speaks, they pay, nobody gets hurt. What's the actual harm? Since Obama isn't actually in a position to give Wall Street any political favors, and since he's a private citizen, why should it matter? Indeed, Debbie Wasserman Schultz told those who might be upset by the speech to "mind their own business."

Well, first, there are some basic issues of personal ethics involved in post-presidential buckraking. There *is* something tawdry about immediately leaving office to go and make piles of money in any way you can, and it's a short hop from doing your inspirational speaking schtick for corporate events to doing it in television commercials or at birthday parties for investment bankers' teenage children. That's why Harry Truman famously refused to serve on corporate boards, declaring that doing so would be undignified. ("I could never lend myself to any transaction, however respectable, that would commercialize on the prestige and dignity of the office of the presidency.") And those who think Obama is being held to an impossible standard (that impossible "do good things rather than simply lucrative things" standard) should remember that Jimmy Carter has spent a productive and comparatively modest retirement writing, campaigning for the basic dignity of Palestinians, and quite regularly intervening to criticize American policy at home and abroad.

Some have said that as a "private citizen," Obama's choices of how to make money should be beyond moral scrutiny. But it's private citizens who could use a lot *more* moral scrutiny. Obama's choosing to become a mansion-dwelling millionaire is not wrong because he used to be the president,[25] but because being exorbitantly rich in a time of great global poverty is heinously immoral.[26] Moreover it defies credulity to suggest, as some have in earnest, that Obama *needs* to take money from this particular source. He is already guaranteed a lavish annual pension of more than $200,000 in addition to expenses and almost $400,000 in further pension money accrued from his time as an Illinois State Senator.[27] He and the former First Lady have just signed the most sumptuous post-presidential book deal in history[28] (worth $65 million, or almost 1500 times the median personal income)[29] and will assuredly spend the next several decades enjoying a standard of material comfort few Americans have ever known, Wall Street speaking fees notwithstanding.

Finally, there's the political hypocrisy. On the *very same day* as the infamous speech, Obama was elsewhere decrying the pernicious political influence of wealth, somberly declaring that "because of money and politics, special interests dominate the debates in Washington in ways that don't match up with what the broad majority of Americans feel."[30] Obama's public posture has always been that he resents the political influence of special interests and financial elites, yet as both a political candidate and a private citizen they have showered him with money he has been only too happy to accept.[31]

Yet Michael Cohen is also partially right: the speech itself is not actually terribly important. It's a mistake to focus on the personal ethics of Obama's actual *decision*, and if we frame the relevant question as "Should Obama have taken the money?" then it's easy to lapse into something of a shrug. So the guy wants to get rich. Fine. He's no worse than every other member of the 1%. They're all indefensible, and as long as nobody continues to maintain the illusion that Obama is any different from any other politician, there's no reason to single him out as uniquely wicked. (One suspects, however, that some people do still maintain the illusion that Obama is different from other wealthy denizens of the political class.)

The most important aspect of the story is not that Obama accepted Cantor Fitzgerald's offer, but that the offer was made in the first place. Indeed, it's hard to escape the impression that certain powerful interests are now rewarding the former president with a gracious thanks for a job well done. Rather than asking whether Obama should have turned down the gig, we can ask: *if* his administration had taken aggressive legal and regulatory action against Wall Street firms following the financial crisis, would they be clamouring for him to speak and offering lucrative compensation mere weeks after his leaving office? It's hard to think they would, and if a Democratic president has done their job properly, nobody on Wall Street should want to pay them a red cent in retirement. Obama's decision to take Cantor Fitzgerald's cash isn't, therefore, some pivotal moment in which he betrayed his principles in the pursuit of lucre. It's simply additional confirmation he has never posed a serious challenge to Wall Street's outsized economic power.

In fact, we've known that for as long as we've known Obama. He was popular on Wall Street back when he first ran for president. According to *Politico*, he "raised more money from Wall Street through the Democratic National Committee and his campaign account than any politician in American history," and in just one year "raked in more cash from bank employees, hedge fund managers and financial services companies than all Republican candidates combined."[32]

Serious economic progressives did not become disillusioned with Obama when he accepted $400,000 for a speech, but when he arrived in office at the apex of the financial crisis and immediately stuffed his cabinet and advisory team with a coterie of alumni from Goldman Sachs (a top donor to this campaign in 2008).[33] At the height of the worst financial catastrophe since the Great Depression, during a time of unique (and completely warranted) antipathy towards rapacious corporate interests, Obama had been elected with the single greatest mandate to implement sweeping change in recent political history. Given the same extraordinary kind of political demand, FDR took the opportunity to proclaim that "The old enemies of peace: business and financial monopoly, speculation, reckless banking, class antagonism, sectionalism, war profiteering...they are unanimous in their hate for me — and I welcome their hatred."[34]

But when Obama was faced with a similar moment of calamity and possibility, he opted instead for the avenues of brokerage and appeasement. He chose not to push for criminal prosecutions of financial executives whose greed and negligence caused the 2008 economic crash.[35] In 1999, Obama's Attorney General, Eric Holder, had proposed the concept of "collateral consequences" (colloquially known as "too big to jail"), whereby "the state could pursue non-criminal alternatives for companies if they believed prosecuting them might result in too much 'collateral' damage" to the economy.[36] Thus, when banking giant HSBC was revealed to be laundering billions of dollars for Mexican drug cartels and groups linked to al-Qaeda, Obama's Justice Department allowed the bank to escape with a fine and no criminal charges, on the grounds that a prosecution might damage HSBC too much and have wider effects on the economy.[37] Top prosecutors had evidence of serious wrongdoing by HSBC, but Holder prevented them from proceeding. A report prepared for the House Financial Services Committee concluded that Holder "overruled an internal recommendation by DOJ's Asset Forfeiture and Money Laundering Section to prosecute HSBC because of DOJ leadership's concern that prosecuting the bank would have serious adverse consequences on the financial system."[38] Yet Holder later falsely suggested that the decision was made by the prosecutors rather than himself. ("Do you think that these very aggressive US attorneys I was proud to serve with would have not brought these cases if they had the ability?")[39] One should note *just how* unjust the "collateral consequences" idea is: it explicitly creates separate systems of justice for rich and poor, because there will always be more economic consequences to prosecuting major banking institutions than individual poor people. The same crime will therefore carry two different sets of consequences depending on how much you matter to the economy.

Holder also institutionalized the practice of extrajudicial settlements, under which "there was no longer any opportunity for judges or anyone else to check the power of the executive branch to hand out financial indulgences" to corporate offenders.[40] Thus even as guilty pleas were extracted from banks and financiers for crimes ranging from fraud, manipulation, and bribery to money laundering and tax evasion, not a single malefactor from Wall Street ended up behind bars. (Meanwhile, America's prisons remained full of less economically consequential people who had been convicted of the same crimes.)

Obama's politics were the same when it came to policy-making. After several years of sustained corporate pushback, aided by both the White House and Congress, the much-touted Dodd-Frank law was whittled down to the status of a mild and extremely tenuous reform.[41] A similar pattern inflected Obama's signature legislative achievement, the now-precarious Affordable Care Act. While undoubtedly improving on the horrific status quo in American health care, Obamacare was notably soft on the insurance and pharmaceutical industries,[42] both of which were extensively consulted during its composition.[43] Far from being the Stalinist caricature of Tea Party fever dreams, Obamacare was based on plan put in place by a Republican governor and sketched out by the Heritage Foundation in the early 1990s. No matter how much the American right may distort the record, Obamacare was essentially a massive corporate giveaway (after all, it mandated that millions of people become new insurance customers), and it manifestly failed to tackle the crux of the problem with US healthcare, which is that market actors are involved in the provision of health insurance to begin with. Obama arguably had the votes to create a public option that would have ameliorated matters somewhat, *even* without his having made any serious attempt at exerting political pressure in favor of one.[44] But instead, he opted to needlessly compromise with the very corporate actors who stand between Americans and the guarantee of healthcare as a right.

This consistently pro-business approach has ensured that Obama isn't the only administration official that corporate America has showered with gratitude. For plenty of Obama's top lieutenants, the revolving door between Wall Street and the corridors of the US government has kept spinning continuously. David Plouffe, Obama's 2008 campaign manager and former senior advisor, now works for Uber.[45] Press Secretary Robert Gibbs is executive vice-president at McDonalds,[46] lobbying hard against raising the minimum wage.[47] Eric Holder, who had left the white-collar defense outfit Covington & Burling to become attorney general, returned in 2015 to once again represent many of the same banks and financial firms he had ostensibly been charged with regulating and prosecuting while in office.[48] (Covington had literally been keeping Holder's office waiting for him.[49] "This is home for me," Holder said of the corporate firm.)[50] And having presided over massive bailouts during his tenure running the US Treasury, Timothy Geithner headed to Wall Street to take up a lucrative gig at private equity firm Warburg Pincus.[51]

This is why Matthew Yglesias was wrong to characterize Barack Obama's speaking fee as a betrayal of "everything [he] believes in."[52] In fact, it was the exact opposite: totally consistent with everything he has always stood for. The point isn't that he's "sold out." It's that, when the soaring cadences and luminous rhetoric are stripped away, Obama never offered any transformative change to begin with. Thus his $400,000 speech matters, not because it represents a deviation from the norm, or a venal lapse in personal ethics, but because it conveniently demonstrates a pattern that has been there all along.

In the Obama presidency, many liberals found the embodiment of their political ideal: an administration of capable, apparently well-intentioned people with impeccable Ivy League credentials, fronted by a person of undeniable charisma and charm, and with a beautiful and photogenic family to boot.

But examining Obama seriously requires acknowledging the fundamental limits of his brand of politics: a liberalism that continues to trade in the language of social concern while remaining invested in the very institutions undergirding the poverty and injustice it tells us it exists to fight; see, e.g., the upper-middle-class liberals who decry educational inequities while sending their own children to private schools.[53] [54] Like the Davos billionaires who "fret about inequality over vintage wine and canapés," Obama denounces money in politics but can't keep himself from taking it.[55] And because he's such a part of the very elite system whose effects he abhors, "Obamaism" was always destined to be a fundamentally empty and insincere philosophy.

Matt Taibbi issued a prescient assessment of Obama all the way back in 2007, when it was still unclear who would win the Democratic presidential primary:

> *"The Illinois Senator is the ultimate modern media creature—he's a good-looking, youthful, smooth-talking, buttery-warm personality with an aw-shucks demeanor who exudes a seemingly impenetrable air of Harvard-crafted moral neutrality... His entire political persona is an ingeniously crafted human cipher, a man without race, ideology, geographic allegiances, or, indeed, sharp edges of any kind...[He appears] as a sort of ideological Universalist, one who spends a great deal of rhetorical energy showing that he recognizes the validity of all points of view...His political ideal is basically a rehash of the Blair-Clinton "third way" deal, an amalgam of Kennedy, Reagan, Clinton and the New Deal; he is aiming for the middle of the middle of the middle....In short, Obama is a creature perfectly in tune with the awesome corporate strivings of Hollywood, Madison avenue and the Beltway—he tries, and often succeeds, at selling a politics of seeking out the very center of where we already are, the very couch where we've been sitting all this time, as an exciting, revolutionary journey into the unknown."*

The real tragedy of the Obama story is that in 2008, millions of desperate Americans cast votes for a presidential candidate they believed would fight for meaningful change. He successfully marketed "hope" and "change" to a country that was reeling from a horrific financial collapse (his 2008 presidential run even won a "Marketing Campaign of the Year" award from the ad industry, beating out Apple and Zappos).[56] But beneath it all was no serious vision of change; the grand speeches, paid and unpaid, turn out to contain little more than well-crafted platitudes. (Christopher Hitchens once pointed out that while everyone considered Obama a powerful and memorable speaker, nobody could ever seem to remember a single specific line from any of his orations, a good sign he'd in fact said nothing at all.)[57] And as Obama biographer David Garrow concludes, "while the crucible of self-creation had produced an ironclad will, the vessel was hollow at its core."[58]

But Obama's weaknesses are not the product of some unique personal pathology. He is simply the most charismatic and successful practitioner of an ideology shared by many contemporary Democrats: a kind of Beltway liberalism that sacrifices nearly all real political ambition, espousing a rhetoric of compassion and transformation while rationalizing every form of amorality and capitulation as a pragmatic necessity. In a moment when militancy and moral urgency are needed most, it seeks only innocuous, technocratic change and claims with the smuggest certitude that this represents the best grown adults can aspire to. In a world of spiralling inequality and ascendant corporate tyranny, it insists on weighting equally the interests of all sides and deems the result a respectable democratic consensus. Bearing witness to entrenched human misery, it wryly declares it was ever thus and delights in lazily dismissing critics with scornful refrains like "*That* will *never* get through Congress..." Confronted with risk or danger, it willingly retreats to ever more conservative ground and calls the sum total of these maneuvers "incrementalism." In place of a coherent vision or a clear program of reform, the best it can offer is the hollow sensation of progress stripped of all its necessary conflicts and their corresponding discomforts.

One could see, in the defenses of Obama's Wall Street speech, just how far this ideology narrows our sense of the possible: it tells us it is unrealistic and unfair to conceive of a president who does not shamelessly use the office to enrich himself. What passes for pragmatism is in fact the most dispiriting kind of capitalist pessimism: this is your world, you're stuck with it, and it's madness to dream of anything better. There Is No Alternative.

We can almost respect Hillary Clinton for embracing this idea openly, and barely even pretending to represent our most elevated selves rather than our most acquisitive ones. The cruelty Obama perpetrated was to encourage people to believe in something better, then give them nothing but a stylized status quo. At least now that he's windsurfing with billionaires and doing the Wall Street speaking tour, there's no longer any reason to keep believing that underneath it all, he was a true idealist whose innermost desires were thwarted by crushing political realities. All along, his innermost desire was to meet Bono over eggs benedict.

The Obama of 2008 was to be this century's FDR, signifying a moment of lasting realignment and transcendent progress — rather than one of growing alienation and despair culminating in the election of Donald Trump. But the liberalism of 21st century America, it turns out, is ill-equipped to achieve the transformative change it once so loftily promised: not because it made a noble attempt and failed but because it never really sought this change to begin with.

While Obama may not have been sincere, a great many of his voters were, and the millions who embraced his message revealed a genuine hunger for transformative change.

Now all we need is a political movement that actually seeks it out.

CITATIONS

"SLAVERY IS EVERYWHERE"
pp. 15-25

1   Whitney Benns, "American Slavery, Reinvented," *The Atlantic* (Sep. 21, 2015).

2   Douglas Blackmon, *Slavery by Another Name* (Anchor, 2009).

3   "International Slavery Convention," Office of the United Nations Human Rights Commissioner (Signed Sept. 25, 1926).

4   Abby Haglage, "Lawsuit: Your Candy Bar Was Made By Child Slaves," *The Daily Beast* (Sept. 30, 2015).

5   "Honduran coffee harvest relies on child workers," *Agence France-Presse* (Dec. 24, 2010).

6   Kate Hodal, "Nestlé admits slave labour risk on Brazil coffee plantations," *The Guardian* (March 2, 2016).

7   Letter to USDA, "Re: Guidelines for Eliminating Child and Forced Labor in Agricultural Supply Chain" (July 11, 2011). Accessed via U.S. Department of Labor.

8   Rishi Iyengar, "Shocking Conditions for Workers on India's Tea Plantations Revealed," *Time* (Sept. 8, 2015).

9   Gethin Chamberlain, "How poverty wages for tea pickers fuel India's trade in child slavery," *The Guardian* (July 20, 2013).

10   Euan McKirdy, "World has 35.8 million slaves, report finds," *CNN* (Jan. 4, 2015).

11   "How many people were taken from Africa?" *Portcities Bristol*.

12   "Children in the Fields," *National Farm Worker Ministry*.

13   Zama Neff, "Child Farmworkers in the United States: A "Worst Form of Child Labor," *Brown Human Rights Report* (Nov. 17, 2011).

14   Marc Bain and Jenni Avins, "The thing that makes Bangladesh's garment industry such a huge success also makes it deadly," *Quartz* (April 24, 2015).

15   19 U.S. Code § 1307 - Convict-made goods; importation prohibited. Accessed via Cornell Law School Legal Information Institute.

16   Anemona Hartocollis, "At Harvard Dorms, 'House Masters' No More," *The New York Times* (Feb. 24, 2016).

17   "Harvard Law School Is Ditching its Controversial Crest Linked to a Slaveholder," *Reuters* (March 15, 2016).

"THE PATHOLOGIES OF PRIVILEGE"
pp. 27-35

1   See Caila Klass and Alexa Valiente, "'Affluenza' DUI Case: What Happened Night of the Accident That Left 4 People Dead," *ABC News* (Dec. 31, 2015).

2   "Profile of Ethan Couch's parents, who attorneys argued spoiled him, made him irresponsible," *CNN Wire* (Dec. 21, 2015).

3   Michael J. Mooney, "The Worst Parents Ever," *D Magazine* (May 2015).

4   Phil Rosenthal, "Ethan Couch, spared by 'affluenza' defense, squanders one more gift," *The Chicago Tribune* (Dec. 30, 2015).

5   Nicole Hensley, "'Affluenza' teen Ethan Couch and missing mother captured near beach in Mexican resort town of Puerto Vallarta," *New York Daily News* (Dec. 29, 2015).

6   "Prevalence of Imprisonment in the U.S. Population, 1974-2001," Bureau of Justice Statistics (2003).

7   "Michelle Alexander: More Black Men Are In Prison Today Than Were Enslaved In 1850," *The Huffington Post* (Oct. 12, 2011).

8   Joe Palazzolo, "Racial Gap in Men's Sentencing," *The Wall Street Journal* (Feb. 14, 2013).

9   Jonathan Rothwell, "How the War on Drugs Damages Black Social Mobility," Brookings Institution (Sept. 30, 2014).

10   Devah Pager, "The Mark of a Criminal Record," *American Journal of Sociology*, Vol. 8, No. 5, (March, 2003), pp. 937–75.

11   Andrew Hanson and Zackary Hawley, "Do Landlords Discriminate in the Rental Housing Market? Evidence from an Internet Field Experiment in U.S. Cities" (2011).

12   S. Nazione and K.J. Silk, "Patient race and perceived illness responsibility: effects on provider helping and bias," *Medical Education*, Vol. 47, No. 8 (Aug. 2013), pp. 780-9.

13   Daniel M. Butler and David E. Broockman, "Who Helps DeShawn Register to Vote? A Field Experiment on State Legislators" (May 6, 2009).

14   For an informative illustration of the gap, see Tami Luhby, "The black-white economic divide in 5 charts," *CNN* (Nov. 25, 2015).

15   Rakesh Kochhar and Richard Fry, "Wealth inequality has widened along racial, ethnic lines since end of Great Recession," *Pew Research Center* (Dec. 12, 2014).

16   "Forest Whitaker Falsely Accused Of Shoplifting; Deli Employee Who Frisked Star Fired," *The Huffington Post* (Feb. 19, 2013).

17   Krissah Thompson, "Arrest of Harvard's Henry Louis Gates Jr. was avoidable, report says," *The Washington Post* (June 30, 2010). See also Charles Ogletree, *The Presumption of Guilt: The Arrest of Henry Louis Gates, Jr. and Race, Class and Crime in America* (St. Martin's Press, 2012).

18   Carmen Rios, "Did You Do These 6 Activities Today? Then You've Got Class Privilege," *EverydayFeminism.com* (Dec. 9, 2015).

19   Mike Pearl, "Why Are Some People Saying Dylann Roof Was Given Special Treatment When He Was Arrested?" *VICE* (June 23, 2015).

20   Jason Silverstein, "Cops bought Dylann Roof Burger King after his calm arrest: report," *New York Daily News* (July 23, 2015).

21   Corky Siemaszko, "Recall Effort Launched Against Judge Aaron Persky in Stanford Rape Case," *NBC News* (June 6, 2016).

22   See Sam Levin and Julia Carrie Wong, "Brock Turner's statement blames sexual assault on Stanford 'party culture'" *The Guardian* (June 8, 2016).

23   K.C. Johnson and Stuart Taylor, Jr., "Stanford sex assault case: Sentence was too short — but the system worked," *The Washington Post* (June 8, 2016).

24   Elle Hunt, "'20 minutes of action': father defends Stanford student son convicted of sexual assault," *The Guardian* (June 6, 2016).

25   Eliott C. McLaughlin, Joshua Berlinger, Ashley Fantz and Steve Almasy, "Disney gator attack: 2-year-old boy found dead," *CNN* (June 16, 2016).

26   "Feminist Says She Doesn't Care About Alligator Killing Toddler: 'So
      Finished With White Men's Entitlement,'" *The Daily Wire* (June

27   For information on the racial disparity, see Death Penalty Information
      Center, "Race and the Death Penalty."

28   See Nathan J. Robinson, *Superpredator: Bill Clinton's Use and Abuse of
      Black America* (Current Affairs Press, 2016), pp. 55-60.

"THE NECESSITY OF POLITICAL VULGARITY"
pp. 37-44

1   Dylan Matthews, "Inside Jacobin: how a socialist magazine is winning
     the left's war of ideas," *Vox* (March 21, 2016).

2   See Amber Frost, "The Pornographic Propaganda That Was Used
     Against Marie Antoinette," *Dangerous Minds* (July 27, 2015).

3   Robert Darnton, *The Forbidden Best-sellers of Pre-revolutionary France*
     (Norton, 1995), p. 21.

"WHAT DOES FREE SPEECH REQUIRE?"
pp. 45-53

1   See "An Act for the Punishment of Certain Crimes Against the United
     States" (Sedition Act), U.S. 5th Congress, 2nd Session.

2   "What Is Ag-Gag Legislation?" *ASPCA*.

3   Hadas Gold, "Donald Trump: We're going to 'open up' libel laws,"
     Politico (Feb. 26, 2016).

4   Louis Nelson, "Trump calls for jailing, revoking citizenship of flag-
     burners," *Politico* (Nov.29, 2016).

5   Alex Emmons, "Trump Already Demanding Leak Investigation and
     He's Not Even President Yet," *The Intercept* (Jan. 6, 2017); Spencer
     Ackerman and Ed Pilkington, "Obama's war on whistleblowers leaves
     administration insiders unscathed," *The Guardian* (March 16, 2015).

6   Brandy Zadrozny and Tim Mak, "Ex-Wife: Donald Trump Made Me
     Feel 'Violated' During Sex," *The Daily Beast* (July 27, 2015).

7   James Risen, "If Donald Trump Targets Journalists, Thank Obama,"
     The New York Times (Dec. 30, 2016).

8   Madison Park and Kyung Lah, "Berkeley protests of Yiannopoulos
     caused $100,000 in damage," *CNN* (Feb. 2, 2017).

9   Nathan J. Robinson, "Let the Kooks Speak," *Current Affairs* (Sept. 10, 2016).

10   "The Palestine Exception to Free Speech: A Movement Under Attack in the US," *Palestine Legal* (Sept. 2015).

11   Elizabeth Redden, "Pro-Palestinian Group Banned on Political Grounds," *Inside Higher Ed* (Jan. 18, 2017).

12   Rachel Bade and Heather Caygle, "GOP lawmaker removes painting of police as animals from Capitol," *Politico* (Jan. 6, 2017).

13   Betsy Klein and Deirdre Walsh, "The controversial painting Congress refuses to brush off," *CNN* (Jan. 11, 2017).

14   Warner Todd Huston, "Congressional Black Caucus to Re-Hang Anti-Cop 'Police as Pigs' Painting in Capital Citing 'Constitution,'" *Breitbart* (Jan. 9, 2017).

15   "What Are Speech Codes?" *Foundation for Individual Rights in Education*.

16   "Exclusive Video: Ben Shapiro Barred From Entering DePaul University!" *YouTube* (Nov. 16, 2016).

17   Monica Wang, Joey Ye, and Victor Wang, "Students protest Buckley talk," *Yale Daily News* (Nov. 9, 2015).

18   Susan Svrluga, "Williams College cancels a speaker who was invited to bring in provocative opinions," *The Washington Post* (Feb. 20, 2016).

19   Abby Jackson, "'Disinvitations' for college speakers are on the rise — here's a list of people turned away this year," *Business Insider* (July 28, 2016).

20   Jillian Lanney and Carolynn Cong, "Ray Kelly lecture canceled amidst student, community protest," *Brown Daily Herald* (Oct. 30, 2013).

21   Conor Friedersdorf, "The Glaring Evidence That Free Speech Is Threatened on Campus," *The Atlantic* (March 4, 2016).

22   "MILO Thrashes Heckling Muslim Women At New Mexico," *YouTube* (Jan. 28, 2017).

23   "MILO At UNM: Here's ICE's Phone Number, Use Wisely," *YouTube* (Jan. 27, 2017).

24   Claire Landsbaum, "Alt-Right Troll Milo Yiannopoulos Uses Campus Visit to Openly Mock a Transgender Student," *The Cut* (Dec. 15, 2016).

25   Nicole Frechette, Luis De Leon, Keaton Walkowski, Jenna Daroszewski and Kaliice Walker, "Transgender Student Tells UW-Milwaukee Chancellor to 'F' Off After Yiannopoulos Speech," *Media Milwaukee* (Dec. 14, 2016).

26   Charlie Nash, "Milo Explains Why Ugly People Hate Him," *Breitbart* (Jan. 25, 2017).

27   Emma Stefansky, "Simon & Schuster Defend $250,000 Book Deal with "Alt Right" Troll Milo Yiannopoulos," *Vanity Fair* (Dec. 31, 2016).

28   Matt Teitelbaum, "I'm A Liberal, And I Want Milo Yiannopoulos On My Campus," *Huffington Post* (Feb. 6, 2017).

29   Tyler Durden, "Berkeley Blowback: Milo Book Sales Soar 12,740% Overnight," *ZeroHedge* (Feb. 3, 2017).

30   Hart Eagleburger and Jack Rusk, "In Support of the Anti-Milo Berkeley Antifa Action," *Left Voice* (Feb. 3, 2017).

31   Paul P. Murphy, "White nationalist Richard Spencer punched during interview," *CNN* (Jan. 21, 2017).

32   Quoted from an image of an email posted on Facebook.

33   Eric Owens, "REVEALED: Gunman Who Seriously Injured Man Outside Milo Yiannopoulos Event Is Strong Trump Supporter," *The Daily Caller* (Jan. 26, 2017).

34   Amber Cortes, "Alleged Shooter Reached Out to Milo Yiannopoulos for an Autograph: 'I'm Outside In Line to Your UW Event,'" *The Stranger* (Jan. 24, 2017).

35   Laurie Penny, "I'm With the Banned," *Medium* (Jul. 21, 2016).

"HOW IDENTITY BECAME A WEAPON AGAINST THE LEFT"
pp. 55-64

1   See Laura Gottesdiener, "The Great Eviction: Black America and the Toll of the Foreclosure Crisis," *Mother Jones* (Aug. 1, 2013).

2   See Tara Culp-Ressler, "Why racism is a public health issue," *Think Progress* (Feb. 3, 2014).

3   See Julia Elliott Brown, "Emotional labour: The hidden tax that's driving women to despair," *The Telegraph* (Nov. 11, 2015).

4   Rachel Weiner, "Obama calls Kamala Harris 'the best looking attorney general,'" *The Washington Post* (April 4, 2013).

5   Michael Sainato, "Clinton Donors Have Picked Their 2020 Democratic Presidential Nominee," *The Observer* (July 17, 2017).

6   Emily Smith, "Dems' rising star meets with Clinton inner circle in Hamptons," *Page Six* (July 13, 2017).

7   Carolyn Lochhead, "Kamala Harris faces high expectations as California's new senator," *The San Francisco Chronicle* (Jan. 3, 2017).

8   Lois Beckett, "Could Kamala Harris revive the fractured Democratic party for the 2020 election?" *The Guardian* (July 22, 2017).

9   "Prisoners in 2015," Bureau of Justice Statistics.

10   Phil Willon, "Kamala Harris should take bolder action on police shootings, civil rights advocates say," *The Los Angeles Times* (Jan. 18, 2016).

11   See Kamala Harris, *Smart on Crime* (Chronicle Books, 2009).

12   Jamilah King, "Kamala Harris Went to Prison So Others Won't Have To," *Mother Jones* (July 18, 2017).

13   Emily Bazelon, "Kamala Harris, a 'Top Cop' in the Era of Black Lives Matter," *The New York Times Magazine* (May 15, 2016).

14   *Id.*

15   Chris Johnson, "Harris seeks to block gender reassignment for trans inmate," *The Washington Blade* (May 5, 2015).

16   Christopher Cadelago, "Kamala Harris picks her fights as criminal justice crusader," *The Sacramento Bee* (May 1, 2016).

17   Maura Dolan, "U.S. judges see 'epidemic' of prosecutorial misconduct in state," *The Los Angeles Times* (Jan. 31, 2015).

18   Quoted in Bazelon, *supra.*

19   Melody Gutierrez, "Kamala Harris: California's 'truancy crisis' must be stopped," *SFGate* (March 11, 2014).

20   Bryce Covert, "Meet the victims of Steve Mnuchin's 'foreclosure machine,'" *Think Progress* (Dec. 1, 2016).

21   David Dayen, "Treasury Pick Steve Mnuchin Denies It, But Victims Describe His Bank as a Foreclosure Machine," *The Intercept* (Jan. 19, 2017).

22   David Dayen, "Treasury Nominee Steve Mnuchin's Bank Accused of 'Widespread Misconduct' in Leaked Memo," *The Intercept* (Jan. 3, 2017).

23   David Dayen, "The Left's Misguided Debate Over Kamala Harris," *The New Republic* (Aug. 8, 2017).

24   Eric Garcia, "Harris Was Only 2016 Senate Democratic Candidate to Get Cash From Mnuchin," *Roll Call* (Feb. 14, 2017).

25   See Nathan J. Robinson, "Unless The Democrats Run Sanders, A Trump Nomination Means A Trump Presidency," *Current Affairs* (Feb. 23, 2016).

26   Andrew Joyce, "Democratic rising star Kamala Harris has a 'Ber-

nieland' problem," *Mic* (July 31, 2017).

27 See @neeratanden, @joyannreid, and @vabvox on Twitter.

28 Brittney Cooper, "Get Off Kamala Harris's Back," *Cosmopolitan* (Aug. 7, 2017).

29 B. Gray, "Bernie Sanders Doesn't Have a Black Problem—He Has a Pundit Problem," *Paste Magazine* (July 27, 2017).

30 David A. Graham, "A Short History of Hillary (Rodham) (Clinton)'s Changing Names," *The Atlantic* (Nov. 30, 2015).

31 Chase Purdy, "The blatantly sexist cookie bake-off that has haunted Hillary Clinton for two decades is back," *Quartz* (Aug. 21, 2016).

32 Tamara Keith, "Evolution Or Expediency? Clinton's Changing Positions Over A Long Career," *NPR* (May 23, 2016).

33 Mark Landler, "How Hillary Clinton Became A Hawk," *The New York Times Magazine* (April 21, 2016).

34 Stephanie Condon, "Hillary Clinton: Single-Payer Health Care Will 'Never, Ever' Happen," *CBS News* (Jan. 29, 2016).

35 "The Definitive, Encyclopedic Case For Why Hillary Clinton is the Wrong Choice," *Daily Kos* (Feb. 22, 2016).

36 Charles Clymer, "The Pettiness of the Angry White Male," *Medium* (May 26, 2016).

37 Jonathan Easley, "Poll: Bernie Sanders country's most popular active politician," *The Hill* (April 18, 2017).

38 Tim Murphy and Pema Levy, "Civil Rights Hero John Lewis Slams Bernie Sanders," *Mother Jones* (Feb. 11, 2016).

39 "Michelle Alexander: 'I Am Endorsing the Political Revolution,'" *MSNBC* (April 5, 2016). https://www.youtube.com/watch?v=tFHN-zlx24QM

40 "Ta-Nehisi Coates Is Voting for Bernie Sanders Despite the Senator's Opposition to Reparations," *Democracy Now* (Feb. 10, 2016).

41 "Erica Garner Endorsement of Bernie Sanders for President," Erica Garner on Youtube https://www.youtube.com/watch?v=oP4X-asc1t7Q

42 Quoted in Sam Sanders, "#BernieMadeMeWhite: No, Bernie Sanders Isn't Just Winning With White People," *NPR* (March 28, 2016).

43 *Id.*

44 "Caucacity," *UrbanDictionary.com*. Defined as "mad wack things only white people would do."

45 See: https://twitter.com/briebriejoy/status/892563406137561090 for a long list of examples submitted in response to a public request for

people to describe their experiences with this phenomenon.

46   Sally Albright on Twitter: https://twitter.com/sallyalbright/status/855647662288318464?lang=en

47   Glenn Greenwald, "The Smear Campaign Against Keith Ellison Is Repugnant but Reveals Much About Washington,"

48   Adam Gabbatt, "Gloria Steinem: women are supporting Bernie Sanders 'for the boys,'" *The Guardian* (Feb. 16, 2016).

49   Elizabeth Bruenig, "Why Are Millennial Women Gravitating to Bernie Sanders?" *The New Republic* (Feb. 9, 2016).

50   Raymond Hernandez, "Surrogate for Obama Denounces Anti-Romney Ad," *The New York Times* (May 20, 2012).

51   Murphy and Levy, *supra.*

52   Kevin Drum, "Take It Easy on Hillary Clinton and the 1994 Crime Bill," *Mother Jones* (Jan. 25, 2016).

53   Patrick S. Tomlinson, "Take In From Milwaukee: Beware of Sheriff David Clarke," *The New York Times* (May 23, 2017).

54   Sarah Burris, "Why Is Bernie Sanders' Overwhelmingly Pro-Choice Record Being Attacked?," *AlterNet* (Jan. 28, 2016).

55   Danielle Paquette, "Why Tim Kaine Can Oppose Abortion and Still Run With Hillary Clinton," *The Washington Post* (July 26, 2016).

56   Jason Le Miere, "Bernie Sanders' 'Colossal Mistake': Backing Heath Mello," *Newsweek* (May 11, 2017).

57   See: "Resources on Implicit Bias," American Association of University Women, http://www.aauw.org/resource/iat/

"MORE LAWYERS, SAME INJUSTICES"
pp. 71-78

1   Sarah Larimer, "'You'll find out how nasty I really am': A judge's seething response to a hostile defendant," *The Washington Post* (June 24, 2016).

2   Nick Romano, "Rick and Morty spoofs Georgia v. Denver Fenton Allen," *Entertainment Weekly* (Aug. 5, 2016).

3   "Clarence Earl Gideon," *The State Historical Society of Missouri.*

4   Ken Armstrong, "What Can You Do With a Drunken Lawyer?" *The Marshall Project* (Dec. 10, 2014).

5   "Right to Counsel," *Southern Center for Human Rights.*

6   Stephen B. Bright and Sia M. Sanneh, "Fifty Years of Defiance and Resistance After Gideon v. Wainwright," *The Yale Law Journal* (June 2013).

7   Dylan Walsh, "On the Offensive," *The Atlantic* (June 2, 2016).

8   "Prisoners 1925–81," *U.S. Department of Justice* (Dec. 1982).

9   "Prisoners in 2014," *U.S. Department of Justice* (Sept. 2015).

"PRETENDING IT ISN'T THERE"
pp. 79-88

1   "Nuclear Weapons: Who Has What at a Glance," *Arms Control Association* (July 2017).

2   Ike Jeanes, *Forecast and Solution: Grappling with the Nuclear, a Trilogy for Everyone* (Pocahontas Press, 1996), p. 301.

3   *Atomic Platters: Cold War Music from the Golden Age of Homeland Security* (Bear Family, 2005).

4   Jerry Brown, "A Stark Nuclear Warning," *The New York Review of Books* (July 14, 2016).

5   Brad Roberts, *The Case for U.S. Nuclear Weapons in the 21st Century* (Stanford University Press, Dec. 2015).

6   Nathan J. Robinson, "How to Justify Hiroshima," *Current Affairs* (May 11, 2016).

7   "Famous 'Daisy' Attack Ad from 1964 Presidential Election," *YouTube* (Oct. 30, 2010).

8   Eric Schlosser, *Command and Control: Nuclear Weapons, the Damascus Accident, and the Illusion of Safety* (Penguin Books, 2014).

"THE SCOURGE OF SELF-FLAGELLATING POLITICS"
pp. 89-94

1   See, e.g., Cassie Baker, "I Am Ashamed To Be Apart Of The Demographic That Elected Trump," *Affinity* (Nov. 10, 2016).

2   Fredrik deBoer, "Admitting that white privilege helps you is really just congratulating yourself," *The Washington Post* (Jan. 28, 2016).

3   "Donald Sutherland 'ashamed' of white privilege," *The Toronto Sun* (Nov. 17, 2016).

4   Michael Moore on Twitter: https://twitter.com/mmflint/status/792436882378465280?lang=en

5   "Women and the Bomb," *Atomic Heritage Foundation* (June 5, 2014).

6   Luke Harding, "Meet the Anti-Germans," *The Guardian* (Aug. 27, 2006).

7   Ali Michael, "I Sometimes Don't Want To Be White, Either," *The Huffington Post* (June 16, 2015).

8   Malcolm X, "Interview With Gordon Parks," *Malcolm-x.org.*

"SUICIDE AND THE AMERICAN DREAM"
pp. 113-119

1   Carlo Alcos, "Story of a suicide survivor: 'The millisecond my hands left the rail it was an instant regret,'" *Matador Network* (Dec. 16, 2015).

2   Matthew Miller, M.D., Sc.D., and David Hemenway, Ph.D., "Guns and Suicide in the United States," *The New England Journal of Medicine* (Sept. 4, 2008).

3   Sabrina Tavernise, "U.S. Suicide Rate Surges to a 30-Year High," *The New York Times* (April 22, 2016).

4   Thomas Curwen, "His Work Is Still Full of Life," *Los Angeles Times* (June 5, 2004).

5   Michael Cabanatuan, "Golden Gate Bridge board OKs $76 million for suicide barrier," *SF Gate* (June 28, 2014).

6   "Update on Suicide Deterrent Net Construction Project," *Golden Gate Bridge Highway and Transportation District* (Feb. 18, 2016).

7   "Suicide and Self-Inflicted Injury," *CDC.*

8   Sarah Boseley, "Unemployment causes 45,000 suicides a year worldwide, finds study," *The Guardian* (Feb. 11, 2015).

9   Gene Sprague, "Saturday, January 10th, 2004," *The Uselessness of Being Me* (Jan. 10, 2004).

10 German Lopez, "Way more Americans are drinking themselves to death. Here's why," *Vox* (Dec. 28, 2015).

11 Sabrina Tavernise, "First Rise in U.S. Death Rate in Years Surprises Experts," *The New York Times* (June 1, 2016).

12 Tavernise, "U.S. Suicide Rate Surges to a 30-Year High."

13 Unconfidence, user comment on *Reddit* (2014).

14 Scott Alexander, "Burdens," *Slate Star Codex* (Aug. 16, 2014).

"THE GREAT AMERICAN CHEMTRAIL"
pp. 127-133

1   The Alex Jones Show, "Did the Chemtrail Flu Kill Prince?" *InfoWars*, (April 22, 2016).

2   Jon Bowne, "Special Report: Was Prince Murdered By Illuminati Record Execs?" *InfoWars* (April 23, 2016).

3   Jane McGrath, "What are chemtrails, and should you be scared of them?" *How Stuff Works*.

4   Nancy Levant, "Passive Democide: Drought and Starvation," *GeoEngineering Watch* (Jan. 27, 2014).

5   A.M. Mercer, D.W. Keith and J.D. Sharp, "Public understanding of solar radiation management," *IOP Publishing* (Oct. 24, 2011).

6   Chuck Norris, "Sky Criminals," *WorldNetDaily* (April 24, 2016).

7   Jessica Firger, "Joni Mitchell and the mystery of Morgellons disease," *CBS News* (April 2, 2015).

8   William Thomas, "Jet Contrails May Be Sickening People Across The US," *Environmental News Service* (Jan. 10, 1999).

9   Richard Hofstadter, "The Paranoid Style in American Politics," *Harper's* (Nov. 1964).

10   Mick West, "Advocating violence against 'Chemtrail' planes, pilots, scientists, and debunkers," *Metabunk.org* (Sept. 14, 2011).

11   Alston Chase, "Harvard and the Making of the Unabomber," *The Atlantic* (June 2000).

12   "Project MKUltra," *Wikipedia*.

13   Amber A'Lee Frost, "Flakes Alive!" *The Baffler* (June 12, 2015).

"WHY JOURNALISTS LOVE TWITTER"
pp. 141-148

1   Nathan J. Robinson, "Keeping the Content Machine Whirring," *Current Affairs* (Feb. 24, 2016).

2   "Twitter Usage Statistics," *Internet Live Stats*.

3   Gyan Yankovich and Mat Whitehead, "28 Tweets About Gymnastics That Are Just So Damn Real," *BuzzFeed* (Aug. 9, 2016).

4   Brian Galindo, "19 Tweets Anyone Addicted To Diet Coke Will Completely Relate To," *BuzzFeed* (Aug. 5, 2016).

5   MojoIOL, "What does being 'woke' mean?" *Storify* (2015).

6   @deep_beige, post on *Twitter* (July 14, 2015).

7   Nathan J. Robinson, replies to Nicholas Kristof posted to *Twitter* (2015-16).

8   Robinson Meyer, "Here Comes the Berniebro, *The Atlantic* (Oct. 17, 2015).

9   @yayitsrob, *Twitter*.

10 Glenn Greenwald, "The 'Bernie Bros' Narrative: a Cheap Campaign Tactic Masquerading as Journalism and Social Activism," *The Intercept* (Jan. 31, 2016).

11 Jamil Smith, "The Sanders Campaign Knows the 'Bernie Bros' Are a Problem," *The New Republic* (2016).

12 Amanda Marcotte, "Bernie Bros out of control: Explosion of misogynist rage at Nevada's Dem chairwoman reflects terribly on Sanders' dwindling campaign," *Salon* (May 17, 2016).

13 Rebecca Caplan, "The Bernie Bro Code," *The New Yorker* (March 29, 2016).

14 Paul Krugman, "Sanders Over the Edge," *The New York Times* (April 8, 2016).

15 Matt Bruenig, "The Myth of the Bernie Bro," *Jacobin* (Oct. 31, 2015).

16 Olivia Nuzzi, post on *Twitter* (June 7, 2016).

"HAMILTON"
pp. 149-159

1   "Captain Dan & His Scurvy Crew (Full Audition)," *YouTube* (June 13, 2012).

2   Ben Brantley, "Review: 'Hamilton,' Young Rebels Changing History and Theater," *The New York Times* (Aug. 6, 2015).

3   Nicole Dieker, "Is 'Hamilton' The Musical The Most Addicting Album Ever?" *Popular Science* (Feb. 13, 2016).

4   Chris Weller, "'Hamilton' is the most important musical of our time," *Business Insider* (March 19, 2016).

5   David Marcus, "'Hamilton' Haters Are Why We Can't Have Nice Things," *The Federalist* (April 7, 2016).

6   Mark Binelli, "'Hamilton' Mania! Backstage at the Cultural Event of Our Time," *Rolling Stone* (June 1, 2016).

7   Clarence Page, "'Hamilton' is even better than its hype," *Chicago Tribune* (July 1, 2016).

8   Eleanor Kagan and Another Round, "14 Things You Never Knew About Hamilton's Lin-Manuel Miranda," *BuzzFeed* (March 8, 2016).

9   Ellie Hall, post on *Twitter* (Oct. 29, 2015).

10 "Listicle," *Wikipedia*.

11 Arielle Calderon, post on *Twitter* (Nov. 4, 2015).

12 "Nerdcore," *Wikipedia*.

13 MC Router and funky49, "Trekkie Pride," *YouTube* (Jan. 24, 2012).

14 Abbie – Kristin Nicole Richie, "I Was on Dr. Phil, and as a Muslim woman, I felt Wrongly Portrayed," *The Islamic Monthly* (July 11, 2014).

15 Jesse Lawrence, "'Hamilton' Is Broadway's Most Expensive Show—Ever," *The Daily Beast* (May 3, 2016).

16 Rebecca Mead, "All About the Hamiltons," *The New Yorker* (Feb. 9, 2015).

17 Ben Zimmer, "*Hamilton* Through the Lens of Language," *Slate* (May 10, 2016).

18 Michael Sokolove, "The C.E.O. of 'Hamilton' Inc." *The New York Times Magazine* (April 5, 2016).

19 Adam Gopnik, "'Hamilton' and the Hip-Hop Case for Progressive Heroism," *The New Yorker* (Feb. 5, 2016).

20 Jody Rosen, "The American Revolutionary," *T Magazine* (July 8, 2015).

21 Jennifer Schuessler, "*Hamilton* and History: Are They in Sync?" *The New York Times* (April 10, 2016).

22 Lyra D. Monteiro, "Race-Conscious Casting and the Erasure of the Black Past in Lin-Manuel Miranda's *Hamilton*," *The Public Historian*, Vol. 38, No. 1 (Feb. 2016), pp. 89-98.

23 Mark Binelli, "*Hamilton* Creator Lin-Manuel Miranda: The Rolling Stone Interview," *Rolling Stone* (June 1, 2016).

24 Quoted in Mead, "All About The Hamiltons."

25 Joanne B. Freeman, "How *Hamilton* Uses History," *Slate* (Nov. 11, 2015).

26 "Remarks by The First Lady at 'Hamilton at The White House' Student Workshop," Office of the First Lady, The White House (March 14, 2016).

27   "Remarks by the President at 'Hamilton at the White House,'" Office of the Press Secretary, The White House (March 14, 2016).

28   "Vice President Joe Biden Visits Broadway's Hamilton," Playbill.

29   Binelli, "'Hamilton' Creator Lin-Manuel Miranda: The Rolling Stone Interview."

30   Jordan Sargent, "Rahm Emanuel Secretly Spent Night After Chicago Teachers' Strike Enjoying 'Hamilton' on Broadway," Gawker (April 5, 2016).

31   Liz Kreutz, "'Hamilton' Musical Teams Up With Hillary Clinton for July Fundraiser," ABC News (June 26, 2016).

32   Erik Piepenburg, "Why 'Hamilton' Has Heat," The New York Times (June 12, 2016).

33   Rupert Murdoch, post on Twitter (March 7, 2015).

34   President Barack Obama and Marilynne Robinson, "President Obama & Marilynne Robinson: A Conversation—II," The New York Review of Books (Nov. 19, 2015).

35   Janice Kaplan, "Why Has 'Hamilton' Become Broadway Gold?" The Daily Beast (Aug. 6, 2015).

36   Gopnik, "'Hamilton' and the Hip-Hop Case for Progressive Heroism."

"HOW LIBERALS FELL IN LOVE WITH THE WEST WING"
pp. 169-179

1   Eliana Dockterman, "Listen to Lin-Manuel Miranda's West Wing Rap," Time (Jan. 16, 2017).

2   Robert Ito, "'The West Wing Weekly,' a Podcast With a Ringer," The New York Times (June 24, 2016).

3   Juli Weiner, "West Wing Babies," Vanity Fair (March 6, 2012).

4   Ibid.

5   Joyce Millman, "'Don't Blame Me, I Voted for Martin Sheen!'" Salon (Sept. 11, 2000).

6   Helen Lewis, post on Twitter (Nov. 9, 2016).

7   Emily Heil, "President Bartlet for Hillary: Actor Bradley Whitford says fictional prez would be for Clinton," The Washington Post (April 5, 2016).

8   Ezra Klein, "Hillary Clinton's 3 debate performances left the Trump campaign in ruins," Vox (Oct. 19, 2011).

"MIKE CERNOVICH"
pp. 181-187

1   Mike Cernovich, *MAGA Mindset: Making YOU and America Great Again* (Castalia House, 2016).

2   Lloyd Grove, "Why Did Fox News Welcome Date Rape Apologist Mike Cernovich?" *The Daily Beast* (Aug. 9, 2016).

3   Mike Cernovich, "The Orlando Shooter Did Not Act Alone," *Danger & Play* (June 15, 2016).

4   Cernovich, "How to Choke a Woman During Sex," *Danger & Play* (Dec. 26, 2011).

5   Cernovich, *Gorilla Mindset: How to Control Your Thoughts and Emotions and Live Life on Your Terms* (Media, 2015).

6   Cernovich, *Danger & Play: Essays on Masculinity* (2015).

7   Andrew Marantz, "Trolls for Trump," *The New Yorker* (Oct. 31, 2016).

8   Margaret Pless, "Mike Cernovich: Potemkin Alpha Male," *Internet Famous Angry Men* (Dec. 31, 2015).

"GEORGE W. BUSH"
pp. 189-199

1   George W. Bush, *Portraits of Courage: A Commander in Chief's Tribute to America's Warriors* (Crown, 2017).

2   Peter Schjeldahl, "George W. Bush's Painted Atonements," *The New Yorker* (March 3, 2017).

3   Jonathan Alter, "Bush Nostalgia Is Overrated, But His Book of Paintings Is Not," *The New York Times* (April 17, 2017).

4   Nathan J. Robinson, "Getting Away With It," *Current Affairs* (Jan. 26, 2017).

5   "George Bush Poncho Video," *YouTube* (Jan. 21, 2017).

6   Jenna Amatulli, "Ellen Asks George W. Bush About His Inauguration Poncho: 'Had You Put One On?'" *Huffington Post* (March 2, 2017).

7   Bobbi Nodell, "Study: Nearly 500,000 perished in Iraq war," *UW Today* (Oct. 15, 2013).

8   *IraqBodyCount.org.*

9   "Civilians Without Protection: The ever-worsening humanitarian

crisis in Iraq," *International Committee of the Red Cross.*

10   John Leyne, "Iraqi Medical Crisis as Doctors Flee," *Common Dreams* (March 24, 2007).

11   Rory Carroll, "Iraq war is blamed for starvation," *The Guardian* (March 30, 2005).

12   Dahr Jamail, "Iraq: War's legacy of cancer," *Al Jazeera* (March 15, 2013).

13   "Looking Back on Ten Years of War, Trauma, Death, & Displacement," *Iraq: the Human Cost* (MIT).

14   Caroline Hawley, "Iraq conflict: Crisis of an orphaned generation," *BBC News* (Nov. 28, 2012).

15   "University Reconstruction in Iraq" (Watson Institute, Brown University).

16   Hawley, "Iraq conflict."

17   "Red Cross: Iraq situation getting worse," *ThinkProgress* (April 11, 2007).

18   "Bush: 'Leave Iraq within 48 hours,'" *CNN* (March 17, 2003).

19   Harry Frankfurt, "On Bullshit," *Raritan Quarterly Review* (1986).

20   Dan Glaister, "Bush ignored intelligence on Iraqi weapons, says ex-CIA officer," *The Guardian* (April 23, 2006).

21   Peter Taylor, "Iraq war: the greatest intelligence failure in living memory," *The Telegraph* (March 18, 2013).

22   Stephen T. Hosmer, *Why the Iraqi Resistance to the Coalition Invasion was So Weak* (RAND, 2007), p. 12.

23   James Risen, "Review: 'Debriefing the President' Tears Into the C.I.A." *The New York Times* (Dec. 18, 2016).

24   Joel Roberts, "Plans for Iraq Attack Began on 9/11," *CBS News* (Sept. 4, 2002).

25   "'Building momentum for regime change': Rumsfeld's secret memos," *MSNBC* (Feb. 16, 2013)

26   Andy McSmith, "Bush 'plotted to lure Saddam into war with fake UN plane,'" *Independent* (Feb. 3, 2006).

27   Richard Norton-Taylor, "Blair-Bush deal before Iraq war revealed in secret memo," *The Guardian* (Feb. 2, 2006).

28   Michael Moore, "Six Years Ago, Chuck Hagel Told the Truth About Iraq," *Huffington Post* (Jan. 5, 2013).

29   "Abizaid: 'Of Course It's About Oil, We Can't Really Deny That,'"

ThinkProgress (May 25, 2011).

30   Michiko Kakutani, "Personality, Ideology and Bush's Terror Wars,"
      The New York Times (June 20, 2006).

31   Suzanne Goldenberg, "Bush ignored warnings on Iraq insurgency
      threat before invasion," *The Guardian* (Sept. 28, 2004).

32   Patrick Cockburn, *The Occupation: War and Resistance in Iraq* (Verso,
      2007).

33   Rajiv Chandrasekaran, *Imperial Life in the Emerald City: Inside Iraq's
      Green Zone* (Vintage Books, 2007).

34   John W. Dower, *Cultures of War: Pearl Harbor / Hiroshima / 9-11 /
      Iraq* (W.W. Norton & Company, 2011), p. 532.

35   Jonathan S. Landay, "Study says violence in Iraq has been
      underreported," *McClatchy Newspapers* (Dec. 6, 2006).

36   Nick Davies, Jonathan Steele and David Leigh, "Iraq war logs: secret
      files show how US ignored torture," *The Guardian* (Oct. 22, 2010).

37   Gregg Carlstrom, "Iraq files reveal checkpoint deaths," *Al Jazeera*
      (Oct. 23, 2010).

38   James Glanz and Andrew W. Lehren, "Use of Contractors Added to
      War's Chaos in Iraq," *The New York Times* (Oct. 23, 2010).

39   Ryan Tate, "Off the Grid," *The Intercept* (Dec. 9, 2014).

40   Seymour M. Hersh, "Torture at Abu Ghraib," *The New Yorker* (May
      10, 2004).

41   Philippe Sands, "The Green Light," *Vanity Fair* (April 2, 2008).

42   Senate Select Committee on Intelligence, "Committee Study of the
      Central Intelligence Agency's Detention and Interrogation Program"
      (April 3, 2014).

43   Daniel Summers, "'Rectal Feeding' Has Nothing to Do with
      Nutrition, Everything to Do with Torture," *The Daily Beast* (Dec. 10,
      2014).

44   Senate Select Committee on Intelligence, "Committee Study of the
      Central Intelligence Agency's Detention and Interrogation Program,"
      p. 4.

45   "Fmr. Army Chaplain James Yee on the Abuse of Prisoners at
      Guantanamo, His Wrongful Imprisonment and Anti-Muslim
      Sentiment in the Military," *Democracy Now* (Oct. 6, 2005).

46   Ray Rivera, "A Witness Comes Forward," *The Seattle Times* (Spring
      2003).

47   "Two Hundred and Seventeenth Day, Monday, 30 September 1946,"

Nuremberg Trial Proceedings Volume 22 (Accessed at Yale Law School, the Avalon Project).

48 Afua Hirsch, "Iraq war was illegal, Dutch panel rules," *The Guardian* (Jan. 12, 2010).

49 Jenny Gross and Alexis Flynn, "U.K.'s Long-Awaited Chilcot Report into Iraq War Criticizes Legal Basis for Invasion," *Wall Street Journal* (July 6, 2016).

50 Ewen MacAskill and Julian Borger, "Iraq war was illegal and breached UN charter, says Annan," *The Guardian* (Sept. 15, 2004).

51 David Hughes, "Chilcot report: John Prescott says Iraq War was illegal," *Independent* (July 9, 2016).

52 George W. Bush, *Decision Points* (Broadway Books, 2011).

53 "Bush Doesn't Care About Black People," *YouTube* (April 17, 2006).

54 Philip Kennicott, "George W. Bush's best-selling book of paintings shows curiosity and compassion," *The Washington Post* (March 12, 2017).

55 Sherryl Connelly, "Guantanamo Bay staff sergeant claims three men believed to have committed suicide were actually tortured to death," *NY Daily News* (Jan. 17, 2015).

"RUTH BADER GINSBURG"
pp. 211-222

1 Irin Carmon and Shana Knizhnik, *Notorious RBG: The Life and Times of Ruth Bader Ginsburg* (Dey Street Books, 2015).

2 Army Corps of Engineers v. Hawkes Co., 578 U.S. ___ (2016).

3 Rumsfeld v. Forum for Academic and Institutional Rights, Inc., 547 U.S. 47 (2006).

4 Integrity Staffing Solutions, Inc. v. Busk, 574 U.S. ___ (2014).

5 Atul Gawande, "Hellhole," *The New Yorker* (March 30, 2009).

6 Davis v. Ayala, 576 U.S. ___ (2015).

7 The Editorial Board, "Justice Kennedy on Solitary Confinement," *The New York Times* (June 19, 2015).

8 David G. Savage, "Justice Kennedy practically invites a challenge to solitary confinement," *Los Angeles Times* (June 19, 2015).

9 Heien v. North Carolina, 574 U.S. ___ (2014).

10   Taylor v. Barkes, 575 U. S. ___ (2015).

11   Plumhoff v. Rickard, 570 US ___ (2013).

12   Samson v. California, 547 U.S. 843 (2006).

13   Kansas v. Carr, 577 U.S. ___ (2016).

14   David Fontana, "Sonia Sotomayor Is a National Treasure," *The New Republic* (April 14, 2014).

15   Mark Joseph Stern, "Sonia Sotomayor Takes a Stand Against Police Brutality," *Slate* (Nov. 9, 2015).

16   Shelby County v. Holder, 570 U.S. 2 (2013).

17   Bush v. Gore, 531 U.S. 98 (2000).

18   Amy Davidson, "In Voting Rights, Scalia Sees a 'Racial Entitlement,'" *The New Yorker* (Feb. 28, 2013).

19   Ariane de Vogue, "Scalia-Ginsburg friendship bridged opposing ideologies," *CNN* (Feb. 14, 2016).

20   Randall Kennedy, "The Case for Early Retirement," *The New Republic* (April 27, 2011).

21   Emily Bazelon, "Stop Telling Ruth Bader Ginsburg to Retire," *Slate* (Dec. 18, 2013).

22   Ibid.

"BARACK OBAMA"
pp. 223-234

1   Leo Janos, "The Last Days of the President," *The Atlantic* (July 1973).

2   "Presidential Vehicles," *National Park Service*.

3   "Frequently Asked Questions," *Marantha Baptist Church*.

4   Christopher Dawson, "Former President Jimmy Carter's 32-year passion project to build homes," *CNN* (Sept. 20, 2016).

5   Sara Rimes, "Enjoying the Ex-Presidency? Never Been Better," *The New York Times* (Feb. 16, 2000).

6   Dana Guthrie, "Which of George W. Bush's paintings is your favorite?" *Houston Chronicle* (Nov. 24, 2014).

7   Sam Byford, "George W. Bush's bizarre bathroom self-portraits laid bare by audacious hack," *The Verge* (Feb. 8, 2013).

8   Nathan J. Robinson, "I Don't Care How Good His Paintings Are, He Still Belongs in Prison," *Current Affairs* (April 19, 2017).

9   "The Board," *Obama Foundation*.

10   David Z. Morris, "Citizen Obama Wants Your Ideas," *Fortune* (Jan. 21, 2017).

11   Deena Zaru, "Barack Obama's kitesurfing adventure with Richard Branson," *CNN* (Feb. 8, 2017).

12   Tierney McAfee, "Bono and the Obamas Brunch in the Big Apple — and Get a Standing Ovation," *People* (March 10, 2017).

13   Glenn Greenwald, "Key Question About DNC Race: Why Did Obama White House Recruit Perez to Run Against Ellison?" *The Intercept* (Feb. 24, 2017).

14   Edward Isaac-Dovere, "Obama wades into French election fight," *Politico* (April 20, 2017).

15   Jean-Baptiste Duval, "Emmanuel Macron veut diviser la recette de l'ISF par deux, mais il devrait toujours le payer," *Huffington Post* (Jan. 2, 2017).

16   James Creedon, "'The best way to afford a suit is to get a job,'" *France 24* (May 31, 2016).

17   "Merchandise: The Trump Collection," *The Trump Organization*.

18   Eric Bates, "Beyond Hope," *The New Republic* (Dec. 13, 2016).

19   Max Greenwood, "Obamas sign with agency for speaking gigs," *The Hill* (Feb. 10, 2017).

20   Jill Abramson, "Barack Obama has a powerful voice. He shouldn't use it for paid speeches," *The Guardian* (April 27, 2017).

21   Adam H. Johnson, post on *Twitter* (April 28, 2017).

22   Michael Cohen, post on *Twitter* (April 25, 2017).

23   @eshaLegal, post on *Twitter* (April 28, 2017).

24   "Imani Gandy," *LinkedIn*.

25   Randee Dawn, "The next Obama family home: Take a tour of their new Washington DC house," *Today* (Jan. 13, 2017).

26   A.Q. Smith, "It's Basically Just Immoral to Be Rich," *Current Affairs* (June 14, 2017).

27   Alicia Adamczyk, "Here's How Much Money Obama and Biden Will Get From Their Pensions," *Time* (Jan. 20, 2017).

28   Constance Grady, "What the Obamas' $65 million book advance actually means," *Vox* (March 2, 2017).

29   "Personal Income in the United States," *Wikipedia*.

30   Jeff Stein, "Barack Obama is betting that young people can save

America — and his legacy," *Vox* (April 24, 2017).

31   Jon Schwarz, "Barack Obama Never Said Money Wasn't Corrupting; In Face, He Said the Opposite," *The Intercept* (April 15, 2016).

32   Joe Scarborough, "Obama's 'friendship' with Wall Street," *Politico* (Nov. 7, 2011).

33   Robert Yoon, "Goldman Sachs was top Obama donor," *CNN* (April 10, 2010).

34   "1936 Madison Square Garden speech," *Wikipedia.*

35   Zach Carter, "Obama's $400,000 Wall Street Speech Is Completely In Character," *Huffington Post* (April 26, 2017).

36   Jillian Berman, "Eric Holder's 1999 Memo Helped Set The Stage For 'Too Big To Jail'," *Huffington Post* (June 4, 2016).

37   "Matt Taibbi: After Laundering $800 Million in Drug Money, How Did HSBC Executives Avoid Jail?" *Democracy Now* (Dec. 13, 2012).

38   Committee on Financial Services, U.S. House of Representatives, "Too Big to Jail: Inside the Obama Justice Department's Decision Not to Hold Wall Street Accountable" (July 11, 2016).

39   "Democratic Platform Drafting Committee Hearing, Day 1, Part 1," *C-Span* (June 8, 2016).

40   Matt Taibbi, "Eric Holder, Wall Street Double Agent, Comes in From the Cold," *Rolling Stone* (July 8, 2015).

41   Matt Taibbi, "How Wall Street Killed Financial Reform," *Rolling Stone* (May 10, 2012).

42   Ben Mathis-Lilley, "Maybe Obama Is Doing Paid Speeches Because He Thinks Big-Money Special Interests Are Fine," *Slate* (April 28, 2017).

43   Paul Blumenthal, "The Legacy of Billy Tauzin: The White House-PhRMA Deal," *Sunlight Foundation* (Feb. 12, 2010).

44   Howard Dean, post on *Twitter* (April 15, 2016).

45   Morgan Chalfant, "Obama advisor David Plouffe beats out Jay Carney for Uber 'campaign manager' job," *Red Alert Politics* (Aug. 19, 2014).

46   Ben Mathis-Lilley, "Obama Spokesman Who Promised to Confront Corporate Interests Is Now McDonald's Spokesman," *Slate* (June 9, 2015).

47   Chris Opfer, "As McDonald's Moved to Raise Workers' Pay, Its Lobbyists Urged Caution on Wage Hike," *Bloomberg BNA* (May 6, 2015).

48   Matt Taibbi, "Eric Holder, Wall Street Double Agent, Comes in From the Cold," *Rolling Stone* (July 8, 2015).

49   David Dayen, "Why Eric Holder's new job is an insult to the American public," *Salon* (July 7, 2015).

50   Tony Mauro and Katelyn Polantz, "Q&A: Eric Holder Jr. Goes 'Home' to Covington, Reflects on Tenure," *The National Law Journal* (July 5, 2015).

51   Gregory Wallace, "For Geithner, a lucrative life in the private sector," *CNN* (Nov. 18, 2013).

52   Matthew Yglesias, "Obama's $400,000 Wall Street speaking fee will undermine everything he believes in," *Vox* (April 25, 2017).

53   Allison Benedikt, "If You Send Your Kid to Private School, You Are a Bad Person," *Slate* (Aug. 29, 2013).

54   Abby Jackson, "What the prestigious $40,000-a-year school that's educated 35 years of presidential kids has to offer," *Business Insider* (Dec. 9, 2016).

55   Peter S. Goodman, "Davos Elite Fret About Inequality Over Vintage Wine and Canapés," *The New York Times* (Jan. 18, 2017).

56   Matthew Creamer, "Obama Wins! ... Ad Age's Marketer of the Year," *Advertising Age* (Oct. 17, 2008).

57   "Christopher Hitchens - Obama Is A Maniacal Narcissist!" *YouTube* (May 16, 2011).

58   Carlos Lozada, "Before Michelle, Barack Obama asked another woman to marry him. Then politics got in the way," *The Washington Post* (May 2, 2017).

ABOUT CURRENT AFFAIRS

CURRENT AFFAIRS IS A BIMONTHLY PRINT MAGAZINE OF political commentary, journalism, and satire. It's a fresh, fearless, and independent antidote to contemporary political media. We focus on challenging preconceptions and undermining orthodoxies. *Current Affairs* showcases some of the country's best contemporary writers, and is edited by a highly experienced team of professionals with backgrounds in law, literature, design, technology, and politics. We bring a sharp critical eye to the absurdities of modern American life, and provide a new and unique set of perspectives on major political issues.

CURRENTAFFAIRS.ORG

91094301R00157

Made in the USA
Lexington, KY
18 June 2018